The 3 Cs

. . . .

Chaos Crisis Confusion

Your invitation to a new life

Alana Fairchild

BLUE ANGEL®
PUBLISHING

The 3 Cs

Published by Blue Angel Publishing®
80 Glen Tower Drive, Glen Waverley
Victoria, Australia 3150
Email: info@blueangelonline.com
Website: www.blueangelonline.com

Edited by Jeanette Hartnack

Blue Angel is a registered trademark of Blue Angel Gallery Pty. Ltd.

ISBN: 978-1-922161-90-1

Contents

· · · · · · · · · · · · · · · · · · · ·

Introduction

· ·

LIKE MOST PEOPLE, I have experienced plenty of pain in my life, including emotional suffering and mental anguish. For a long time I believed that life was just a never-ending series of obstacles and hurdles. I didn't feel excited or empowered by life. It just seemed like something I had to fight against constantly to survive. I was plagued by anxiety, confusion and doubt. I was so exhausted in body and mind that one day I even felt a stab of vicious jealousy towards my cat as she slept contentedly in my top desk drawer whilst I laboured over a hefty legal textbook I had little interest in. I had no idea how – or if – anything could change for the better. I hated what I was doing and where I was going. I didn't fantasise about a future filled with excitement and fulfilment. I couldn't even imagine such a life for me. I just felt bleak at the prospect of a dreary future with a never-ending workload and an absence of genuine peace, happiness, wellbeing and pleasure.

I had done everything I thought was 'right' so that I could have a wonderful life. I worked hard, I made smart choices about my career path and, on the outside, I seemed to have many things going my way. But inside, I felt miserable. I became depressed every Sunday afternoon because Monday – and the start of the working week – was about to begin.

There were many other things I wanted to change in my life too. Health, finances, love life … well practically all of it, really. It seemed like a big task. I didn't even know for sure that it would be possible to change my life so dramatically, but I was willing to give it a go. I had learned something useful from my mother, which was to never give up: if something isn't working, look for an answer and don't let anyone dissuade you until you find out what you need to know. Just keep going until you find it. So I did just that. I went on a quest to work out how to not feel depressed, miserable and deeply unsatisfied with my life!

That's when my life began to change. I thought it would change for the better – and eventually, it did in a dramatic and meaningful way. That didn't happen by taking a simple step from miserable to mended however. It was a journey filled with chaos, crisis and confusion. Sometimes on that journey I worried that I had wandered so far from the familiar (though unhappy) path that I was once on, I might never find my way out of the confusion and into a new life. All I knew was that I was letting go not only of the pain of my past, but also of what was familiar and certain in my life. For someone who was far more comfortable being in control and planning her life, this was rather uncomfortable for me, to put it mildly.

Then I realised something that changed my perspective entirely, allowed me to embrace the process and learn the rules of the game I didn't even realise I had been playing. I was visiting a herbalist for a health matter. She prescribed a herbal mixture for me and cautioned me that, in taking the herbs, I might have a healing crisis. It would be like a detox effect, she explained, where I would probably feel worse before I felt better. She told me not to worry because without it, healing couldn't happen and it would pass.

I did go through exactly that. I felt awful for a while, much worse than before I started taking the herbs. I could have stopped at that point, deciding that not only was the treatment not working, but it was making things worse. But I didn't stop. I figured it must be the healing crisis my herbalist had mentioned, and I was desperate enough for positive changes in my health that I decided I would stick it out and see if it got better. After a little while the detox ended and I felt better than ever.

Something clicked in me. I wondered if a healing crisis could happen not only in my body, but in my life too. Was the confusion in me and the chaos in my life a sort of healing crisis? I had been willing to take steps to walk away from a career I hated – law – even though I didn't really know what I was supposed to 'do' with my life. I knew in my heart that I needed to walk away though, even if I didn't know where I was supposed to go exactly. I mostly just felt confused! I knew what I didn't want, but what about what I did want? That wasn't so clear to me, but I was determined to figure it out.

As soon as I tried to improve some area of my life though, it seemed like that part of my life got worse. All the problems seemed to 'rise up' to the surface and it was an absolute mess. Chaos. Crisis. Confusion. Despite my best intentions to live a better life, everything was falling apart.

Rather than feeling despair about this, I decided to see if it could be a healing crisis – just like I went through with my body when I took those herbs. This meant that things might get worse because they were about to get better. So when something seemed to go wrong, and I felt confused, upset, angry or defeated, I chose not to think of the situation as bad. Instead, I treated it as if I was going through a healing crisis. I expected that things were ultimately getting better – even if that meant the situation appeared to get worse in the short-term. Maybe if I just treated those emotional reactions as symptoms of a life-healing crisis, they would pass eventually and I would feel better. If I was in a healing crisis, then I must be doing something *right* because healing was taking place. That meant that a better situation would happen eventually. I just had to learn how to get through the crisis part first!

Instead of becoming depressed and fearful, I started to feel more optimistic – sort of like at the end of winter when you know spring is going to come, even though it hasn't happened yet. I just felt like something good was going to happen. I had hope for the first time in a long time and I began to dream of a more positive and happy future for myself. I might not be comfortable with the changes, but at least things were changing, and that is what I wanted. When situations became messy and confusing – which they often were at that time of transition for me – I took it as a sign that they were about to change into something better. I had a new belief: things fell apart so they could come back together in a new and improved way. I started to feel more empowered and confident that life was helping me get to what I wanted instead of believing that life was just something I had to push against. I began to trust in what was happening, even when it seemed confusing, rather than resisting it. I gained more energy, started to feel some happiness, and kept changing my attitude and dealing with my life from that different perspective. My life situation kept changing, and improving too.

So when a big challenge arose, I realised that the bigger the challenge, the bigger the improvement that was waiting for me on the other side. Instead of believing that a challenge was life saying no to me, I began to see it as life believing I was capable of more, and to step up and go with it because in overcoming that challenge, I would experience more happiness, confidence and empowerment. You could say that instead of hating the journey of life, I started to trust in it and love it.

I realised that I had to give up certain personality traits if I was going to be free from anxiety, depression and fear. Believing that the only way to be safe was to be in control was one of those things. I saw that chaos, crisis and confusion were natural signs of growth and I was only uncomfortable with those experiences when I didn't trust life. When I did trust life, and I believed it was trying to help me to be happier, I went through these growing phases more willingly. Chaos, crisis and confusion were growing pains. They didn't have to be so painful if I remembered to trust and chose to see them as a transitional phase helping me let go of what wasn't working in my life to embrace a life that was more suitable and satisfying.

So eventually I learned how to work with chaos, crisis and confusion, and realised that they were an invitation from my destiny. It was like I had a future self who was living a much better life, waving at me and calling out to me, saying, "Hey Alana, you'll enjoy your life so much more over here. There's some stuff that's going to seem like a challenge, but it will teach you things that will help you join me and live your better life much sooner!"

It can be the same for you. You have a future self living a better version of your life, which you'll enjoy more than you might have believed possible. That future self will call to you, just as mine did, through chaos, crisis and confusion, to help you get to your better life.

Perhaps you have already heard that call and your life seems to be spinning out of control, or you can't quite seem to find your way through confusion, or there is one crisis after another, and another, that seem to find their way to your door. Whatever is happening for you, no matter how much you may think that this is all there is, I can promise you that it is not the final story. It's just one chapter in your life drawing to an end so a new one can begin.

In this book I'll teach you how to answer the call to your better life, how to begin that next chapter, so that the story of your life becomes one you enjoy more and more. I'll show you simple steps you can take to get through your chaos, crisis and confusion, and into the better life calling you forward. You'll feel more confident, trusting and optimistic. You'll enjoy the changes in your life, and you'll probably inspire others to live with less fear and more wisdom too. I hope that with this book, you'll find the process quicker and easier to figure out than I did, and begin to enjoy your life that much sooner.

So let's begin ...

A NOTE ON WORKING WITH THE GUIDED EXERCISES

The guided exercises included in the workbook section – Chapters 7 to 10 – have been designed to help you easily and effectively integrate the teachings of this book. It might seem really strange to do those guided exercises. You might wonder if they are doing anything at all, or if you are doing them correctly, especially if you tend to be a more intellectual than intuitive personality. If you feel that way, it's completely normal and understandable. The exercises have been designed to work beneath the conscious mind, encouraging a reprogramming of your subconscious mind, and even the cells of your body. That might sound quite dramatic, but information goes into our subconscious minds without us really thinking about it all the time. Have you ever had an advertising jingle stuck in your head and couldn't stop singing it for a while? Imagine having positive and helpful thoughts running through your mind constantly instead of songs about foodstuffs. You'd feel happier, more energetic and more optimistic almost instantly!

If you have ever tried to do something consciously and with a clear intention, only to end up doing something else – perhaps the exact opposite, such as starting a new diet by eating a cheesecake! – then you will have had firsthand experience of the power of the subconscious mind. You mean to go one way and you end up going another without knowing why. That is because the subconscious mind is what moves us. When it 'matches' our conscious intention, we make great strides, but when it doesn't, we feel like we want something to happen but just don't get there. Maybe we even seem to undermine ourselves by negative thinking or behaviours, even whilst we try to 'be positive' and make a change in ourselves or our lives.

That's okay. That's part of the (interesting!) journey of being human. It's just that when what we want to do and how we want to live seems *not* to be what is happening, then the subconscious mind needs an adjustment. It is useful to work with the conscious mind too, of course, with explanations and stories, to help us change the way we think and behave. But working with the subconscious mind through the guided exercises will amplify the transformation that this book can bring you, thereby helping you and your life change for the better that much more quickly and easily. You won't have to fight so much to bring about a happier way of being. It can just happen more easily and naturally. That being said, if a guided exercise feels right for you, do it, but if you don't feel like it at a given time, that's fine too. Perhaps you can go back to it in a day or so when you are ready to give it a go. There's no need to force things. Trust yourself.

In terms of actually doing these exercises in a practical sense, you can either read them as you go, or record them on the recording note-taking function of your mobile phone and play them back to yourself. If you are working through these exercises with a friend (or group of friends or colleagues, for example) or a family member, you may even like to have one person read the exercise aloud whilst the other completes the guided exercise.

Also, do not worry about if you are 'doing the exercise right'. Even just reading through it whilst paying attention is powerful enough to get the subconscious mind programmed with the sort of thought patterns and ideas that are going to help you. If you can read it aloud, all the better. If you can actually do the exercise as well, then that is wonderful too.

CHAPTER 1

The Call

· ·

GROWING OLDER OR GROWING UP?

Growing up is not the same thing as getting older. If you have ever known a fully-grown adult who lacks emotional or psychological maturity to 'match' their age, you'll understand this. Or maybe you've met a person who seems so much wiser and older than their years. Maybe you are one of those people. These sorts of old-before-their-time people are often called 'old souls'. There is a sort of old-age maturity to them, even when they are young. Perhaps this is because of responsibilities or struggles they went through earlier in life that forced them to grow up before their time.

Growing up instead of just getting older requires more than the passing of time. Growing up means that it isn't just your body that changes, but also your mind and your emotions. It means that you evolve as a person. That requires change on the inside, not just the outside. It is the difference between the caterpillar that remains a caterpillar, and the one that becomes a butterfly.

THE CALL OF THE WILD

The call of destiny for you and me is not so different to the force of nature that compels caterpillars to become butterflies, or winter to become spring.

It is natural that living things grow. Different spiritual traditions from around the world urge us to realise that the only thing that is constant is change itself. Life is constantly changing and nature is always growing. Even when the natural world is apparently in decline, it serves a purpose to prepare and fertilise for a new life cycle. Compost heaps can make for very abundant gardens!

Even though growth is natural though, it isn't always comfortable. A caterpillar goes through the process of breaking itself down into mush within its chrysalis in order to become a butterfly. This end result is extraordinarily beautiful, but the process is certainly not something that you'd imagine to be particularly pleasant or comfortable, no matter how cosy that chrysalis might be. The call of the wild is just that; it's wild. It isn't tame and we won't feel in control of the process of natural growth that happens within us. It's more about choosing how to respond to it as best we can with an understanding that although it might feel unsafe sometimes, it is actually helping us become what we are destined to be.

So whilst the idea of transforming into a butterfly – a symbol for your most beautiful and inspiring and extraordinary self – might seem appealing, in reality, when change starts to happen, you'll feel out of control. That is not something that most people find easy to experience or particularly appealing at all. Feeling out of control can trigger all your otherwise hidden suspicious, paranoid and fearful tendencies. Living life on the wild side can certainly take some getting used to, even if it is a way of life that will eventually allow for more happiness, wellbeing and satisfaction than you ever thought possible. It took me a while to learn how to enjoy living that way. I hated it at first and tried to use my will to force life to play by my rules rather than learning to play the game of life. It was a futile struggle, but I just didn't know any better at the time.

You might have a similar response to the feeling of your own life being wrenched out of your hands by circumstances beyond your control. If you are a strong sort of personality and a bit rebellious (like me!) you might try to force things to go the way you want them to go. Rather than learning to navigate the path of the river, you might try to force it to go in a particular direction. You try to direct nature rather than learn to let her guide you.

There is a myth from ancient Greece about a daring young man who has a dream. His name is Icarus. He wants to fly. He makes some wings, straps them on, and off he goes. It goes great for a while, but when it's time to return to earth, as all human beings are meant to do, he isn't interested. He gets hooked on the powerful rush of soaring and instead of honouring the natural law of 'what goes up must come down', he wants to play by his own rules. He thinks he can outsmart Nature's law of the wild, and so he begins to fly higher and higher. He feels so high (pun intended) that he decides he will fly to the sun! What a legend he will be! He does turn out to be a legend, just not in the way he expected. What he doesn't think about is that his wings are held together with wax. As he flies higher and higher, the heat of the sun melts the wax, his wings fall off, and well, you can imagine how that all ends. The law of 'what goes up must come down' won in the end after all. It's not the most intelligent moment in human history, but we can learn from his mistake though.

There is nothing wrong with wanting to fly high and be free. Isn't that one of the great gifts in becoming a butterfly? It's just that resisting the natural process and trying to control it, to make it happen in the way we want it to happen, won't end well. That is the story that Icarus, the brave and slightly stupid young man, can teach us. Life knows what it is doing. We need to learn how to accept life, to trust where it is leading us and not let our minds get carried away with what we think should happen. Instead, we need to learn to participate with more relish in what is happening. We can dream big and life means to support us in growing into our dreams. But for that to happen, *we have to grow through it to go through it*, not fight against life in the process, even if it sometimes seems to be leading us somewhere we don't want to go (like back down to earth).

This might sound passive, like we may as well just spend the rest of our lives tucked under a blanket on the lounge, eating chocolates and watching the latest television series for hours at a time, and not really do anything. That's not what acceptance means though.

Accepting our lives means showing up. It means saying yes to whatever is happening and working our way through it – like working through a puzzle, a mystery or a game. It's about being willing to participate in life, not just watch someone else's on television (even though that may be entertaining at times).

Eventually I learned what Icarus might have found helpful to realise before his adventure in flight. I had to stop trying to use my strength of will to force things to work out the way I wanted. Instead, I could use that inner strength to respond to life as though it was my friend, rather than my enemy. Then things could work out according to a better plan, and actually in a better way than I could have imagined for myself. Sure, tough love would happen sometimes, but my friend loved me and wanted to help me in the best way possible. So if that was through tough love at times, then it's just that tough love was needed then. I realised that my life would change (for the better!) if I was willing to change my approach to life.

Now I realise that it's a good thing I didn't get my way – I would have missed out on a lot of happiness actually. I did learn that we don't need to worry and it's safe to trust in life, that things are actually sorting themselves out at the time even when you don't think so. When you choose to change your attitude and approach to life, things will change. Some of the changes – even some of the losses – will be a relief. It's also likely that some of the changes will seem like the worst things in the world, and you'll wonder how you are supposed to make lemonade out of the lemons life seems to be handing you.

There will be times when we are confronted with losing something we would rather not lose that needs to end for us to grow. We'd rather not have to grow at all, preferring to stick with what we know, and remain a happily hungry caterpillar rather than go through all the ups and downs required to become a butterfly. Yet if it's your destiny to outgrow your caterpillar-ness, then it's going to happen. Just like winter is going to become spring, and spring will become summer, and so on. It is nature. It is life. It's your destiny.

Now sometimes destiny lures us to her with a sweet song, and we willingly dance to her tune, but sometimes we are hiding so much from her, so afraid of what she might ask of us, that the only way she can get through is to give us a mighty kick up the behind. It can hurt at the time, but it also gets us moving in the right direction.

If the trigger for your growth is something you don't want – like a loss of some kind – then it can be hard to be grateful for it, to see the positive side and move through it willingly. You may feel like life is forcing you to do something you don't want to do. That's understandable. I have felt the same way at times, but the force of nature is a powerful thing to resist. Trying to do so leaves us feeling sick and exhausted and way off course in our lives. We also miss out on the benefit of a helping hand lurking behind the things that happen in our lives – even those things that feel more like a slap than a tickle.

Rather than trying to resist life, it's smarter that we learn how to cope with the inevitable changes that will take place in the best way possible. Otherwise it would be like sailing our little boat on the ocean, when a storm starts to whip up some huge waves. Do you think that throwing a tantrum and saying, "Stop, I don't like those waves; they are too big!" is going to do much? It would be more helpful to put your energy into remembering how to swim. Maybe we can even learn to enjoy the transformation. Maybe we can realise that that storm is moving us to a new and exciting destination, even if we do get a little damp in the process. When we realise that change is natural, resisting it can seem a bit silly. It's sort of like frolicking about in a sundress in the middle of winter because we don't want the summer to end. It makes more sense (and ultimately feels better) to change our attitudes (and our wardrobes) and learn to enjoy cosy, cold winter evenings in front of the fireplace for the duration of winter instead.

Or maybe you don't resist the changes starting to happen. Maybe they are things you want and you get excited about it. You may even want it to happen faster. You might be very keen to become a butterfly. You want to feel free and fly. It sounds great! Then it can be a matter of letting your inspiration come down to earth and going through the small steps day by day that need to happen within you, which may be confronting some fears and making some choices that intuitively feel right for you, even though to your mind they may seem risky. Your positive attitude will become the sail on your ship so that life's gusts and breezes make your journey to your destiny a quicker and smoother one.

BEEP! BEEP! BEEP!

Inside each one of us there is a timer, something like an in-built alarm clock. That alarm clock is set to wake us at a particular time. You could call it the alarm clock of your destiny. When it's your time, it rings and you (and your life) get stirred up.

For some people, it will start ringing when they are very young, and seem to keep ringing for most of their life! This will be either because they find it hard to embrace the idea of change, or that they are changing but are capable of even more change and life wants them to keep going and growing. These are the people who will go through many changes in their lives, sometimes to the point that it feels like living a completely different life having changed so much from the person they once felt they were and how they once lived. Often there will be a lot of challenges as the 'triggers' for those changes happen. They might feel like they go through the process of being a caterpillar and becoming a butterfly more than once in their lifetime.

For others, the inner alarm clock might suddenly 'go off' later in life. Everything has seemed pretty 'normal' and then all of a sudden, they are thrown into a spin where life goes anywhere but according to plan. They might think they are too old to be questioning life or going through midlife crises or some such thing, but actually, they are just growing because destiny is calling them and it's their time. It doesn't matter if life seems to be perfect or seems to be a mess; when it's time for change, it comes. Our job is to respond to the natural urge for growth and not try to fight it from a place of fear.

Although our inner alarm clocks might go off at different times, what we all have in common is that they are persistent. It's a bit like a phone ringing, but instead of it ringing for a little while and then stopping and going to voicemail, this call of destiny just keeps ringing. And ringing. And getting louder. And more obvious. This continues until it becomes too loud to ignore.

What that looks like in your work is when there's an issue that you know with an inner 'niggle' isn't quite right. But for whatever reason, you try to sweep it under the carpet and hope nothing comes of it. Eventually the niggle turns into a realisation that if you don't do something there's going to be trouble. If you still avoid responding to that, then the niggle turns into trouble and keeps getting bigger. It's sort of like a snowball that started with a single little rock but is now the size of a small car heading right for you! So an example could be that you might start off feeling unhappy at work, but don't take the steps to leave and perhaps retrain in a different field. Maybe you are scared that this is the only job you'll get and that fear keeps you prisoner in a situation that actually isn't right for you. So you end up with anxiety, or depression, or eventually some sort of accident or illness that prevents you from going to work at all. That's some tough love from life to get you to change course into something that's right for you.

In a meditation class one evening, a participant shared a story from her life with the group. She was a workaholic. More than that, she just couldn't sit still. Her body and mind were so tightly wound up and locked with tension that she was not ever really able to feel happy or relaxed. She wanted to learn how to feel happy and relaxed though. That's why she ended up in meditation class. Learning meditation made her more observant and aware of herself. She realised she was always *doing* something. She couldn't just give herself even a little bit of time off to relax and enjoy herself. She always had to be working or be busy with some project or other. Working in her three jobs, refusing to give herself some slack, she eventually had an accident and broke her arm. Well, she couldn't drive to work then. She sat at home with limited movement and, as you might imagine, it was rather difficult for her. Weeks of doing nothing much loomed before her and she couldn't stand the thought of it. So she decided that with one broken arm she could still paint the house. Yes, that's right. She got on a ladder and began painting. She got through a portion of the first room and, of course, fell off the ladder and broke her other arm. That finally got the message through to her. It took two broken arms before she would give herself a break of a different kind. She decided that even if she couldn't stand the idea of taking a rest, she'd better get used to it because otherwise she might break a leg or two and not be able to stand at all!

Now this is a rather extreme example, and in over a decade of working with clients I've never heard another story quite like it, but I included it here to let you know that you really don't want to get into tough love with life if you can avoid it. Sometimes you can't avoid it and there's a challenge that you need to face, but in the case of the workaholic woman, she knew what she needed to do for herself and although it was hard for her, it wasn't impossible. She was so strong-willed though that she didn't respond to the gentler hints. There was no other way she was going to stop working herself into an early grave. She actually had a sense of humour about the whole situation. And she chose to learn from it.

You certainly don't have to be frightened of what life will bring to you. You just need to listen to yourself. If you are unhappy, you are meant to do something about it. If you are miserable, then you need to do something about it before it turns into depression or despair or worse. You don't have to be scared, but you do have to be real with yourself. When it's time for change, you'll know it. You'll feel it. It's not usually a comfortable feeling. It can be exciting, it can be terrifying, or a mixture of both, but you'll know that a new life is calling you. And if you listen to the call, it is actually going to be to your benefit, not just in avoiding further unhappiness or suffering, but also in the increase of happiness and satisfaction that the new life wants to bring to you.

A VERY HUNGRY CATERPILLAR

Let's go back to our caterpillar friend for a moment. He's cute, green and lives happily enough munching on whatever juicy green leaves he can find. He doesn't think too much about what's going on around him, unless something or someone comes too close in which case he'll scurry for cover or curl up in a little ball. Then once danger passes, it's back to munching on green leaves and growing plump.

Then one day, his world changes – just like that. He is drawn into a strange and overpowering process. He withdraws from his little world of leaf-eating and growing plump, and begins to wrap himself up. He creates a chrysalis around himself. His world is no longer green and lush, but a tight and shiny cocoon. Within that cocoon he begins to fall apart. It feels a bit crazy, a bit like dying, but something in him cannot resist it. He just has to do it. He has to answer the call of his destiny.

Eventually, he is no longer a caterpillar anymore. He doesn't feel like much of anything, except a puddle of mush. But from that mush, held together by the chrysalis, something is growing and changing. The same force of destiny that drew him away from the lush world of green leaves, and into his chrysalis, and into mush, is the same force transforming him, growing his antennae, his new body, his new legs, his new wings! Yes, wings! He is destined to become a butterfly!

The truth is only revealed at the end of the process. All the way through, this little caterpillar was very brave and trusting, even when it seemed like his world was ending – which it was! But it wasn't that the end was really THE END. It was actually the start of something new.

When the butterfly emerges, he is transformed. He can fly. He sees the world and experiences it in a much more open and free way. He is beautiful. He makes people laugh and brings them happiness. He is light and joyful. He is alive. It seems utterly impossible; it must be a miracle. Actually it's just the call of destiny. Acorns become oak trees. Ugly ducklings become beautiful swans. Caterpillars become butterflies. You become the being you are destined to be.

THE CALL OF DESTINY (OR WHEN EVERYTHING SEEMS TO GO WRONG)

Imagine how strange it is for that caterpillar, happily eating green leaves for most of his life and then just suddenly thinking, *I'm done with this. Time to stop doing the thing I love the most (eating) and go cocoon myself in darkness.* It's a bit weird. Other caterpillars might wonder what's wrong with him. Why has he become so antisocial? Does he think he's too good for that leaf-eating life now? What's so special about him anyway?

He and the other caterpillars don't know he's going to be given an amazing gift at the end of his unexpected withdrawal from life as they've known it, unless one of them happens to be a caterpillar blessed with psychic ability. All he knows is that he has to leave his life behind, no longer do what he found familiar and pleasurable and, instead, go and do something downright confusing and chaotic (become caterpillar mush, grow wings and longer legs etc.) so he can be reformed and reborn as something new. Seems sort of crazy really. If you didn't know it happened in nature all the time, you probably wouldn't even believe it was possible.

When that same force of destiny calls us, we might feel rather like the caterpillar. The things we once knew and enjoyed might not hold the same appeal for us anymore. We might feel like we've outgrown our old lives. Maybe we cocoon ourselves intentionally. For some reason we withdraw from the world, don't want to socialise, or maybe feel depressed and not much like being in company. Or maybe we try to force ourselves to still go out and play but it doesn't feel as good as it used to because it's a bit forced, rather like running from something. We might lack the same amount of energy as we used to have for life and wonder if there's something wrong with us. We might feel anxious in social settings, not really as sure of ourselves as we would like. We are meant to be cocooning, and if we try to force ourselves to live life the way we would when we aren't in our chrysalis, it won't feel quite right.

People might wonder what's wrong with you, just like those judgemental caterpillars thumbing their caterpillar noses at our soon-to-be-a-butterfly friend. You might wonder what's wrong with you too! But there's nothing wrong with you. You are just growing. When destiny calls you, it means things are due to change. You are due to change. It's your time, and you are going to have to leave behind what you have known, to embrace a new stage in your life.

Sometimes the change in you or your life is so obvious, shocking or powerful that you know you can't go back to how things were. Sometimes an event will happen, or a person will say something, or you will have a moment where you see the truth in a situation, and it just changes everything. You can't undo it. Maybe it changes you instantly from the inside and you get 'mad as hell and not going to take it anymore', and you stand up for yourself and refuse to be a doormat. Or you just can't stay living in a house or town where you are constantly reminded of what isn't in your life anymore, and even though you've loved it, you have to move on. Or it might be a crisis that makes you question what you believe in, changing how you view the world and how you want to live your life. It might be an event beyond your control that shakes up your world, turning everything you have known upside down – a natural disaster, a relationship ending, a job dismissal, a loss of a loved one.

Even if the people around you don't seem to be changed by it as much as you, you cannot pretend you are the same anymore. This doesn't mean you are weak or that there's something wrong with you. It means that for you, this event was part of your inner alarm clock going off. It was meant to wake you up, to shake you up. It might not be the right time for others in your life to change, but when you have received your call from destiny, you won't be able to go back to your life as it was before. If you try to, it will fail you. Either it will not be there for you in some way and you'll feel that even if you wanted to, you aren't going to be 'allowed' to go back to it, or if you can go back, it will feel fake as though you are just going through the motions and lying to yourself because it's not who you are anymore. Eventually you'll need to let it go and step into the adventure life is sending your way instead.

Of course, it might not feel like much of an adventure at first. Whilst some of us are blessed with an adventure that is a dream come true, for many of us, getting to the place of happiness requires a tour of duty through some fairly confronting changes first. In that case, the adventure can seem more like a nightmare. Often this is because you are being pushed to confront your worst fears.

Our fears are where we hold ourselves back. If there is an opportunity that can change your life and help you become more of who you are and there is a fear between you and it, then you can guarantee that your destiny is going to push you to deal with that fear. Not because it is mean or not loving, but because it wants you to have what you want and that fear has to be removed so you can receive the goodness headed your way. You might feel as though whatever you have tried to avoid is right up close and personal. You might fear many things: not having money, being rejected, losing your status, feeling alone, being discovered to be a 'fraud', the loss of a loved one, falling out with a family member, business failure, or an idol falling from grace leaving you wondering if you'll ever be able to find your way through the mess and feel happy, secure, safe and peaceful ever again – or even for the first time. These 'bad things' are a sign that life is trying to give you something great and that whatever is 'failing' for you is getting in the way. You need to clear that out and be open to receive something new (and improved) instead.

For some people, the call to adventure is a little less like a brass band blaring in your ear and more like a soft flute in the distance. It is there, but just not so blatant or sudden. Perhaps you just feel confused and not sure why; it might have been building up for a while. Maybe inside you there is a niggling doubt. You try to push it down but it always manages to sneak back into your mind when you aren't expecting it. It might be a doubt about your marriage, your work, about how you are living your life. You might be terrified of getting into that doubt for fear it will just wreck everything and then you won't know what to do. But of course, life will help you find your next step, as if dropping breadcrumbs along your destined path, providing a guiding hand to help you take step, after step, after step, even if it feels sometimes like driving on a foggy night when you can't see much of the road ahead of you.

So your call to adventure might be a huge event, big and life-shatteringly dramatic, or quiet, internal and only noticeable to you and those that know you well enough to spot when you are not feeling quite right. Whatever you need to grow is what will come to you. Some of us are meant to take a very transformational journey in life, where our fortunes change dramatically and we seem to become a completely different person. The people in your life may expect you to act the way you did a year ago, and yet once you start your adventure, you won't want or need to act like that anymore. You won't feel like that person. You won't want to munch on green leaves, you'll want to be flitting about the sky testing your wings instead.

Even if your destiny seems to be asking you to do something that seems less dramatic than a complete transformation of who you are – like perhaps forgiving someone, or learning to relate to a loved one in a different way – it is still just as important. When it is important to you, it is important. Don't think that if you are asked to think about your daughter-in-law differently, accept your son's sexuality or to forgive your ex-wife and get on with your life, that this is small potatoes compared to needing to change careers or move to the other side of the world. What the most challenging thing is for you – whether on the surface of things that seems big or small – is what destiny will bring up when you get the call to new life. That's why it feels so chaotic, like a crisis, so incredibly confusing. You will be tested to let go of whatever you fear the most, whatever is going to make you feel like mush. Then you will be free to let go and allow life to move you into your destiny.

"HI, I'M DESTINY," SHE SAYS. "GREAT TO MEET YOU!" (AND THEN SHE KICKS THE FRONT DOOR DOWN)

The reason we feel chaos, crisis and confusion in our lives is because the call of destiny rarely walks up to us, like a charming flight attendant, and says, "Hi, I'm Destiny. Your flight will land as planned, but we are hitting some turbulence … please don't worry, here's a stiff drink and remember to stay calm."

More typically, she appears like a knife-wielding ninja in the middle of the night, waking you up with a start and looking rather grim and perhaps even a bit terrifying! She's not there to harm you though. She is planning to use that knife to cut free the binds you have tied around yourself. Those ties might be beliefs holding you back which need to be challenged so you can be freed, or situations that feel familiar but keep you locked in habits preventing you from reaching the next stage in life.

You might not want to leave the comfort of what is known, and yet, if you don't, you'll end up stifled and blocked. It's a bit like refusing to move from the crib and into a bigger child's bed when it's time to move on. In time, you'll end up cramped and uncomfortable if you try to keep sleeping in that crib (or it will just fall apart because it won't be able to hold your weight). Sometimes it's just time to venture beyond what you've known, even if it has been appropriate for you in the past.

You might wonder why the whole experience has to happen unexpectedly. Often it's simply because if you saw destiny coming along, clear as day, you'd think, *Oh no, that's gonna hurt! I'm getting outta here!* Then she'd have to chase you through back alleys in Chinatown, dodging crates of chickens and vegetables falling all over the place as you scramble to get away from her hot pursuit, climbing through someone's apartment as the family quietly tries to eat dinner, hiding behind large potted plants, telegraph poles and fire hydrants, and all sorts of ridiculous cinematic-style faffing about which just wastes time, just trying to elude her.

So when Destiny comes knocking at your door, or kicking it down (as she sometimes prefers), it is rarely something you anticipate. You might not have a lot of time to think about it, and certainly not much time to work out how to avoid it. You just need to deal with what is happening.

What will be happening is that something you are holding on to will fail you in some way. It's failing you to free you, but of course we don't typically feel that it is at first. So it could be a marriage, a career, a business deal, a hero, your health, an identity you've held on to or a religious or political affiliation that seems to have 'feet made of clay' and disappoints you, lets you down, falls from grace or otherwise generally leaves you feeling abandoned, betrayed or rejected. The world you have known suddenly feels too small or has fallen apart. Maybe you still love the people in your life but can't relate to them like you used to, or perhaps they suddenly seem superficial and you wonder if there could maybe be more to life than you once thought. When this happens, blame often emerges. It's a way to postpone processing the inevitable pain of loss, even if at some level you accept it's needed. So that could mean blaming someone else for not behaving as you want them to, or blaming yourself because you think you've failed somehow. You may wonder if you could have or should have done something differently in the past – maybe worked harder, or tried to fit in more, or something! Then perhaps you could have avoided whatever is happening.

It is wise to learn from your behaviour so that you repeat the things that work and learn a different way for the things that don't work so well. But even if you did all that you could do absolutely perfectly, when Destiny comes a-knocking, life is going to get messy, no matter how much effort you put into trying to keep things neat and ordered. As the saying goes, 'if you are going to make a cake, you'll have to break a few eggs', which means that when you are going to cook up a truly delicious life, you are also going to have to do some cleaning up.

ETERNAL OPTIMISTS AND CHOCOLATE BARS

Once upon a time, there lived a king in Africa. He had a close friend who travelled with him everywhere. His friend was an optimist. No matter what happened, he would say, "This is good!"

One day the king and his friend went hunting together. The friend loaded up the king's rifle and handed it to him. They didn't realise that he had loaded it incorrectly. So when the king fired, he lost his thumb!

"This is good!" exclaimed his friend. The king, who was now missing a thumb, decided his friend was not only dangerous but an idiot as well. He had him locked up in jail.

Some time later, the king went hunting again, but this time on his own!

Africa was a dangerous place however, and he was captured by a tribe of cannibals who took him to their village, stoked a fire, and began to tie him up. They tied his legs and tied his arms. Then they noticed he had no thumb. They were a superstitious people and would not eat anyone who was less than whole, so they set the king free.

Feeling grateful and remorseful, the king went to his friend in jail and apologised for locking him up, saying that his lost thumb had actually saved his life. But his friend just said, "Don't worry – this is good too!"

The king was very puzzled. He asked his friend, "But how could spending this past year in jail be good?"

And the friend replied, "Because if I wasn't in here, I would have been hunting with you, and that tribe would have eaten me instead!"

We can choose to view what happens in our lives with optimism. Perhaps we can't quite pull off the same level of unquestioning and radical optimism as the friend of the African king, but we can certainly give life the benefit of the doubt.

Whilst it's great to celebrate the things going right in life, you'll actually experience even more of those good things when you are willing to see the things that seem to be going wrong in a different way. This is what it means to give life the benefit of the doubt.

You could imagine it like this. You are eating a yummy chocolate bar. You are happy eating it. Then suddenly it is snatched away from you. You are shocked and upset. You want it back! You might try to fight the hand that took it away, grabbing for it even whilst it is disappearing from your view. You might feel angry and wonder why it had to happen. What did you do? You just want what you had before. It isn't fair! You miss that yummy sweet chocolate!

When you give life the benefit of the doubt you say to yourself, "Okay, this has happened. I didn't want it to happen like this, but it has. Maybe there is some benefit in this experience for me. Maybe, even though I don't understand it, I can choose to trust it and just *wait and see what else might happen* and how this can be for the best for me."

In time, you may see that there was a good and helpful reason why that chocolate bar was taken from you. You were still hungry. So you went looking for something else to eat. You found a nourishing – and actually rather more delicious – feast. It was better for you, tasted better too, and satisfied you far more. To be motivated to go looking for it though, you had to get a little hungry. If you were 'allowed' to simply continue to eat your chocolate, you might take too long to realise what you were missing (or you might not have realised it at all) and missed an opportunity that was destined to come your way at a certain time. Hence the intervention of the chocolate-grabbing hand of life.

Of course when it isn't a sweet snack, but perhaps a relationship, a high-status job, financial security, a healthy or slim body, or comforting sense of familiar identity whisked away from you by circumstances beyond your control, then the pain can seem far worse than a tantrum over a sweet being taken away.

The best way to deal with destiny yanking something out of your hands is to trust in what is happening, even when it is painful or you don't understand it. Have faith that if something is taken away, there is meant to be an even better option soon to replace it. You don't have to like it. If you have lost something, you still need to mourn it – and even get angry or feel whatever else you feel such as fear, doubt, guilt, uncertainty – but you do not allow these things to become the final analysis. They are not the end of the story. They aren't even the end of the chapter, just the first few sentences. There is a whole series of events that are going to unfold from that one loss designed to give to you something you are destined to receive, the feast that you can only receive when you are willing to give up the snack. That means mourning the loss, but not getting stuck in it. If you spend the rest of your time on this green earth whingeing about the loss of the snack, you'll get bitter. And go hungry! Why not give life the benefit of the doubt and as soon as you can summon up the courage, venture out in search of a feast instead. Life will help you find it. Just follow your nose! When something smells right, go for it. If it doesn't, it's not for you so steer clear.

This is easier said than done, no doubt, at least until you get used to it. You can learn how to trust and be guided by life by experimenting with different ways to be, rather than trying to hold on to how things once were. The more you allow change to happen – startling and abrupt as it may be at the time – the more you are saying to the universe, "I know you've got my back. I know you are cooking up something here, and I trust that you are trying to show me the best way to fulfilment of my own destiny." That is giving life the benefit of the doubt.

When alternatives present themselves – opportunities, new chances – we accept, provided they 'smell right' to us. If they don't seem quite right, we wait, knowing that our invitation to the feast is already issued and that it's only a matter of finding our way there now, with less distractions (the chocolate bar has gone) and more motivation because of that.

Typically, we won't know what the bigger plan is at the time destiny stomps into our lives. We'll just know that change is happening. If you feel like you are being asked to let go of many things, perhaps more than others, then know it's because there's a bigger pull to new life for you. The more dramatic the transformation of you and your life is meant to be, the more chaos, crisis and confusion will precede it.

WAKING UP

Sometimes we feel the call to a new life within us, but we do our best to ignore it for a while. We huddle under the covers when she appears in the middle of the night, and try to pretend that it's not really happening. This is what is going on when we stay in a relationship we know we are meant to leave behind, or don't quite understand why that job is slowly driving us into depression, or refuse to stand up to that 'friend' who drains the very will to live out of us (because, you know, that might not be a 'nice' thing to do).

Eventually however, that inner alarm clock becomes something we can no longer ignore. My personal experience of that was when I was working for a management consultant. She was not a person I enjoyed working for, nor was it a job that I enjoyed *in any way at all*. I stayed in it for around nine or so months, which was rather a long time to be in something you didn't like at all, but not as long as five years at university studying something you didn't like, so I figured I was at least improving in my life choices somewhat. Being in that job felt like a pregnancy in a way, a sort of giving birth to myself, like the caterpillar. I had left a legal career behind and was growing into readiness to step onto a path as a healer, which is where I wanted to be. That job was advertised as looking for a person 'with heart' and the culture of the organisation – at least in theory, if not in the reality that I experienced – was about raising consciousness and innovation, all of which appealed to me.

Then one day, after virtually every single day during those nine months feeling pretty damn awful (it felt a lot longer than nine months, let me tell you), something burst. Maybe I was giving birth to my new self and it was the waters breaking, metaphorically speaking. It certainly felt like an inner tsunami of emotion I couldn't fight against. I just remember standing at the threshold of the office door and thinking so vividly, *If I keep forcing myself to walk through this door, I think I am actually just going to start screaming and never stop!*

Through sheer bloody-mindedness and force of will, I did walk through that door that last morning, without screaming, but not without resigning. Even though there were so many uncertainties in my heart about leaving, one of the primary ones being that I was in more debt than I had ever been (for me, misery loved shopping) and I had no other source of income, I knew within every cell of my being that I just had to walk away from that job. It seemed completely crazy to every part of me, except my heart that just said loud and true, "Leave!" So that's what I did.

After the absolute exhilaration of feeling free and utterly relieved about never having to step foot in that office again, I began a new adventure. That was the adventure of how on earth was I going to support myself financially without a regular job! I will talk about how that crisis sorted itself out, because of course it did, later on. For now, it's enough to say that in the moment of wondering if I was actually going to be physically able to walk through that office door on that last day, my inner alarm was beeping so loudly I couldn't ignore it anymore.

When our inner alarm clocks starts ringing, it's wake up time. We are being asked to be honest about where our lives aren't working. Sometimes we use false gratitude as a way to avoid being completely honest with ourselves. We might hide behind 'oh it could be worse, I could have the life that so-and-so has … ' or that old stand-by, 'think of all the starving children in Africa'. If you are really moved by starving children in Africa, do something constructive to help their quality of life, perhaps through making a donation to a legitimate charity, but don't use their plight as an excuse to not live the best life you have been lucky enough to be given. Gratitude is great, but trying to stick with what isn't working because it feels safer to be with the 'devil you know' is not gratitude. It's just not being as brave as you could be.

If we keep ourselves locked in a job we hate, or in a relationship that makes us miserable (even if love is supposedly involved), or if we keep acting in ways that make us feel unwell, unhappy and unfulfilled, then the call is going to become louder, and louder, and louder, until we are forced to answer it. By the time it reaches that stage, it will feel like the situation is completely out of your control, and you will have to do something about it or it will all end rather badly. You could say that sometimes life is going to get our attention – to lead us into a better life – whether we like it at the time or not!

UNVEILING A HIDDEN POWER

When you admit that something isn't working as well as it could – your career, your relationships, your health, your finances, your direction in life and so on – then you give yourself a surprising power. This is the power of choice and of change. You cannot change anything if you don't admit to there being an issue in the first place. If you are in denial, pretending everything is okay when deep down you are feeling depressed, anxious, unhappy, frightened or unfulfilled in your life now, then you are also ignoring your power.

Most of us think that powerful people are the ones with a lot of money, high-flying corporate jobs and perhaps an island hideaway, a team of lawyers and accountants, or even a Swiss bank account or two stashed away somewhere. Yet no matter whether someone is highly educated, or wealthy, employed or not, every person has inner power. Inner power is more important than things that look powerful on the surface. Many wealthy people will tell you that fortunes can change – and even be completely wiped away – in an instant. A great career can take a nosedive based on one bad decision. A divorce may cut your circle of powerful friends and contacts down to none, casting you out of a glamorous life with social status virtually overnight. Life is anything but predictable and there is no guarantee that the things that seem to give people power today will be there tomorrow.

To think otherwise is a bit like building an incredible sandcastle. It might be the most amazing, spectacular, impressive and huge sandcastle anyone has ever seen. You might spend absolutely ages building it. People might gravitate towards it and simply stare, saying, "Oooh how wonderful! Wouldn't life be so incredible if I had a sandcastle like that!" Every person on the beach comes by to look at it and feels jealous and wants one of their own!

Then a great big wave comes along and it's gone in about two seconds.

Fortunately there is a power within us that cannot get washed away. Every time there is a wave on the beach washing away some person's sandcastle, or even our own, that inner power actually gets *stronger*. In fact the only thing that weakens it is when we forget it's there and neglect to use it. But even then, it doesn't go away; it just waits for us to come back to it. It's sort of like a truly hardy and forgiving houseplant. When we pay attention to it, it grows and thrives.

Or you could imagine your inner power like electricity. You are the lamp that is plugged into the power point on the wall. Electricity is flowing, but it isn't until you flip the switch that it flows into the lamp and presto – you have light. Suddenly you can see in the dark and although you still may not see all there is to see, you can at least see around you. Life becomes a bit easier to fathom and navigate. That electricity is always there, but if you don't flick the switch on to get it flowing, the lamp remains in darkness. You can't see a damn thing and it's harder to find your way. It's not impossible, but harder than it needs to be.

The way you flick the switch to access your inner power is with your attitude. You choose to see life as guiding you, not out to get you. You believe that you can grow through whatever comes your way. That sort of attitude of trust in life and trust in yourself gets your light glowing and inner power flowing. Everyone has it within them; the only difference between those trying to see in the dark and those that can see more clearly is whether they are holding the right attitude. And as our attitude is one of the few things completely within our own control, this is something to feel confident about.

Our inner power gives us the ability to choose how we respond to the sandcastle-destroying waves of life. Instead of only noticing what that wave is washing away, we can also keep our eyes open for what it might be washing onto the shore. Sometimes life will have us at the top of the mountain, and at other times, right down at the bottom and starting all over again.

Our inner power gives us the courage to deal with anything that comes our way, whether we are flying high (though hopefully not quite as high as Icarus) or landing flat on our behinds after taking a tumble (when we do get a bit too Icarus-like). It gives us the guts to be honest and admit when things are not working. It gives us a positive attitude, so we believe we can tackle any issue in our lives. It makes us brave, adaptable, and clever enough to learn from our mistakes. It makes us humble enough to laugh when we truly stuff something up (because, you must admit, sometimes our mistakes are pretty funny – perhaps not right at the time when they are happening, but as dinner party conversation sometime later? Hilarious!).

You can enjoy the sandcastle while it lasts, of course. Why not? You want to enjoy what life has to offer. With the guidance of this book, you'll naturally start to develop an even more positive attitude, and from that place, you'll naturally start to attract many more of those gifts because you'll be more trusting and therefore more open to receive. It's hard to give a gift to someone who is so guarded that they are huddled up in a ball waiting for something bad to happen. If you put a lovely gift next to them on the ground, they won't see it all huddled up like that.

I live in a part of the world that is surrounded by trees and bush reserves, and about two feet outside my front door is a miniature bushland with a rock face and dripping water. It's practically a tiny rainforest. So often enough, I get little visitors of the creepy crawly variety venturing inside, even though they would be more at home outside. I usually grab a piece of paper and gently scoop them up before depositing them back in the forest we share between us. Sometimes I do this so gently they hardly realise it's happening. One minute they are crawling over my carpet, the next moment across foolscap with my scrawling handwriting on it, and a moment later onto fresh forest mulch in the tiny forest garden again. Everyone is happy.

However, sometimes a little visitor senses that the carpet is not quite the same as the foolscap paper, or they just don't like my writing, but whatever the reason, when I scoop them off the carpet and onto the paper, they curl up defensively and my job of compassionate relocation becomes more difficult. First of all, they roll. So I am not only trying to open the screen door with my elbow whilst balancing a piece of paper, I am also trying to gently manoeuvre the paper back and forth to keep the curled up little critter from rolling about excessively (it makes me think they'd get really dizzy and it wouldn't be a pleasant experience), or rolling off the edge altogether and falling what would be rather a long way for such a little creature. The whole process becomes more stressful for him and trickier for me.

Of course, he doesn't know I am not seeking to hurt him. Maybe he's survived for a long time with those defences intact; however, when it comes time for something good to happen, such as a relocation to the forest floor, those same defences turn an otherwise helpful event into an experience that is frightening.

When we are in touch with our inner power, we are confident enough to handle things. Because the light is on, we can also see when the hand of life is reaching out to assist us, and accept that help rather than bite the hand that feeds, so to speak. We stay more open to life. It's not like you can't defend yourself if you need to from such an open state. In fact, because you see more clearly (rather than from behind many walls of protection, or with your arms crossed over your face), your ability to perceive a genuine threat to your wellbeing, as opposed to a compassionate intervention by life, becomes more accurate. You won't respond with fear to things that don't need to be frightening. If fear is a helpful response – for example, you fear for your safety and quickly move out of harm's way if a car suddenly swerves too close – then you'll be able to react appropriately, more swiftly too, because you can see more clearly. When you are in defensive mode, you can't see clearly. Nor can you really tell the difference between a genuine threat and something making you uncomfortable but that is actually very helpful, and which may even be the very thing that saves your sanity. In defensive mode your reactions and decisions are not going to keep you safe. They just keep you in the dark.

It is your inner power you can rely upon to enable you to respond in a smarter way to what life delivers to your door, even when those deliveries might seem most unexpected or even unappealing at first glance. It is your inner power that gives you the ability to engage and transform whatever life sends you into something helpful and constructive, especially if you are getting a kick in the pants from life to move forward.

In such moments, it can be too easy to curl up like those little creatures I mentioned and feel afraid. But when you are in touch with your inner power, you can acknowledge the pain and then ask yourself how you can grow and become happier through the experience. At first, the only thing you might think of is, *Well, I survived it!* So you'll gain some confidence in your strength. That's an important realisation. Good for you! Yet I promise you there'll be something more in the experience, something more wonderful, but you may just need to walk a few steps along your life path before you can look back and see the benefit of what took place. Then it can become something you are happy to have experienced (and not just because it makes for entertaining dinner party conversation). You'll be grateful because with your inner power flowing, you'll be able to see more clearly. And so, even if it takes months or years to understand how the situation helped you, you will do so in time, even if what happened to you seemed like the toughest sort of tough love at the time.

Being able to feel safe and trust in life isn't about where you begin in life, the privilege that you have socially or financially, or even how much you have earned. It's all about your attitude. Don't think that having more money, a better body, a more impressive job title or successful relationship is going to prevent destiny from giving you a kick sometimes. People with the super fantastic-looking sandcastles actually have the same sorts of problems that other people do. What solves problems and changes you and your life in a good way, is having enough inner power to allow for growth. Throwing money at something doesn't bring growth. Using your influence to try and manipulate people through fear doesn't bring growth. Your inner power brings growth. That is what makes you brave and smart enough to face whatever life sends your way and even turn adversity into opportunity, simply through a good attitude. If you believe that your power comes from external things that can change – jobs, relationships, wealth, health, and status symbols – then that's like trying to move into that sandcastle on the beach and then feeling devastated when it gets washed away (which of course, at some stage, it will).

When things don't go the way we want and we feel out of control, it's easy to forget about that inner power. We can react in ways that aren't so helpful. We might think we are being punished, that we have bad karma or that life is too hard and that we might as well give up. We can become defensive, like that person huddled up in a protective little ball or one of those crawly creatures I seek to relocate out of my house and into the little forest, and maybe feel we are getting too big for our boots, dreaming too much, and that it serves us right to be knocked down. Or we might just get scared, and try to go back to what we know to avoid the pain of disappointment in future.

These are reactions of people who essentially believe that the sandcastles on the beach are their power. When you realise it's great to enjoy a sandcastle but it's not your real source of power, then you are able to respond to challenges in life in a different way. This is important. Sometimes people will try to avoid change and just keep rebuilding the same sandcastle, even if they know it is going to get knocked down again! It's a bit crazy really. They try to solve the same problem with the same solution that didn't work before, quite possibly 'ignoring the situation' with the result, of course, that nothing gets better. I've tried that. It doesn't work. As the expression goes – 'insanity is doing the same thing and expecting a different outcome'.

It's a better idea to look for genuine power, the power within, rather than the outward appearance of it. This book will help you learn to recognise that power within and how to use it to create more happiness, peace and fulfilment in your life. It will help you flip the switch from defence to trust, so that you can receive more help from life, and enjoy your journey more along the way.

When it feels like life is throwing down a gauntlet and issuing a challenge you really don't want or aren't sure you can handle, then you know you are meant to be moving ahead. This situation is going to get you where you need to go.

When it seems like a big challenge, you'll probably quake in your boots. You might be excited about it too, but also terrified enough to quake nonetheless. When you find yourself in such a place, even while you quake, be proud. Those moments when we face something bigger than we think we can handle – whether the situation seems to promise us heaven or hell – comes with a message from life. We are a bit like the bird at the edge of the nest (of what we have known and felt comfortable with) and it's time for us to stretch our wings into new ways of being, feeling, dreaming and living. We might wonder if we are ready, but when life is happening, you *are* ready. Life is telling you, "Hey there! You are up for this!" You will probably doubt that – *a lot*. Being ready and *feeling* like you are ready can be two completely different things. But when the call of destiny comes to you, through gentle invitation or a kick to get you moving, you actually are ready.

Whether you like the terrain that your life takes you through or not, there is always a loving intelligence in why things happen the way that they do, even though sometimes you are going to have a snowball's chance in hell of working out what that could be. No matter how painful something is – and it takes courage to accept the pain of life and move through it – there is a purpose behind it.

A lot of people are very confused about their purpose in life. Some may want a job that will tidy that confusion up for them, give them a sense of meaning and help them feel they are on the right path in life. Or some, perhaps, seek a sense of purpose through helping others – as a parent for example. Whilst there are jobs and life roles that can help us feel fulfilled and purposeful, our real life purpose, the reason for us being here on this planet is actually to become all of what we can be. Like a plant, you are destined to grow into yourself. You might not have any idea that your current version of yourself – perhaps acorn-like – has the potential to become an oak tree. That's quite a transformational process. But if it's in you, then it's going to happen. Life knows it, even when you don't.

Great loss, challenge and upheaval is always a sign that you are becoming more of what you are destined to be. Knowing this doesn't take away the pain of the challenge, but it does give it context. We need that bigger picture, that realisation that there is a reason for our struggles and that something good can come of them so we don't become overwhelmed by the process.

When the change that is seeking us out is really dramatic, it can feel like a part of us is dying. Even though we cannot control life, we do have the power of choice (we'll explore this further in the chapter on confusion (Chapter 4)). For now, it's enough to say that we get to choose how we are going to deal with any situation in our lives. Will we pitch ourselves forward on the path, even through the worst and most confusing and ridiculous times, and just take the journey?

If you've got a truly intimidating challenge before you, then consider yourself notified that you have a lot of potential! Most of all, we have to believe in ourselves. Life offers us what we can handle, although admittedly, it will be at our growth edge and there are going to be times when we'll wonder. In those times, when it seems like something is beyond your capacity to deal with it, you can be sure that you've not been accurate in your estimation of yourself. You are capable of, worthy of, something more.

CHAPTER 2

Chaos

EGGS, CAKES AND KITCHEN RENOVATIONS

"No chaos, no creation. Evidence: the kitchen at mealtime." – Mason Cooley

Chaos has a purpose. It might seem like a random and evil thing, intent only on causing upheaval, laughing at your despair, and then whirling away to wreak havoc in some other poor soul's life. But chaos has goodness in it. It causes a mess, but it is the mess that allows for creation. It is the destruction that makes way for something new.

Trying to keep eggs intact when they are needed to make a cake is only going to result in a recipe for failure. As the saying goes, 'if you want to bake a cake you are going to have to break a few eggs'. Chaos is a force of nature, a force of life. It is the breaking of the eggs and the making of mess. If you remember what you are seeing in the first place – the making of the mess – is not the final outcome, not the whole picture, only part of a bigger story, then you'll find it easier to accept. If you want something good to happen, then you have to be willing to allow it to happen. That means some things that aren't working will need to be broken down and rebuilt into what will work better. They fall apart so they can come together in a new form.

Chaos in our lives is pretty much like the chaos of a house renovation. A renovation starts with a promise of a better home. It might seem like it's 'planned or controlled' chaos at first, but anyone who has ever done a home renovation will tell you that plans fly out the window almost immediately, along with meeting scheduled deadlines, and the process of destruction and re-creation takes on a life of its own. It is chaos.

Let's say you have a dream of an amazing kitchen, beautiful and functional, and a place where you simply love to be, and that would increase the joy you feel in cooking. You cannot renovate the kitchen, however, without some demolition first. Nor can you avoid disruption to your life whilst the demolition and rebuilding takes place. You'll be washing dishes in the laundry and trying to cook everything on the BBQ outside or learning to love raw foods for a while. Maybe from sheer habit you'll saunter into the unusable kitchen one morning to prepare breakfast and then remember all over again that you can't use that room for the time being. There will be dust everywhere and you'll probably be feeling a bit crazy, dispossessed, without the safe sanctuary of your home intact. That will probably make you feel restricted, annoyed, inconvenienced and downright frustrated. You'll possibly feel tired, 'over it', and be counting down the days until you have your lovely, shiny new renovated home (at which point, you shall say, "Oh it was all worth it! But I still hope we never have to do that again!"). You might even have moments where you'll become fearful and have some doubts about whether you will ever 'get your life back' from the mess.

However you probably won't be afraid of the actual renovation process itself, because you will understand it. You will know what is happening. You might not like it. You might be looking forward to when it is all over. You might remind yourself of how wonderful your new home will be to help you have patience and peace through the process, but you won't shriek in terror when a delightfully muscular builder traipses through the front door, heading towards the kitchen, unless he happens to be trampling mud on a carpet that wasn't covered with drop sheets of course. Or unless you don't actually trust the builders you have hired, believing instead that they may not know what they are doing and the structure of your renovations may be unsound, then you might be very nervous indeed.

So to be able to get through that renovation with some degree of sanity remaining, there are two essentials. You need to understand what is happening and why (demolition for a new and improved kitchen), and you need to have trust in the process (that there isn't some shoddy workmanship happening, but safe and sound renovation that will improve the value of your home).

This chapter will help you understand how chaos in your life – or as I like to describe it, 'When the wheels are falling off the car as you are trying to drive' – is like a home renovation. When you understand why it is happening, and what it is all about, you can actually choose to relax and trust in the process, knowing that it is actually not something you need to fight against but can accept as a gift (especially when it's over and the 'home improvement' in your life has been completed).

FEAR – FRIEND OR FOE?

One of the trickier emotions to deal with in life is fear. Life is mysterious at times, absolutely unfathomable at other times. Fortunately, you don't have to understand why absolutely everything happens the way it does in order to trust it.

Imagine going to a tribal village for an eco-safari holiday. You might not understand the ways of that tribe. Their ways might seem rather strange to you. Your ways might seem rather strange to them! You might not understand each other at all. And that's just what's happening on this one planet that human beings share. Earth is just one planet amongst many. Life is very vast – it flows through solar systems and galaxies. We can assume that it knows what it's doing, even when we don't. There will be many things we don't understand, but that doesn't mean we have to feel afraid.

If you feel a jolt of terror when you notice a person running into your local bank, waving a gun in the air and wearing a balaclava, then listening to that fear and deciding not to go into the bank at that time (and perhaps also calling the local authorities) is going to be a smart course of action. Likewise, if you are about to cross the road and suddenly a car swerves in front of you, your survival instinct is going to have you jumping back out of the way. Or if you meet someone who seems charming, but something about them just feels a bit 'off' or makes you nervous, then trust your gut, and step away.

Fear in that instinctive sense can be useful in modern life. We might not need to run away from wild animals on a daily basis, like our ancestors did, but there are situations in modern life where listening to that inner alarm bell ringing – and acting on it – can save us from experiencing unnecessary pain.

That sort of fear is natural. It is the same fear an animal in the wild would show. Wild animals have far more threats to their survival than we do, and yet they are less anxious and panicked than most humans are. Ever seen a nature documentary showing a leopard resting on a tree branch, tail flicking lazily? Or sleepy lions passed out in slumberous bliss on the African savanna? Of course! Fear arises instinctively in a wild animal when needed for their survival, and then it passes and they rest.

Human beings are meant to work in a similar way. Fear arises naturally if we need it. Then it is meant to pass and we feel rested and serene. Unfortunately, our minds tend to get in the way and then fear can stop helping and start hurting us. We start to disconnect from what is really happening – the helpful hand of life guiding us along our merry way – and begin to fear *what might happen*. This is a case of the mind 'getting the better of us' and creating pain when there is nothing actually there to cause it – except the nightmares our own negative imaginations create. Then fear becomes a constant in our lives, instead of something that comes and goes only when genuinely needed. We start to believe that we need fear to be safe all the time, that we cannot trust life, and rather than being a reaction that helps us deal with unusual situations in our lives, we believe that life is a war zone. We believe we are always under at least the threat of attack and expect that terrorism lurks around every corner, and we forget how to let it go. It is utterly exhausting and saps the joy and spontaneity out of our souls. We start to hold on to what we know, even if the familiar isn't actually right for us anymore and life is urging us to move into greener pastures. Life becomes more difficult – and it's all through a trick of the mind. Yet it doesn't need to be that way.

There are lists that have been compiled of the things people fear the most. I remember reading one such list and it rated public speaking as more terrifying than being mauled to death by a shark! Whilst I found that rather unexpected, it did confirm something I already knew – fear that we create in our minds is not particularly logical and not particularly smart. It is very different to the fear that naturally rises and falls, spontaneously, instinctively and naturally, when needed. We don't think about that fear, it's just there when there is a genuine need for it, and it goes when there no longer is.

So how and why does the mind get itself all worked up into a fear frenzy creating such a nightmare for us? The problem occurs when the mind cannot tell the difference between an actual threat and a perceived threat. One of the greatest perceived threats the mind seems to hold on to, especially in the Western world, is feeling out of control. Somehow the mind has equated this to being a dangerous thing that must be avoided, which is utterly ridiculous because no human being controls life. It would be like a drop in the ocean trying to control the waves. To imagine that we control life is a false form of mental security. We have to teach our minds how to think smarter and not make life harder! We have to learn to think *differently*. That means gently but persistently encouraging our minds to give up one worldview, to slowly but surely learn a new way to think. Part of that new way to think will be 'drummed into your mind' (lovingly!) through this book. Part of that new way to think is to realise that not only is control over life not possible, it's not even necessary to feel safe. We need to teach our minds to realise that whilst we can work on controlling our choices, making them as helpful and positive and useful as they can be, we don't actually need to try and control the world around us to be safe.

If we don't learn to respond to the fears the mind conjures up with a firm, wise and loving adjustment, then we set ourselves up for far more misery than we ever need to experience. Your mind can make fear seem more important and more constant than it needs to be. Your experience of fear then becomes unnaturally prolonged. Our bodies and minds were not built to cope with this unnatural way of being. Our quality of life actually decreases if we are unnaturally afraid. We become more stressed. We have more panic and anxiety, even when we know there isn't actually anything we could 'put our finger on' that is bothering us. If it goes on for long enough, we start to feel negative about life generally. We lose our sparkle and our sense of cheekiness, play and humour. Depression can follow. Life becomes a struggle in trying to control the uncontrollable and it's tiring. Exhausting, actually. We forget how to relax, how to trust. Distrust and fear become the 'normal' way of living. I've been there. Perhaps you have too. It ain't fun!

If we are in that place long enough, we start to forget there is even a choice about it, that there could be another way. We think that that is 'just the way it is'. It's like living in a city and breathing in polluted air, day after day. After a while you get used to it. Everyone else is doing it. You don't really think about it much. You take it for granted and assume 'that is the way life has to be'.

Then one day you go on a mountain escape for a holiday. The air is clean. It's sweet! Sweet air! Who knew such a thing existed? Suddenly breathing becomes so much more than something you just do to stay alive without really thinking about it. You start to notice it. It's pleasurable! You want to breathe deeply and fully because it just feels so good. You change. You love that clean sweet air and you want to breathe it all the time! You try to go back to the land of dirty air, but you don't want to breathe its air anymore. You KNOW that there is something so much nicer and more enjoyable and that is what you want to experience all the time.

That sweet mountain air that makes you want to breathe deeply and fully is what life feels like when your mind isn't clouded with fear. There is an exercise for this in Chapter 7 to help you 'clear the clouds of fear' in the mind. When you are more trusting and relaxed about life, you'll find that if you need fear (to avoid oncoming cars or for remembering to turn the gas stove off) it will be there for you to urge you into an instinctive reaction to take necessary action. The rest of the time, you'll simply not need it.

The way to help your mind make the transition from fear to a more relaxed and trusting attitude is to remember that fear needs a response from you. It doesn't need to be denied or ignored. You don't need to judge yourself if you feel it. You just have to decide if you are going to choose how to run your life or if you are going to let fear make you run from life.

There is no fear greater than your capacity to overcome it. None. That is whether we are talking about fears of bugs or flying, or fear of death, being alone or unloved, or a sort of general fear that you can't quite put your finger on – maybe about darkness or evil or some such thing.

There is no doubt that there is challenge in life, and sometimes our problems and struggles can seem like very tricky puzzles to try and work out. Here's a secret that not everyone knows, but that everyone can benefit from: for every puzzle and problem that life creates, it also creates a solution. Often many solutions, actually.

When you choose to make fear the chance to *face everything and rise (rather than fear everything and run)* you activate the law of attraction. The law of attraction is a natural force of life. It is a magnetic phenomenon whereby we attract what we are seeking. From a fantastic parking space to the new 'toy' that you wanted to buy (on sale!), to a buyer for your home or clients for your business, from a relationship to information you need with which to solve a puzzling situation, the law of attraction is the helpful hand of life in action. It helps put you in the right place at the right time for all sorts of goodness and assistance to unfold in your life. Now, if you are hell-bent on getting to Point B from Point A, but really, what you want is going to be found at Point C, then the law of attraction is going to be guiding you straight to Point C (perhaps through the 3 Cs!).

When you are relaxed and trusting, the law of attraction can help you more easily – like the person once huddled up in a fear-driven ball and now open and receptive and willing to accept what life delivers because they realise it is actually helping rather than hindering. When you are in that trusting and open space within your heart and within your mind, you engage the law of attraction and draw to you exactly the help you need at the perfect time to get you to the solution to whatever issue is in your life. It might not look like a solution at the time. It might well look like … you guessed it! Chaos! That will happen when the solution to a problem requires a big change in you or your life. You'll like where you end up through that process. You'll have an improved life situation and the problem will be resolved. That will make you happier.

But you will have to learn how to confront your fear so you don't run from chaos – and the solution it is bringing you! You learn how to allow yourself to go through the experience and remain open so you can get to all the good stuff on the other side. There is a process to do this, and we'll go over it in Chapter 7. It will help you distinguish between perceived and actual threats, and learn that it *is* safe to feel relaxed.

As you learn to confront rather than run from your fear, it will become clearer to you exactly what you are frightened of – and most of the time that's like discovering the big scary monster you thought was lurking behind the curtains at night is actually a light breeze floating through a window you forgot was open. The more you break down your fear response, you'll realise you are afraid of things that aren't going to happen – you're afraid you will be left alone, you won't be loved or you won't be safe.

Until you face these fears and reassure yourself that, actually, you are going to be okay and everything's going to work out (a tip – *it will!*), your fears will keep popping up. You might feel you are being haunted by your own fears or anxieties, but actually it's just life saying to you, "Hey, can you please have a look at this! I want to help you but this needs to be put behind you now! Come *on*, there's a lot of living left in you. Let's enjoy it!"

If you don't face those fears, they tend to grow and become distorted. Instead of leaving a relationship behind you so you can experience love in a new way, you become terrified that you are going to be alone for the rest of your life, have a terrible time in your later years and try to hold on to a relationship that isn't healthy or good for you now. Your life flow gets aborted and you are stuck in a phase that's not helping, when actually, you could be free from that and feeling more in love and happier *if only you would let go and trust*. Those sorts of fears aren't about anything real. There's no oncoming car you need to avoid. Such fears are the unresolved anxieties deep within trying to get your attention. It's not till you investigate, and realise what is really going on, that you can respond to them with love and reassurance, overcome their grip on you and your life, find some peace of mind and live the life that is meant for you. In Chapter 7 we'll work through some ways for you to do just that, together.

RISING TO THE OCCASION

My first long-term romantic relationship was with a kind-hearted man who was sociable, funny and talented at music. He struggled in life though; for even with all his talent, he found it hard to believe he would ever cut a break. At some level, he identified with being the underdog. When a movie would show someone triumphing over difficult odds, the underdog actually winning in some way, he would surreptitiously wipe away a tear or two and then 'man up' by doing something practical afterwards. But his soul was genuinely stirred by the portrayals of those that could rise up and conquer a challenge in their lives, perhaps because he had encountered a lot of obstacles in his early life and was learning how to feel that he was powerful. I learned valuable life lessons from that man. He taught me how to love unconditionally, something that he was able to naturally do. I also learned how important it was for human beings to feel self-esteem and self-confidence by facing their fears and realising that they could overcome adversity if they were willing to give it a go – and not give up (no matter how many falling-down-on-one's-face episodes happened on the way) until they got past whatever was in their way – otherwise, so much talent and happiness would simply never see the light of day, and that seemed a shame to me.

Sometimes the greatest gift of encouragement you can give yourself is just to remember that success is possible. Great and wonderful things can and will happen if you allow life to help you be in the right place at the right time. Sometimes you won't want to pack up your bags, or leave excess baggage behind, and yet if you do it anyway, because deep within, you know it is what is being asked of you by life, then you'll get to exactly the right place at exactly the right time for you.

There can be so many challenges – even just in daily life trying to handle all the things that need to be done. There are so many obstacles to get through (ever tried to get a straight answer and a problem resolved with a public service office, like the local council, or a telephone company?) that you can start to feel defeated by the end of a day and when you haven't really even tried to do that much. It can wear you down without you even realising it. You can start to feel that life is a battle and you have to keep fighting for your life – utterly exhausting. No wonder we want to watch movies sometimes where the little guy stands up to apparently insurmountable odds, kicks them to the kerb, and perhaps manages to get a nice-looking, sweet-hearted girlfriend in the process too. There is a part of us that might be afraid of that sort of courage, and that part tries to tear people down who seem to us to be successful, maybe judging them or looking for flaws to show they are just human after all (of course they are, we all are). But there is also a part of us that craves the heroic, wants to have victory, wants to experience that high of taking a leap and landing somewhere amazing, even if we land in a few puddles or heaps along the way.

Recently, a story circulated across social media about a little old lady called Edith Macefield who was asked by a big property developer to sell her home so they could build a shopping mall. It was to be built across several properties, hers being one of them. She refused. They offered her a million dollars. She refused. In a bizarre twist, the shopping centre was built around her home on three sides, her little house remaining right in the centre. At eighty-four years old, she loved her little home and didn't want to move. When she died, around two years later, she left it to one of the building workers she had befriended with the suggestion that he sell it to pay his children's college tuition fees. The property was valued at around a hundred and thirty thousand dollars and eventually put up for auction.

Reactions to this story are as interesting as the story itself. The Pixar film studio loosely based their film, *Up*, on the story. The public reaction to the situation ranges from idealising the house as an uplifting symbol of an individual beating a corporation and being happy in doing so, to being criticised as a ridiculous choice on Edith's part, given that her little home was eventually surrounded on three sides by a massive concrete mall and that she turned down a lot of money. However, she saw the last of her days out in a place she called home and that seemed to be what made her happy. Photos of her in the media show an utterly cheeky and laughing woman who quite likely found the whole situation, and all the attention it brought, to be amusing indeed. She was certainly in touch with her inner power, and her sense of humour.

No matter whether you agree with Edith's decision or not, it's hard not to be inspired by her sassy attitude and willingness to stay true to what she felt was right for her at the time, even when a great challenge presented itself. Maybe she didn't even know exactly how empowered she was until turned down the offer, stayed put, made a friendship so valuable she would leave her home to him upon her passing, and decided she would enjoy the rest of her days in the way she chose for herself, no matter what happened. It's no wonder her home has been something of an inspirational landmark, gifting many thousands of people with hope. Life gave her a big lemon, and she turned it into enough lemonade to tend to the thirst of thousands.

It can be a quirk in human nature to focus on the negative. You might have a whole room full of people who love and admire you, and there could be one person staring at you with a disapproving expression or saying something mean about you, and don't you just know, that one person can easily seem more important to you than the other hundred people in the room. In the exercise on training your brain in Chapter 7, we'll learn how to undo that tendency to dwell on the negative so you can allow yourself to partake of that medicine for the soul, the strengthening tonic for your body and mind, which is hope. Hope helps you find your way through even the hugest and most chaotic situation in your life because it prevents you from giving up until you get through it!

For now, if you acknowledge that you have a tendency to focus on the negative, you can use it to your advantage. I love to take adversity and make it the way that I gain the upper hand in a struggle in my life. You can too! So if you know that you give the negative more focus than it needs to have, out of proportion to what is happening, you will be very smart indeed. You will be catching the mind at its own game. What you think and feel is negative is just a habit that you've learned, and a habit that you can unlearn. It is not something you have to believe in. So then you can rise – you choose not to give power to the naysayers and haters in the world, or to the voice of fear within you, and you try laughing instead of ranting when you are on hold for half an hour with the telephone company and the situation still isn't resolved. You don't let negativity get a grip on you. You don't need to run away. You can face everything, and rise – one step at a time, for as long as needs be.

CHAOS IS HIGHER ORDER

Deciding to work through your fear and face the chaos in your life requires that you learn to find the eye in the centre of the storm of upheaval.

When it comes to hurricanes, the bigger the storm, the bigger the calm eye at its centre. It's possible when there is a lot of change going on that you can find a spot within your life where you just stay calm and let it happen. It's only if you try to grab on to whatever the tornado is ripping up and pulling in to the power of its spiralling force that you'll get sucked up and thrown about along with it. If you are willing to stay centred and allow the process to complete itself, you can remain surprisingly peaceful through it all, and then just deal with whatever needs to be dealt with once the storm has finished. It is about learning how to surrender. You allow life to show you its hand, so to speak, in the game being played. Then you know how to respond.

Surrender might sound passive but it's not. It is an active choice. Surrender means each day, when you get up and your life seems like a shambles because you don't feel in control and things seem to be happening that you just don't understand, you say to life, "Okay, I'll do what I can today, but I trust that you know what you are doing, even when I have no clue what you are up to! So I surrender. I'll try not to judge the things I am finding challenging and instead, I'll get on with doing the best I can in whatever circumstances I find myself in … " And then you go about your day, doing just that.

Sometimes this is enough to create a surprising feeling of peace within you. With true surrender, you do everything you can, but you give up worry. So you'll feel calmer, as though you are in partnership with life to create the next version of your life, and it's exciting and good and you can enjoy it more than you might have imagined.

Other days, surrender will seem stupid and you won't want to accept what is happening at all. Maybe you won't want to 'stand up for your rights', or face a fear, or let go of something or someone you know is no longer meant for you. In such moments, you'll be resisting rather than surrendering. You'll be choosing to fight (or bite) the hand of life. That tends to feel like throwing an almighty tantrum because you are beyond the edge of what you feel capable of handling. You might just want to switch off, numb out, and tune out, ignoring everything and either getting drunk or high on chocolate cake, sedating by marathon television or computer-game viewing – or some combination of this plus other activities designed to dissociate you from what's happening. The problem with these activities, apart from their toll on your health and relationships, is that they aren't very constructive. They don't actually help you get a better grip on your reality and feel happier about what's going on in your life. You actually do have a choice to feel happier, even outside of your comfort zone. That happens by *growing* your comfort zone so that you learn to feel happy and at peace in places you weren't able to previously. We'll go over how to do that in the exercises in Chapter 7.

HI! MY NAME IS CHAOS, AND I AM HERE TO RIP THE RUG OUT FROM UNDERNEATH YOUR FEET … READY, SET, *GO!*

Chaos may come into your life in the guise of an event outside of your control. It might be a person who enters your life, or a situation that happens, and you are thrown into a spin. Life seems different, your perspective is changed and you can't go back to the way things were before. You may feel alive, lost, exhilarated and terrified.

At other times you'll feel as though the chaos is within rather than something outside of yourself. Maybe your old beliefs are clashing with new ideas. Perhaps you want to take a leap of faith in some area of your life, but you feel held back by your own beliefs about yourself or life. You might want to change careers, but you doubt your abilities or demand for them, or you buy into the ridiculous but socially accepted belief about a person only being productive and employable up to a particular age. Or maybe you want to change your health or lifestyle, but there seem to be so many choices, so much information, that you only get so far before you feel overwhelmed. You give up and just go back to what you know before realising that what you already know isn't enough for you to be really well and happy, and so you are thrown back into chaos again.

Even if the chaos does seem to be within you rather than through something happening outside of you, you still won't feel in control of it. That's how you know it's chaos rather than laziness on your part! If you can deal with something you deal with it, get it sorted out and the problem is resolved. Chaos that leads to something new and better is not the mess you cause by refusing to take responsibility for the things you *can* control. You can control the attitude you choose to take, choosing to care for your possessions or let them fall into disrepair. You can control taking responsibility for how you treat the people you invite into your life and how you allow them to treat you, instead of complaining about it, maybe trying to blame someone else instead of stepping up and doing what you can. That sort of mess is caused by laziness, unwillingness to honour what you have in your life, and immaturity. Your quality of life will be diminished by that sort of behaviour. It is not the sort of life-changing chaos that pushes you to grow and brings positive change. That lazy sort of chaos is what leads you into crisis instead. It's not the only thing that causes crisis, but it's certainly a fairly common one. From that crisis you'll then be pushed to grow until you learn how to take responsibility for what is in your life – and then the positive change can come. We'll learn more about that in the next chapter.

THE IMPORTANT STUFF HAPPENS WHERE IT CAN'T BE SEEN

Chaos is only frightening to the extent that you believe you have to be in control in order to be safe. Here's a secret that will quite likely add good quality of life to your years, and years to your good quality of life: you don't have to control life. Chaos is the opposite of control – in our human view of things. But as far as life is concerned, it is just nature taking its course.

Have you ever considered the process of growth from the perspective of a plant? It starts as a seed. Being a seed doesn't seem very exciting or glamorous. It isn't like the fruit phase that is so obviously delicious. We know that without the seed, all that other stuff – like bearing fruit – can't happen. But there's more magic to the seed than that. Deep down in dark earth where we can't see it, there is so much happening within that seed as it goes from dormancy to cracking open and sprouting. It is the beginning of life of a plant, all in that tiny little capsule and all beneath the surface of what can be seen. Eventually you get a tiny shoot. If there is enough chutzpah in that plant, it will grow and grow until it develops further, perhaps eventually creating a strong stem, leaves and perhaps even a trunk and branches, maybe even some flowers and fruit. What a journey! It's full of chaos and courage, and creativity, and triumphs over great odds. Yet it happens every day. If we stopped for a moment and considered it, we'd realise that growth is a crazy, challenging and amazing process. How much chaos there is for the plant that starts as a seed, and grows in the dark, before rising up and changing form so dramatically.

And we are the same. Not just in how our bodies are created, but also in how we grow as people, how our spirits get their flavour – joyful, wild, free, fighting … and so on. We have to crack open, and reach into unknown darkness, rely on our inner strength, all of this before we can even begin to show 'results' for our efforts, above the surface, where they can be seen.

So chaos – when the order of our lives is disrupted and even when things appear to 'go to seed' – is not a sign of an end, but of new possibilities. Those new seeds can bring about a new order, a new phase, a new stage, a new cycle in our lives. As the Zen proverb puts it, 'What the caterpillar calls the end, the master calls the butterfly'. We just have to be willing to spend some time in the dark to go through it.

Just like in nature, in our lives there is a time for winter and a time for spring. Sometimes we have to let things go, so that when the time is right, we are ready to emerge into a new phase. That might be the ending of a relationship, or a career, an identity (such as when kids leave the nest of home and you might not feel like the same mother who is so needed anymore or when you graduate from school or college and need to become more of your 'own person'). For everything that begins, something ends. It is natural. It is the way of life. It's that seed that becomes a plant which eventually returns to seed again.

Part of retraining our minds, re-educating them, is to remember this. Instead of simply focusing on what seems to be falling away, we encourage a different perspective, a viewpoint that takes nature into account. Maybe something more like, 'this is sad because something is ending, but also this is exciting because something new must be beginning'. The mind – for all its ability to imagine the most terrible outcomes – actually lacks genuine imagination. It tends to respond only to what has happened in the past or dwell on the negative possibilities. If we want our minds to create more positive energy, we have to train them to do so. We will explore that in the exercises in Chapter 7.

The choice to rise instead of run is simply that, a choice. We can choose to be cowardly or courageous every day. You don't have to push yourself or make yourself wrong when you just can't quite summon the courage to let go of negative thinking or doubts and fears. It's best to be kind in those moments. Use your courage in that way, then you'll have more energy and love within you to think braver, bolder and more positive thoughts in the hours and days that follow. Most of the fear and negativity that exist within us is simply there because it is familiar. Maybe that is what we learned from the world around us, and we didn't even know we had the choice to think differently. By the end of this book you'll have a more empowering point of view. Even just by reading this book you'll get zaps of positive energy from the words and ideas on the page. You'll be healing whilst you are reading, reprogramming your mental habits from resistance to trust.

It is enough to just get some inspiration, some positive thinking, from the page of a book to start a positive transformation of attitude within. It doesn't take much, but you do need to be consistent. It's kind of like healthy eating but for your mind. The exercises in the book will help you with that, but so will just picking up a positive inspirational book or affirmation card each day – even if only for a few minutes. It is enough to lay the foundation for a different way to be in yourself and in the world. It's sort of like a snowball that starts as a single pebble rolling down a mountain. The constant motion attracts more and more snow and soon enough it's a mammoth snowball rather than a piddly pebble. Fear often grows in this way. We start off with one fear and then we think, *Oh, but then this could happen*, and then you have two things to be afraid of, and so on, until you are a nervous wreck with anxiety and can't even venture outside the house to go a party without feeling that all sorts of terrible things might happen. Or you soldier on with your life but are so defensive that you cannot allow anything new or exciting into your life either.

Fortunately it isn't only fear that can be a snowball gathering momentum and force in you and your life. It can also work with positive energy, hope and inspiration. In the aftermath of the 9/11 attack on the Twin Towers in New York, a lot of people struggled with processing the experience, feeling shaken to the core. It was utter chaos. A story then circulated through social media. A boy was speaking to his grandfather about dealing with all the things he felt – sometimes hopeful, sometimes angry. He felt confused and his mind and emotions were in chaos. His grandfather listened to him thoughtfully and then told him that he had two wolves in his soul, one on the left side, one on the right side. One wolf was fighting for fear, hate and anger. The other was fighting for love, forgiveness and compassion. The boy asked him which wolf would succeed in his fight. His grandfather replied, "The one that you choose to feed."

We always have those wolves inside of us. We choose which one to listen to every day. During the intensity and upheaval of chaos, which one you choose to feed with your attention becomes more important than ever because that is when you are going to need all your courage and positive energy the most.

Your mind can gather good thoughts and inspired energy, or drudge, judge and sludge. It's your choice, but simple little steps each day will add up and eventually become a powerful force within you. Remember, that massive snowball starts with just one little pebble. Personally, I think if you are going to create a force within you, it may as well be one that you enjoy and feels good, is positive and helps you enjoy life.

EVERYONE'S A WINNER, BABY

So what is this higher order that chaos brings as it pulls the rug out from under our feet and tosses us into upheaval and change?

Some people call it 'higher will', some people simply call it life. I like to think of it as growth, the natural impulse within every living thing to become what it is meant to be, no matter how improbable that may seem. Inside every living thing there is a sort of map, a plan, something akin to an architect's blueprint. It's the grown man that the boy will become. It's the butterfly waiting within the caterpillar, destined to be at the right time. It is the oak tree that is the invisible and yet powerful potential for the acorn. It might be the dancer in you, or the parent, the voice you have inside that is meant to be expressed with confidence so it is heard in the outside world too. Your potential is unique and so much more than your biological destiny. The plant grows, but it also feeds the human soul with its beauty and the human body with its nourishment. It has potential not only for what it can become, but for the way its becoming can be a constructive presence in the world.

Our potential is not something outside of us that we might dream of happening, if only we were lucky enough or had a life like a celebrity. Your potential is a real force that exists in your cells, in your DNA, in your heart. It is an inner knowing and an inner genius in the sense that it not only knows what you are supposed to become, but also how to get you there – with the helping hand of life and nature. This happens by growing.

So if you have a dream of something so wonderful that it makes you tingle or involuntarily smile, fills your heart or feels like it would be 'perfect' for you, then that's a moment when you have connected with this part of you. You are getting a glimpse of what your potential is meant to become. You know when that happens because those sorts of moments make you feel alive and inspired. They make life seem worth living. You might wonder, *Could something as wonderful as that happen for me?* Yes, if you are willing to go through the adventure of life, and grow, it *will* happen for you. It's your destiny. It's never too late. You are never too old (just think of Edith causing a storm of inspiration at the young-at-heart age of eighty-four). You are just meant to be and become all that you are, and life is always going to help you get there. Always.

It took me a long time to work this out. I had a mixed up way of thinking about things. I thought I couldn't have what I wanted because everyone else would be in competition for it and everyone couldn't win. It wasn't until I realised two things that I finally let go of that mistaken way of viewing the world.

Firstly, I realised that the things that sounded so wonderful for me (being on stage, singing, dancing, and doing unscripted and spontaneous public speaking on spiritual topics – and I mean without prepared speeches – for hundreds, if not thousands, of people) would be a nightmare for some other people. But for me it just felt natural and exciting and even the thought of it just made me feel happy and peaceful inside. So the first thing I worked out was that we each have our own unique dreams. There might be some things our dreams have in common with other people's dreams, but essentially, the things that will make our hearts sing are unique to us. So there isn't any worry about stealing someone else's dream, nor is there any competition for that one dream that lives inside of you. Do you think the tomato can't become a tomato because there's a pear growing somewhere else? Of course not. Nature loves variety and diversity. You only have to look at the insect kingdom to get a sense of how much of a kick Mother Nature gets out of having an abundance of creatures thriving in life. We are meant to be (bee?) a part of that too.

This understanding led me to my second realisation: there don't have to be winners and losers in life. Everyone can win.

This might not seem important but if you really 'get' this, it will change your life. You'll realise that the desires in your heart, the things you would dream about doing in your ideal life, are not just the stuff you daydream about when you get a moment away from your 'real life'. They are actually the potential within you, the higher order, your inner blueprint, giving you some clues about what life can hold for you if you are willing to show up and take the journey. You don't have to fight anyone else for it. You being happy and successful doesn't take away the opportunity for another person to also be happy and successful. If anything, you living your life and having it get better and better is going to inspire other people to believe that it's possible for them too.

So the higher order that chaos pushes you into, and imposes upon your life, is actually that inner blueprint or natural growth process within you. It is your own inner growth process happening. It is you growing from caterpillar to butterfly. It's a crazy and strange journey at times, that's for sure, but it's beautiful, natural and wild and most of all, even though it might seem like the most dangerous and destructive thing ever, it's safe and you can trust it.

YOU ARE A VERY CREATIVE BEING

You might think that creativity really belongs only to the realm of artists and musicians and the like. But you are creating your life experience – invisibly, powerfully, without always being aware of it – every day. With the thought patterns you think, with the choices you make, you add ingredients into the recipe of your life. Sometimes those ingredients are well past their use-by date, and have much to do with what happened some ten or twenty years ago and not much relevance to what is happening now. It's best to just throw those away or you'll end up with stomach cramps and feeling miserable! Other ingredients might be sweet, tart or even sour. You get to choose the types of thoughts you have. (Yes, it seems like when it rains and you want sunshine, the only thought you can have is disappointment, but you can train yourself to remember that you need rain for rainbows and smile!) You get to add to the recipe of your life. You can know that you are going to be cooked and served up by life (I bet you'll be delicious!), that much you cannot control. But you do get to choose how sweet or sour that dish is going to be by what you add into it.

When chaos is upon you, it's a bit like life has taken the mixing spoon out of your hand for a while. Imagine you are in the kitchen of life with your grandmother, and you are a beloved child. You can do certain things on your own, but other things will be a bit beyond you and Grandma will need to take over for those tasks, probably involving hotplates and sharp implements, oven timers and the like. For a child it might seem all a bit mysterious and confusing, although the delicious treat at the end of the process may be appealing enough to inspire trust and some patience for the process. Of course the child may throw a tantrum and want to do everything herself, in which case the cooking process might take a little longer and be a little less pleasurable for all involved, but it will happen nonetheless.

When Life needs to take over, she will. She'll stir things up for you, but you always add your part to the recipe of your life experience.

Philosopher Friedrich Nietzsche put it nicely when he said, "You need chaos in your soul to give birth to a dancing star."

In creation myths from traditional cultures from all over the world, chaos is prelude to the creation of a new world. It is like a womb of sorts; nothing is formed yet, but it holds the space for that potential to become what it can be.

Whenever you are at a stage in your life where something new is ready to emerge – a new identity, a new sense of self, a new and healthier body or a new insight, idea, career or discovery – there will be chaos beforehand. That's your sign. That's how you know something good and juicy is on your horizon. The bigger that sense of chaos, the juicier that new start will be.

When you remember this, when you use the exercises in this book to train your mind to think in a different way (it will *love* you for it), you will find it easier to drop the fear about not feeling in control, and instead learn to become curious about what is going to come into your life.

WHAT IF … ?

Some of the best discoveries in our lives happen when we imagine something different. What if this wasn't the only way? What if there could be something better? What might it look like? What might it feel like? What if I could put this note paper on the wall and not have to use sticky tape? Voila! Post-it Notes.

It takes courage to stop going back to what already is and assuming that is just the way things have to be. Habit can be such a powerful force that we confuse it with reality. We think the past is the future and forget about the natural world and how much we are a part of that, that we are meant to grow and change. We might think that nothing much changes and history will just keep repeating itself, but reality is far more stretchy and flexible and *fun* than that. Lives can and do change – dramatically. You might have been miserable every day for the last forty years of your life, but that can change if you wish it. It can change completely and utterly so that you, who were perhaps the most negative and miserable person that anyone ever saw, can become the most radiant, positive and happy person that anyone ever saw. You can take delight in pleasantly shocking all your friends and relatives and just live a different way. It doesn't often just happen overnight (most of the time), so we do a little work each day and something new is born in us when the time is right for it to sprout.

Habit is just what we have learned to do. No matter if everyone else around us seems to have the same habits and every single person we know believes this habit has to be this way (this way of living or thinking or being in the world), we can choose something else. Go on and find the rebel in you! Dare to be different, to break away from the crowd and be your own person. You have the courage and guts to do it. You'll feel respect for yourself in doing so.

Habits, even the most powerful ones, *can* be unlearned. *And* powerful and positive and constructive new habits can be learned to replace them. Your mind can become your best friend rather than your worst enemy, a cheerleader rather than a creator of nightmares. You just need to know how to work with it effectively. It's actually not very hard to do if you know how. In the workbook section you'll be guided through exercises to help you know how to unlearn habits and learn new patterns.

The power of positive imagination, or some people call it 'creative visualisation', is immense. There are sporting legends like pro golfer Tiger Woods who reportedly wouldn't take a single golf swing unless he could see it clearly in his mind first. The power of the mind to set an intention and carry out an action is a mighty and powerful way to work with your mind. You can develop this ability too, even if you aren't a visual person. That's why I like the term positive imagination rather than only creative visualisation. For many people, it's easier to feel or imagine rather than see an image clearly in their minds. If you are one of those people who can see clearly, then that's great, but if you are someone who feels or imagines rather than sees in their mind, then that doesn't need to hold you back at all. In the guided exercises we will use positive imagination and guided visualisation so you can just choose to work with what works for you.

There was once a man called Mahatma Gandhi. He had studied law but left the courtroom behind to become a freedom fighter for the people of India. He managed to cause great changes to the face of economic and political interactions between India and Britain without ever resorting to violence. He believed that people were fundamentally powerful and didn't have to use violence to attain great change and justice in the world.

One of his most powerful teachings was to 'be the change you want to see in the world'. This means, rather than waiting for things to change, you become willing to become the change, to feel it inside and to live it, and then the world outside changes in response to you. This is the next step beyond creative visualisation and positive imagination. You don't just imagine or see a change, you begin to act as if it is real now, to really feel it in your bones, training your mind to think as though it were already happening. It's not denial of what is, but a willingness not to keep repeating what you have done and instead to offer an invitation to what could be through your attitude.

Often we believe it needs to be the other way around. We believe we have to wait until something happens outside of us before we can be happy on the inside. These are usually things like losing weight to feel beautiful or attractive, having a relationship in order to feel worthy of one, being wealthy in order to feel happy and trusting in life, or successful in our careers before we feel like we have value and so on.

But this is a disempowering attitude. It not only makes us put our lives on hold until 'some day', but it slows down that 'some day' becoming 'this day'. The more you are able to 'be the change', to act and feel *as if* it has already happened, the quicker and more powerfully you'll draw that reality to you.

This is the law of attraction that we spoke about earlier. It's a good 'cheat' to a new life. Actually, it's the only way to a new life really because if we just keep doing what we have been doing, we'll keep getting what we have been getting, and if you want a positive change in your life, obviously repetition of the past isn't a smart strategy. It is more effective to use your power of positive imagination and act *as if*.

So when faced with a choice in your life, imagine, like the Christians would say, "What would Jesus do?" but ask, "What would successful, happy, healthy me do?" Imagine you are that future version of yourself you dream of, but in the here and now. How would you behave differently? What sort of attitude or action would you take if you already felt safe, secure and successful, trusting in life, loved and appreciated for who you are? That's good, nourishing food for thought and far better than the junk food that popular media tends to dish out, causing a lot of self-esteem issues through the idea that we should compare our lives to others, perhaps celebrities, and maybe find them to be wanting, or recycling yet another story about why we should be afraid of some crisis or other. Being healthy includes our mental diet, especially when so much of the mainstream mental food is just junk and not good for your health.

DARING TO TAKE THE PATH LESS TRAVELLED

Chaos entered my life in the form of health issues. Some of my most vivid early memories were of being unwell as a child. Doctors at the time didn't seem to be able to help very much and my mother, being of a somewhat rebellious and stubborn disposition (something I inherited), decided she would not limit her search for improving her child's wellbeing with the orthodox medical approaches. She also sought out alternative health care practitioners, even martial arts trainers, with a view towards giving my body a chance to heal itself. In a maelstrom of difficult symptoms, which turned out to be based on a blood sugar problem, I remember visiting various practitioners for herbs and tinctures, dietary advice, guidance for lifestyle and exercise, removing allergens and toxins, and all sorts of varying instructions.

Over time, my health did improve. It wasn't, however, a case of simply one day I was sick and then I was better. The first steps were about healing childhood asthma (karate classes seemed to help with that) and then improving chronic sinus conditions (emotional healing work actually really helped with that) and later on, it was about learning how to overcome fatigue and chronic neck and shoulder pain (chiropractic and massage helped there) and so on. Over the years, it was like peeling back layers, dealing with one issue, and then realising there was something else underneath that needed resolving. My mother always had a very holistic view of health, rather ahead of her time, and I benefited from her open-minded attitude.

Eventually, I wasn't just looking for how to stop getting sick (I seemed to have a lot of flu and infections when I was very young, despite my mother's vigilance over keeping a clean house and dosing me up with vitamin C – the fact that I didn't like taking the tablets as a child, and sneakily shoving them between gaps in the skirting boards until I got 'found out' probably didn't help either of us much). As the main problems I struggled with as a young person were overcome, I eventually found that my focus naturally shifted to wanting to just feel more 'well', to have more energy and be able to keep up with all the things I wanted to do.

I started with joining a gym and becoming – I'll be the first to admit – fanatical about exercise and diet. I was so obsessive that I lost connection with why I started (health) and ended up with adrenal exhaustion and eventually, chronic fatigue. It got to the point where I couldn't even leave the house for more than twenty minutes without becoming exhausted and needing to go home and lie down. I had been training excessively and punishing rather than caring for my body and mind. Despite this, virtually everyone around me encouraged me to keep going.

"You look so good!" they said, and I realised then just how messed up our culture was – especially in that gym at the time. It didn't matter if you were damaging your health as long as you sweated hard and looked good in the final analysis. It wasn't until I met a personal trainer with a more moderate approach who basically said to me, "Alana, do you want to die a few years earlier and a few kilos lighter, or live a longer, healthier and happier life?" that I finally felt like someone understood that being thinner and exercising more wasn't always better *or* healthier.

However, even with that moderate approach, I was still in that gym community. It wasn't until I wanted to move house that I was forced by distance to give up that community altogether. It was hard for me. It was giving up an addiction. However, I was also giving up a social group that I had found sustaining. I had many friends at the gym. To leave it behind left me feeling so socially isolated, not to mention going through the 'getting worse before it gets better' health recovery process where I couldn't chase my highs with exercise, and put me into depression for a while.

Recovering from chronic fatigue took more than a year. However, that wasn't even the worst of it. The over-exercising and undernourishing of my body had thrown my endocrine system into disarray and created suppression of feel-good hormones in my body. It took over ten years of trying different approaches to eating and exercise before I found something that seemed to work well for me, that I could do moderately and with good effect. It took more than ten years to get my weight back down to a similar level to what it was when I was training hard.

During those ten years, I suffered mentally and emotionally. I didn't feel happy with my weight being higher than I felt comfortable with, but I couldn't use diet and exercise to reduce it in the way I knew how because of the health issues they had created and that I was still recovering from. Gradually I healed myself from the inside out. I found my way to yoga and eventually studied nutrition to learn about eating well rather than dieting. I learned about rest and recovery and how the body works. Rather than trying to push it to do what my mind wanted, I started to learn to listen to my body and the more I did that, the more my health improved.

At each stage of that long and painful journey there was chaos. I thought I had found my answer only to be presented with a whole slew of disastrous consequences. It was necessary though. Every step of the process was one step further to the answer I needed. I had to take all those steps to learn how to take care of myself in a way that worked for me. What was created out of that painful process was what I wanted all along – an increased sense of wellbeing and a healthier mind and body. I just had to learn how to do this via a different route. I'll talk about that side of it in the next chapter.

You may not have health matters to contend with; maybe your issues are with love, or money, or work. I have had to deal with all of those matters in my life. Chaos has preceded positive change in every single one of them.

What I have noticed through all of it is a repeating pattern. I find an issue. I decide I am going to sort it out. Utter chaos happens! All the habits I had come to rely on were obviously not working, so I had to begin to let go of those habits, even though they had become how I lived. Suddenly, all the things I had relied upon as my basic way of living were 'not allowed' if I was going to feel better and heal myself. I would research new information and experiment with applying those new ideas and theories until I found what would work for me. There is always a lot of information I end up rejecting and some that I feel is worth trying. There is a lot of confusion and overwhelm in that process. Even just sorting through so many different opinions about health, relationships and the like can feel overwhelming at times. During my research phase, where I am trying to get the information I need to make better choices, I typically have no idea what I am doing. Without my old habits to fall back on, I feel quite adrift and it's not really a pleasant feeling. I am swimming in an ocean of new potential, and it feels like pure chaos every time I have gone through such a phase – which I have done many times.

Whilst exploring yet another new level of my health or any other issue in my life is not necessarily easier than what it once was, I am more familiar with the process itself, and I accept that chaos is a part of it. That makes it not only less confusing, but somehow more comforting. When things seem to be falling apart I actually know that this is because they want to come together in a new way and so I am not worried and anxious about that. Instead I trust that when it's time, I'll come up with a new way of being. It will be an improvement on the old way, and that will suit me best, until it doesn't anymore, and then I'll need to learn something else. And so I go through the process again, from an order that doesn't work, into disorder of being 'in between' the old and the new, to allow for new order to eventually emerge.

Chaos always precedes creation. It is always a sign that a new order, a different understanding, is breaking through. It might combine with crisis and confusion and you'll really have to grow and transform to find your way through, but life will help you. When you learn to embrace that, and accept that if you are going to have a better time going through this process rather than fighting against it, then when chaos shows up at different times, you'll be curious about what is going to start anew for you rather than fearful about what is going to end. When you relax and take the journey, the new order that chaos is bringing will show itself more quickly and easily. It might take months, but considering the fact that it would have taken years if you had resisted the process, that's actually something to be welcomed.

CHAPTER 3

Crisis

· ·

READY, SET … GO!

I have always been sensitive to stress and anxiety, never more so than when I was a little girl. During my early schooling years, I was required by the school to participate in many sports competitions. I detested them. Running races and swimming carnivals (though I felt the word carnival was oddly misplaced – they didn't seem colourful or fun, just chlorinated and anxiety-ridden) were the things I liked least.

I didn't mind running (though I preferred dancing) and I enjoyed swimming, but the psychological and physical stress of competition was something I hated because of the extreme anxiety it gave rise to. I felt sick with nerves waiting for that moment on the starting block when a race was about to start, with every sense stretched taught, listening for the fire of the starting gun. Once the race was on, I just got on with it. Sometimes I won ribbons or medals, at other times not.

The worst part of it was that starting gun moment. No matter how much I knew it was coming, or how many times I was in the situation of waiting for it, it never became something I found thrilling. If I was going to be in the race though, that was a part of it I had to accept.

Crisis is a lot like that starting gun. It is a wake-up call. It doesn't necessarily feel good, especially if you are a more emotional or sensitive type of personality, but whether you are cool in a crisis or not, the point is, it's not the end. It's a beginning.

HISTORY DOESN'T HAVE TO REPEAT ITSELF

When the starting gun of life fires and your race is on, your mind needs to be in the right place. So often, human beings look to the past for reference. We see what has been and build expectations based on that as to what the future will look like. This expectation of continuation is what crisis is trying to dislodge from your mind.

Think of it this way. If someone was in shock and jabbering on, unable to come back to the present moment, they might need a swift, sharp slap to bring them out of that hysterical state and into the now. It hurts but it's over pretty quickly and the purpose is served.

Crisis doesn't feel good because it is a jolt. It is a slap. It is the universe saying, "This isn't working. It's time to shift you into what is – pay attention!"

NAUGHTY OR NICE?

Sometimes, for no apparent reason, I'll have a song from childhood pop into my head with incredible vividness, or an advertising jingle, just as vivid but rather more annoying. Anyone who has had an irritatingly catchy childhood nickname they just can't shed will know that sometimes, the apparently silly little phrases we don't seem to pay much attention to can become surprisingly persistent voices in our heads. We'll learn more about this in the next chapter, including how to evict some of those unwanted voices and introduce new ones instead.

For now it's enough to realise that if you grew up on the notion that Santa Claus brings presents to the good children only, if you end up with a crisis in your Christmas stocking rather than a Ferrari (though those two things can go together, but that's usually a different sort of crisis involving an approach to midlife), you'll think it's because you've been naughty rather than nice. The crisis will feel like a punishment if you believe that (a) it's not a good thing and (b) good things happen to those who are good (therefore you'll assume you've done something wrong).

So apart from making the mistake of thinking that when crisis hits it is all about the ending rather than a whole new race that is beginning, humans can easily make crisis even more painful by making it mean things that it really doesn't.

Most of us were conditioned as children to equate unpleasantness with punishment and pleasure with reward. When something difficult is upon us, it seems to be an in-built reaction for many to wonder why God or life is punishing them. Have they done something wrong? Is it bad karma catching up with them? It is rarely seen as the slap on the wrist that moves our hands away from the hotplate. It's just the sting of the slap that is registered.

TANTRUMS DON'T ONLY HAPPEN TO TODDLERS

We live in a culture where immediate gratification can become a way of life. I only have to have a slower-than-desired internet connection to know I can be just as caught up in this as anyone else at times. We want what we want, and we want it now.

I understand impatience. If there is a quicker and more effective way to do something, I am all for it. However, as financial whiz Warren Buffett has said, " … some things just take time. Getting nine women pregnant won't make a baby in a month."

If we allow our desire for immediate results to become more important than trusting in the process, we won't be able to see where sometimes short-term pain or displeasure will actually yield far greater happiness and fulfilment in a not too distant future.

One of my chi gung masters sums it up pretty well. If a student is impatient to be making more gains in their practice, and wishes they were at the fourth year of training rather than the second, he asks them if in two years time, they'd rather be two years worth of training better than they are now, or as they are now, but with the clock just wound forward two years. Sometimes you have to accept that the process, the journey, is just as valuable as the destination.

NOBODY LOVES ME, I GUESS I'LL GO EAT WORMS!

When I was a kid there was a bizarre song the children in my primary school classes used to sing sometimes. It went something like this: 'nobody loves me, everybody hates me. I think I'll go and eat worms'. It was something of the pre-pubescent ode to self-pity.

Sometimes we forget that we are supposed to grow out of that mindset. It's not that you are wrong to think that way or feel self-pity, it's just that if you choose to think like that more than once in a while, you will make life harder than it needs to be. The best way to avoid self-pity is to learn not to take things quite so personally.

A WOMAN ALWAYS RESERVES THE RIGHT TO CHANGE HER MIND

One of the ways to work through a crisis effectively is to be able to not take it personally. Even if it will affect you personally, you don't have to take it personally. You might reject this idea at first. You may feel you are entitled to get mad if life doesn't go your way, to feel rejected or betrayed, disappointed, abandoned, angry and depressed. You may even be perfectly justified and reasonable in feeling such a way. Emotions such as these aren't bad. Keeping your chin up and ignoring how you feel is not a way to good emotional, mental or physical health in the long run. Holding on to emotional responses and believing they are the only truth, however, is not a good idea either. Emotions are energy. They are meant to come and go. If you find it hard to recognise your feelings or perhaps the other extreme, you find it hard not to become overwhelmed by them, then you'll benefit from the exercises in Chapter 8.

Whatever your initial emotional reaction to a crisis, you have the power within to choose what your next response will be. No matter how long you might hold on to an emotional reaction, no matter how long it takes you to work through it, there will always be a 'next response'. You never have to be stuck in one emotional reaction as though your first response to something is your only choice. If you are going to be happy in life, you must always give yourself permission to 'change your mind' and change your emotional responses. That means that whilst you accept the truth of your feelings in one moment, as you move through those feelings – perhaps anger, fear or doubt – you will also be able to see and experience things in a different way after those feelings pass. This requires walking the line between feeling your feelings, and remaining open-minded enough to see things in a different way in time. *When you allow that to happen* and don't hold on to whatever the story may be about the crisis in your life – that you've done something wrong and are so bad as a person, you blame someone else, or fear that life isn't safe and so on – you become willing to change your frame of mind, whether or not you are a woman!

This doesn't mean that certain emotional responses are bad. Any and every emotion is a feeling and a response to life. We are meant to feel them, perhaps learn a message from them. Anger might be telling you that someone is taking advantage of you and you need to set some boundaries and stop allowing your time or energy to be used by another person. Sadness might be telling you that it's time to let go of the past and start afresh. Fear might be telling you that you are at the edge of what has been comfortable and you are about to break through into a new life cycle. Frustration might tell you that you are pushing too hard and need to learn some patience. Anxiety might tell you that you need to look after yourself differently, perhaps with stronger boundaries so you can make choices that work for you, instead of perhaps trying to always please others.

Emotions are clever intuitive communications from within. They are triggered by our life experiences, and they hold messages for us to listen to and learn from. If we neither ignore nor try to hold on to those emotions, we benefit from them – even the apparently negative ones like anger. The reason we want to feel our feelings and then let them go is that holding on to them won't be good for us. It's unnatural. It's like trying to pin a wave on the sand. It's like capturing a butterfly because it is so beautiful, pinning it on a board to admire it. It's lovely but it's dead. The gorgeous craziness of its lightness in erratic flight is lost. Emotions are meant to flow like water. If they aren't allowed to flow, instead of a cleansing flush, you end up with a stagnant pond that starts to smell after a while.

Emotions can be a source of energy if you learn to relate to them in a healthy way. That means listening, responding, but not holding on and turning them into an excuse to create stories that star you as a victim of bad things happening to you, or that you are a bad person being punished, ignored, denied your slice of pie, or that life is terrible, and so on. If you allow negative thoughts and reactions to plunge you into a spiral of depression, for example, then instead of your emotions becoming a source of energy to help you get moving in life, you will have turned them into something that pulls you down and stops you. You will feel drained, stuck and depressed. It's up to you if you want to take the gutsy action of learning to deal with the enormous power of your emotions (it's a bit like taming an invisible but powerful wild beast at times!).

You'll do yourself a favour if you learn to listen to your feelings and choose to take positive action on them. If you try to ignore your emotions on the one hand, or indulge them as giving you permission to complain about life and feel victimised, you do yourself a disservice. Refusing to deal with your emotional life in a mature way will allow your emotions to run amok and wreak havoc with your quality of life instead of supporting it. You might think that trying to ignore a feeling so you don't feel it makes it go away. But life is food for the soul and emotions are part of our digestion process. What would happen if you ate food but tried to hold it in and not let it out through elimination? It would become toxic in your system and you wouldn't feel very good!

I once had a beautiful, fluffy orange cat who was a peculiar and amusing creature. One of his quirks was that after going to the toilet, he would bounce around like a spring lamb, happily frolicking, freshly relieved and leaving his litter tray behind him as a distant memory whilst he sprinted around the house. His glee was very enjoyable to witness. It always made me giggle to see him prancing about (which coincidentally was a way to take the edge off the unpleasantness for me then needing to change his kitty litter). His delight was a natural and unaffected expression of how happy and well he felt after eliminating yesterday's dinner, ready for whatever morsels would come his way today. No wonder there are so many tongue-in-cheek books written about cats being guides to enlightenment. My feline friend's ability to let go of the past and take joy in the now seemed pretty enlightened to me!

If you allow your emotions to flow – and the exercises in Chapter 8 will help you learn how to do that – you'll find that your point of view will naturally shift and change too. Even if your initial reaction is absolute despair or a truly frightening interpretation of a crisis (perhaps making it mean that you'll never be happy or you have to give up because you'll never succeed – both very scary and very untrue propositions), if you remain unattached to your emotions, they will change naturally. You can move from anger to peace far more quickly than you may realise. You might worry that if you don't hold on to your anger, someone is going to 'get away with something', but you can rest assured that life keeps score and you don't have to do so. All you need to do is act on what feels truthful for you in the moment. If that means that you go from anger to forgiveness to peace in a matter of moments instead of years, then that makes your life easier and happier. Where's the negativity in that? By using the tools in Chapter 8, you can end up in a peaceful place quite quickly. You'll be using your willingness to let emotions flow, rather than trying to hold on to them, to tap into that inner power of yours. Your inner light will switch on and you'll suddenly have more light on the subject, and be able to see through some of the darkness. You will find your way more easily.

Sometimes we need to feel jolted into changing our attitudes and our world. Change takes energy. A crisis can get you up and moving with more motivation and energy than you might have otherwise known you had! Heard of people lifting cars off a trapped child or other stories of incredible feats performed when the chips were down? Though you might not be bench-pressing trucks, the appearance of a crisis in your life is rather like the universe lighting a match underneath you. You are going to get up and get moving!

Once you get the message, and the motivation for movement sets a process of change in motion, you can put your energy into taking the steps before you. You do want to act so that another crisis to get you moving isn't needed, but you also want to give up the stress of that initial crisis moment; otherwise, you can start recycling it in your mind over and over again and create a state of fearful distrust and apprehension about your future. (*What if there is another crisis? Oh no! How would I deal with that again?!*) It's more helpful to focus on the fact that you are getting through the situation and on a journey to solve whatever needs to be sorted out. After the initial emotional turmoil has passed, coming to a place of peace can help you have more energy to just do what needs to be done. Although we often need an emotional push to get moving in the right direction, the journey from that point on is usually more pleasurable and productive if we are coming from a more centred place within. There's a swift and easy tip to make this shift from emotional reaction into a centred place in Chapter 8.

Remember too that the less you trust in the inherent goodness in life, the harder it is going to be to give up negative emotional responses like betrayal and fear. Again, those feelings aren't bad, but they are just meant to be one step in a process of growth, not the final say on the matter or a way to live more generally. There is an expression from the Bible that goes like this – 'faith the size of a mustard seed can move a mountain'. What that means to you and me is that a little bit of trust goes a long way and is very powerful. Trust punches well above its weight. When you choose to trust, especially in those things that happen in life where you think you really shouldn't trust (that's when trust really matters most), then you'll begin to see life in a different way. You'll find the reassurance and happiness that comes with the realisation that life is ultimately trying to help you become your whole, incredible self – not trying to wear you down until you fall in a defeated heap not giving a damn about anything anymore. If a crisis has found its way to your door, then it's just life saying to you, "Okay, you are in a race. Are you going to flop along behind the pack, complaining the whole time, or are you going to be brave and bold and run up front where you belong?"

"Seeds of faith are always within us; sometimes it takes a crisis to nourish and encourage their growth." – Susan L Taylor

I'LL DO IT TOMORROW

The power of procrastination, denial and inertia should not be underestimated. Putting off to tomorrow what we could reasonably enough do today is not wise. Only people who ignore death would behave in that way. Life is short. As my manager says, "We are here for a good time, not a long time." This doesn't mean he fails to work hard. It means he looks for enjoyment and pleasure in life, whilst getting on with what needs to be done and doing what can be done now, now! This isn't about running around so busy you don't know if you are coming or going. At times, what is needed will be rest, reflection, taking a pause. These things are constructive and help us reach our goals, get through challenges and live a happier life when they are balanced with reasonable daily action. Reasonable daily action is not trying to control things you cannot or should not attempt to control (such as other people and the greater timing of how your life unfolds). Reasonable daily action is doing what you can do, when you can do it. This kind of approach makes you more productive, and often more rested too, because sometimes, what needs to happen today is letting go.

This is most important in the face of a crisis because the first thing we tend to want to do is put out the fires, so to speak. In other words, we want that crisis to just go away. We want ourselves or our loved ones to not be sick. We want our relationships or our lifestyles to suddenly be okay as they are, even though they may actually be toxic and most definitely needing an overhaul. We want life to 'go back to how it was before' which is the catchcry of a person who isn't quite getting the opportunity a crisis is presenting.

"You never let a serious crisis go to waste. And what I mean by that it's an opportunity to do things you think you could not do before." – Rahm Emanuel

A NEW RACE, SOMETIMES AN ENTIRELY NEW EVENT

You'll remember from the previous chapters, the idea that the bigger the change happening (even in a 'negative' or challenging sense), the bigger the reward or pay-off headed your way. Big transformation can be scary to imagine, and it's normal to cower in your boots at the prospect of dramatic change in your life. For you that might be selling a house and moving to a new area. For someone else it might be changing jobs, leaving a relationship, changing a lifestyle or even renouncing one religion in favour of another. What is big for you might not be such a challenge for another person and vice versa. Life is adept at finding our weak spots and pushing on them, like a really good sports massage therapist. Oh the pain! And then, afterwards those tender spots have been released. Oh my, have you ever felt so good?

Crisis is the bit where our tender spots are pushed upon. I have been in situations where I knew certain changes were needed, but even with all my courage and strength of will (which some naysayers call stubbornness, but I prefer to think of as determination) I couldn't bring myself to make those changes until situations had got so bad that I was at a crisis point. I needed the jolt of feeling that my hand was forced to make changes I knew I needed, but didn't really want to make.

"I really do think that any deep crisis is an opportunity to make your life extraordinary in some way." – Martha Beck

FORTUNE FAVOURS THE BOLD

When crisis presents itself to you, it is not a time to be timid or think small. You are being given an opportunity by life, an opportunity couched in crisis, but an opportunity nonetheless. Unfortunately, if we are in resistance to what is happening, we might just want to focus on making the situation as minimal as possible. But sometimes it's really a matter of facing up to what is happening and thinking bigger, bolder, braver.

"When written in Chinese, the word 'crisis' is composed of two characters.
One represents danger and the other represents opportunity." – John F Kennedy

The situation that I was referring to above – the one where I didn't want to make a change until I really, really had to – was a romantic relationship. I truly loved a man with all of my being and we spoke of spending the rest of our lives together, and that is what I wanted. Yet the relationship with him was not an emotionally healthy one. I tried every way I knew how to change that situation. After several years, I realised that it wasn't going to change, no matter how much I tried to make it work. Although I wanted to be with him, and I was grief stricken at even the thought of leaving him, the only way I was going to feel truly happy was if I went through the painful process of separation and began my life again on my own. I was in a crisis of my own consciousness. To put it bluntly, the situation sucked.

The day I left him, I had the bizarre experience of feeling so devastated at the prospect of life without my loved one by my side that I dangled at the edge of an emotional breakdown; and yet at the exact same time, I was feeling an inner sense of peaceful happiness and relief. Those strange emotional bedfellows of deep, heart-wrenching grief and a lightness of spirit that I hadn't felt in years continued on in me for over a year. On one level I was grieving a loss that at times felt more painful than I believed I could bear, and on another level, I was being given an opportunity for new life. I decided – with my usual moderate approach to life (ha!) – that I wanted nothing short of a complete and utter transformation for myself. If I was going to have to go through all that pain, I was damn sure I wouldn't be letting it go to waste. I was going to use all the strength it took me to walk away and channel that into learning how to love myself, care for myself and live in a better, more mature, more wise, empowered and happier way than I had ever done before. I was utterly determined.

There is a saying that 'When we embark upon our correct path, the heavens become gentle'. Whilst life didn't suddenly become 'a piece of cake', as the expression goes, I certainly did feel that I was helped in so many ways once I made the choice to work through my crisis. Life more than met me half way with helping and guidance, whilst I did my part to just get through the pain of the experience and into the blessing of a new life calling me.

Many challenges presented themselves but compared to what I had been through, I saw them in a new light. So I just tackled one after the other and grew in confidence along the way. Within eighteen months I had grown in leaps and bounds, successfully tackling issues in me and my life that had plagued me for decades. I figured that if I was strong enough to give up someone I had loved so deeply, which was the one thing I never imagined I'd be able to do, then there wouldn't be anything else that could stop me. I used my crisis to build confidence. I decided if I was going to be kicked by life onto a new path, I would do my best to hit the ground running and get as far along that path as I possibly could. I had bold expectations of love and happiness for myself and knew that I would only be asked by life to go through that sort of suffering if it was necessary to receive a great blessing. With that sort of attitude, I worked hard and attracted a lot of help for my journey. Good things happened I just knew in my bones wouldn't have otherwise been able to happen, and I continued on with my life.

Of course this sort of bold attitude doesn't always come easily, especially if you have learned to toe the line and try not to make others uncomfortable. Funnily enough, I have found that the more dramatically challenging a situation is for someone, the more a spirit of defiant heroism seems to rise up from within them. There is a boldness in the heart that seems to say, "Well, I could go down fighting, but it will be in a glorious blaze of fire!" All that boldness – even though it feels like a great risk – inspires success.

"Until one is committed, there is hesitancy, the chance to draw back, always ineffectiveness concerning all acts of initiative and creation. There is one elementary truth, the ignorance of which kills countless ideas and splendid plans; that the moment one definitely commits oneself, then providence moves too. All sorts of things occur to help one that would never otherwise have occurred. A whole stream of events issues from the decision raising in one's favour all manner of unforeseen events, meetings and material assistance which no one could have dreamt would have come their way. I have learned a deep respect for one of Goethe's couplets: 'Whatever you can do or dream you can, begin it. Boldness has genius, power and magic in it. Begin it now!'" – W H Murray

If your crisis hasn't quite reached 'code red' status as yet, you might not believe you need boldness. Perhaps you could find a way to make your hideously depressing job less so, perhaps just by taking longer lunch breaks.

I remember working in a continuing legal education department for about six months. I am surprised that I lasted that long. I had been offered a prestigious position at one of the top commercial law firms in Sydney and I turned it down. I hated every moment of the summer clerkship I had done in that law firm; well, apart from the socialising. People thought I was crazy to turn down a decent-paying job that would guarantee me a glittering legal career. But I couldn't stomach it. I hadn't yet worked out how I could translate my passion of all things 'New Age' into work, so I looked for less demanding part-time work whilst I tried to figure it out. Unfortunately, the jobs I found myself in with such an approach weren't the best fit for me. In the continuing legal education job at my former university, I was so utterly demoralised by the experience, which I found mind-numbingly dull, emotionally dissatisfying and even physically uncomfortable (sitting at a desk and computer in an enclosed office space with no windows, no fresh air, no natural light and my personal bugbear, fluorescent lighting, was not so good for me). I usually got into work at 8.30 am. By 10.00 am I was thinking about how soon it would be to get to a lunch break. By 3.00 pm I was wondering if I could leave early. I spent time browsing New Age bookstores online, and did the bare minimum of work required.

This was appalling behaviour. You'd never know I have an exceptionally strong work ethic from the way I behaved in that job. I was resisting the crisis of needing to leap into a different career. I was resisting the need to leap so deeply that I was behaving in ways that ran contrary to my personal integrity – such as working hard. Instead I was trying to buy myself some time. Depression and despair were closing in around me. I hated that job. I didn't like the people I worked with. I doubt they really liked me much either. My boss was young and something of a power tripper, snapping her fingers at her team to get their attention. It was repellent behaviour but no justification for my behaviour either. I was trying – and failing – to improve a situation that really wasn't going to be improved. I wasn't in the right place for me. I needed to leave. I needed to think bigger, to be bolder, to find my rebellious spirit and refuse to do things according to my logical mind only. I needed to become braver and more willing to trust in my heart. Eventually my sabotaging behaviour forced a situation where I was asked at the end of my contract – rightfully so – not to return. It is the only time I have been sort of fired. I was mortified and relieved at the same time. I hadn't yet summoned up the boldness of spirit required to take the initiative myself and leave that job, but eventually I was pushed into it. It was the first of several leaps I would need to take before I landed into the work I felt I was destined to do. Each leap required that I trust my heart even more than my logical mind, and let go of what wasn't working to open up to what would be more suitable for me. Life showed me every step of the way, but I was still the one that had to take each step.

CRISIS MEANS IT'S TIME TO STAND FOR SOMETHING

I once drove by a church near my home at the time in southern Sydney. At the front of this church was a billboard. The local minister would change the words on the board every week. He seemed to have quite a sense of humour. My favourite by far was the day I saw, 'If you are looking for a sign, this is it.'

During a counselling session, I remember one of my clients saying, "If only there was a map for my life! I would know what to do and follow the steps. Things would be so much easier."

I know that she isn't the only person to feel this way. Whilst there is appeal in the idea of being able to choose whatever we want with absolute freedom, most of us like the idea of having a wise guiding hand to help us stay on track in our lives – perhaps even a clear set of instructions to follow, sort of like a recipe book for our life success. Sometimes the confusion, chaos and crises in life are enough to make even the most daring of us dream – at least for a moment – of giving up our free will and power of choice to just be able to live a more quiet and harmonious existence for a while!

I have 'climbed the wrong mountain' (law school being an example perhaps) on more than one occasion. The lack of happiness I gained from that 'success' made me yearn to be wiser in my choices in future, to invest effort into what would bring me meaningful, enjoyable returns. Of course, even if we did have a map with a big skull and cross bones indicating danger if we pursue a certain path, we still have the power to choose to do it anyway. I tend to be one of those people who, when told that the hotplate is on and it will burn, like to check by singeing my hand on it, just to see if it is true for myself! You might also be the sort of person who likes to figure things out for yourself. Or perhaps, like me, you have learned how to balance that with also allowing yourself to learn from the mistakes other people make rather than just your own.

We do actually have a type of map, that inner blueprint for our potential, our destiny, which I mentioned earlier. But there's not just one way of following that map. There is in life pretty much always a hard way and an easier one, and then about fifty million other possibilities in between.

I visited the sunny, club-hopping, hippie-loving island of Ibiza in Spain for the first time in 2012. There were many things I loved about that island, in particular the energy of the place that just felt like it was ready to break into a dance at any moment, something I often felt like myself. I also enjoyed the laid-back attitude of the locals. Having spent months previously working in Holland – which has a completely different culture and attitude, with a rather more strict, organised and structured approach to life – to soften down into the relaxed Ibiza vibe was a tonic.

There was also a funny quirk in the road signage of the island, quite possibly due to its small size. Almost every crossroads would have a street sign bearing the name of the town you were heading towards – San Rafael, Santa Gertrudis, Santa Eulalia and so on. Arrows would then point you in the right direction so you knew which way to turn at the street sign to reach your destination. Nothing so quirky about that until you notice that the arrows on virtually every street sign point straight ahead, and also to the left and also to the right. You can take any path and *still* end up at the town. It never ceased to make me giggle. It felt like the whole island was saying, "Hey you'll get to where you want to go. Just pick a way that feels right and it'll work out for you." It resonated with my philosophy of life.

A crisis in your life – whether big or small – is a signpost on your map. Sometimes there will be one obvious way to move through it. Those are the moments when we know we do have to change course, perhaps quite dramatically. It feels like there is a big arrow flashing above our heads saying, 'Walk away!' and that's all there is to it. At other times, you'll feel more like me, bemused at the Ibiza street signs that are supposed to be directing you but actually just say you can go any way and you'll get there. All we need to do is just take one step, and then another and then another, even if we aren't sure where those steps are leading, or even if they are in the right direction. Sometimes there is just one direction, and that is progress. Taking a step; that's how we take a stand in life, using our feet, one step after the after.

THE ROAD LESS TRAVELLED

In his poem, *The Road Not Taken*, Robert Frost speaks of that moment where the path diverges and we have to make a choice. We can continue on the way that most people do, where the leaves have been worn down on the road by footsteps of other people, or we can choose the lesser known path, the one where the leaves crunch fresh under our feet.

It is a new way. We don't really know what's going to happen on either path for certain, but on this lesser known one there will be more latitude for creativity, for difference, for change because it is not yet set by the expectations of society, or even ourselves, as to how life should be.

There is a saying, 'better the devil you know'. I love sayings, as you can probably tell from how often I use them in this book! I grew up in a household where various ones were oft repeated. This one rarely was, however, because I don't think any of my family really believed it was true. All of my family members have broken with tradition and carved lives of their own, in their own ways, going against the stereotypes of what should be and surprising me (and perhaps themselves too at times) with how their lives have unfolded. I am the same. I have been on some bizarre and amazing journeys in my life. Sometimes there is a new level of fear to break through in order to leave what I have known behind and embrace yet another new world within me and around me. My work in particular – where my creativity gets free reign – has been quite the path less travelled. Because of this, I do know this is not always an easy choice to make, to break with what you know, with what you can see or feel most familiar with, to take a different path in life.

Earlier on I mentioned that moment when I was just starting upon my ill-advised career as a lawyer. I was sitting in an office of one of the most prestigious law firms in the country, with the human resources manager interviewing me to find out which law partners and areas I would best be suited to and describing what the trajectory of my career would be. The idea of such certainty was completely foreign to me. I wasn't even certain I wanted to be a lawyer, and yet here she was telling me what was going to happen in my professional life five years on. I didn't know whether to be soothed by this knowledge or feel somewhat curbed by it. Even if you are of a steadier disposition and like the idea of seeing where you will be in ten years and how you are going to get there, when a crisis shows up in your life, there will be a better way for you via an alternative route. It might seem scarier – if the unknown frightens you as it does for most people – but ultimately it will be more helpful.

Remember the trust factor? If you are going to be able to read the signs in your life, you have to trust that the sign maker isn't a devil with a perverse sense of humour, wanting to lead you astray at every possible opportunity and then laughing sadistically at your misfortunes! You need to know that life, the universe, the great spirit – whatever your belief system might encompass – is about growth. Growth happens in nature. Nature is what happens when human minds don't make things confusing by thinking too much! So look to Nature to understand life. She grows. Some beautiful things (like spring) end. Some less appealing times (like winter, unless you are a skier, or fond of a cosy wood fire with a cup of hot chocolate) end too. Leading back to the warmth and new life of spring – if you only see winter without the context of a seasonal cycle, you'll find it hard to trust in the goodness of life. But if you see winter as a way to allow for a new spring to emerge, you'll realise that life is about growth. Endings are a part of that.

When a crisis hits you, you have run right into a sign. The sign is saying – 'best for this way to end now, it's time for a new pathway'. You always have the power of choice.

You can of course, continue to wear your springtime clothes all year round. You may well end up sick and frozen and miserable all winter if you do so however. If you choose to change and adapt, to grow with what is happening in your life, you'll become wiser, and happier in the process.

THE MOST DIRECT ROUTE IS NOT ALWAYS A STRAIGHT LINE

In the midst of my exercise obsession, which spanned my late twenties and early thirties, I was training to the point of exhaustion – and to be honest, beyond that on a regular basis. To be fair to myself, I didn't really know any better. I had always been reasonably active, but never to the levels of very high fitness I had achieved during my most rigorous training program. I became addicted to the feelings it brought me – not only the high of training, but the psychological confidence that came with being able to do things that I didn't realise I could do.

I remember during that time going running with my friend and her new boyfriend, both of whom were ten years younger than me, in their early twenties. We went to the sandhills of Cronulla Beach. My friend and I were used to training together and putting each other through our paces. The young man had no idea what he was letting himself in for!

"You girls are pretty fit," he said, before bending over to throw up because he had pushed himself so hard to keep up with our warm-up – which consisted of running up a moderate-incline rubble pathway towards the sandhills. I remembered the first time I had run that path. I didn't throw up, but I did wonder how on earth I was going to manage a sandhill after that 'warm-up'. I even remember looking at that first sandhill with absolute incredulity. I saw the same shock in that young man's eyes when we realised the hill he thought was our workout was just the beginning of what would seem like a very long hour for him.

Even thinking about it now, there are things I miss about that lifestyle. But it cost me too much. It plunged me not only into confusion, but also chaos and eventually a health crisis. I had to outgrow so many thought patterns and behaviours to find my way through the mess I had unintentionally created. Though there are times when I miss the thrill of super-fitness, I certainly do not miss the damage it did to my particular constitution, including the dizzying highs and depressing lows that accompanied that sort of lifestyle. For me at least, it depleted my thyroid and immune function, leaving me feeling bleak, depressed, rarely sleeping well and prone to catching whatever cold or flu was going around at the time.

My health and wellbeing did improve dramatically over time, but it took a prolonged state of health crisis for me to be forced to let go of the socially-accepted way to be fit and healthy – eat a low fat, 'healthy' diet and always build your fitness with exercise. I had to change my mind, and take some steps in different directions, learning how to eat healthy fats and get adequate rest. It took me years to find the information I needed to understand how to improve my health, and then more years to integrate that and apply it sensibly. It was a process – and a long one at that – when really I just wanted to know what to do to get the results I wanted in a few months. I learned that no matter how hard you are willing to work, sometimes you just need to accept that certain changes require time and patience in order to come together.

Given my own personal experience in this matter, I have mixed feelings about the trend for high-intensity, military-style training programs. If they are conducted as exercise, rather than punishment, then perhaps there is value there, but the mindset of either the program creators and/or those drawn to them, rather reminds me of how I used to think – and we all know how that turned out!

A friend of our family recently trained for a fitness event that fell into the category of these sorts of training programs. The event was a sort of obstacle course. She trained for a year to be ready to complete the course. During the event, whilst climbing over a building constructed of metal, which became extremely hot during the middle of the day in summer, she slipped. She fell on her leg and injured it. However, in the mindset that seemed true to the culture of the program she was in, she wanted to be tough and not give up. So she kept running on it. I'll spare you the details of what this did to her body, except to say that her doctors have now told her that she'll not only never run again, but she'll need reconstructive surgery and have to relearn how to walk.

We are so often taught that strength of mind can overcome anything, and too, I believe in the power of the mind and the mantra of 'just keep going'. However we have to apply these things with wisdom. Trying to use strength of mind to overcome a wounded body, for example, is not strength. It is foolishness. It is the trap our high-flying friend Icarus fell into – the refusal to use our strength to set healthy limits so we can truly succeed.

Limits and boundaries aren't very sexy in the 'you can do anything if you believe' mindset, and yet they are the very thing that balances boldness and transforms a dreamer into a living inspiration. Strength of mind applied here would have us say no to the voices within or around us that are interested in pushing us beyond what is right or good for us. Just because you can do something, doesn't mean you should! Strength of mind would have you saying no to such forces and yes to your truth. Keep going, yes, but do so in a way that is about responding intelligently to life, not blindly ignoring the signs that tell you to slow down as if they are not for your benefit. When you believe that life is trying to help you rather than prevent you from being successful in whatever matters to you, then you'll realise that even the slowing down can be helpful. Sometimes you'll avoid unnecessary suffering, or learn something helpful you would have otherwise missed, and then when it's time to quicken your step and take advantage of an opportunity, for example, you'll be better prepared.

I only learned this as I got older, after I had pushed for things to happen according to my own opinion about how life should be rather than trusting in where life was leading me and how it was doing so. Eventually I realised I needed to upgrade my version of the truth. Instead of standing in the truth that only I would look out for what I needed, I began to trust that life would help me grow into what I wanted to create for myself and my life.

I could trust in that process, even when my mind told me not to do so because things seemed risky, or out of my control, or I didn't understand what was happening. Instead, I decided to trust and surrender on a daily basis, using my strength to keep trusting and acting on my intuition, and when I didn't know what to do – to wait and let life show me the way when it was meant to do so. In short, I learned to live in a different way.

I learned a lot doing that. I learned that the intelligence of life is incredible and that its genius is hardly one we can fathom at times, yet it always works things out so beautifully, if we allow it to do so. That is about trusting in the *when* and also in the *how* and the *whom*.

To overcome the health crises I kept evoking through my own choices – although I was doing the best I could – I needed more information. I also had to be ready to hear it, and to be honest, the information that came to me was fairly simple, and sensible, but up until a certain age I just wasn't ready to hear it. I thought that things had to be more difficult than they actually needed to be. The idea of eating more fat to lose weight seemed ridiculous. Yet when I was ready to hear it, it made a lot of sense. Of course, the body wanted to know that if it was going to give up its precious fat stores, it was going to have good, healthy, healing fat of the natural, organic and nourishing sort coming in. That was common sense. But I still needed to unlearn what I had learned through mainstream diet culture over more than twenty years to accept that simple and vital piece of information. Then I had to be willing to overcome my doubts and fears and apply it and see what happened – likewise with an approach to fitness that was more moderate and wouldn't create unhealthy fatigue, but the good sort that promotes rest and healing. Life has a lot to teach us, if we are willing to learn. Despite our fears that it might be out to teach us that we aren't so great, that we have a lot to learn (in a fearful or unpleasant way), what life can teach us is actually how to be well, happy, fulfilled and at peace with ourselves and our place in the world. We can learn to feel truly loved, and safe, as we let life be our therapist, teacher, friend and guide because if we are willing to let ourselves be taught by life, what we will learn is how to *live well*. And that creates happiness.

One of the tricks with letting life do its part, whilst we do ours, is to realise the most direct route isn't always the most obvious one.

So in my case, in the pursuit of wellness, going about it in the fastest and most socially-accepted way didn't help me out. The fact that I am more well in my forties than I was in my twenties is unusual. But it is also because I listened to the crises (eventually!) that came into my life and decided to try different pathways – simply because I felt I had to. I didn't want to continue my life in such an exhausted state, barely unable to leave the house. I knew something was wrong, I just had to figure out how to fix it, even though I wasn't exactly sure what it was. My crises were the hand of life saying, "Stop with this. Enough now. You won't find what you think you are going to find if you persist on this path."

Around that time I had a dream. I have always believed that dreams give us messages, like some secret handshake between us and our inner genius.

In my dream I saw a shiny, black bicycle and a steep mountain and I felt very excited by the thrill of that challenge. Then Jesus rocked up. I am not a member of any one religion; I appreciate different aspects of many religions, but I am happily a spiritual person with security in my own personal belief system. I have had spiritual figures from many different religions show up in my dreams to help me out. In this dream, Jesus saw me looking at the thrill of the challenge, and then instead of encouraging me to take it, he walked a beautiful horse towards a cathedral made of mud, shining with golden light. It was a much gentler path – not as thrilling to me at first, but very intriguing. I woke up wondering what that dream meant.

The meaning of that dream unfolded over many years and helped to guide me to a new way. I believe that at one level, the horse was my desire to literally run free. It was the thrill I felt in my spirit when running up a hill or overcoming a physical limitation. It was the part of me that felt excited about the adrenaline rush of jumping on that bike and climbing the mountain. In my dream, Jesus was suggesting a gentler approach, to temper that freedom-craving spirit. The free spirit in me could climb the mountain, if I wished. The choice was there for me. But so was the cathedral made of mud that shone with gold. I felt that was my body. I needed to learn to bring my freedom-loving spirit to my body to find the beauty not just in the thrill of what challenge I could overcome through effort, but to experience the pleasure and the joy through my body too.

This dream brought me a sort of healing medicine. As I wondered about its meaning, my approach to fitness began to change. Instead of hours on treadmills, pounding pavements, *StairMasters* and spin classes, constantly pushing my body and clocking up more and more hours on endurance training, I took up yoga. I began to dance again, something I had always loved since I was a little girl, and I had been a podium princess dancing in clubs as a young woman. I found more joy in movement because instead of zoning out during exercise, I became more present. I began to get a sense of how to balance working hard enough to have some fitness and strength, without working so intensely that I depleted myself beyond the point of being able to recover within a reasonable amount of time. Instead of just going for it without thought of the repercussions, I began to listen and interact, allowing my feisty spirit and gentler body to learn to know each other. It wasn't always easy. The old ways still lured me sometimes, but I also liked the feeling of my body being happier and enjoying exercise for a change too.

Apart from that, something most unexpected happened. As I got more in touch with my body, I discovered my childhood love of singing again too, something that has brought me so much joy and happiness as an adult. If I had to choose between thrashing my body in workouts for hours a week, or the joy of a more balanced lifestyle that includes singing and feeling the happiness that this creates for all involved, then I'd choose the latter. Actually I did have to choose – my crisis forced me to do so. And I am so grateful that it did.

There is an intelligence in a crisis that is beyond the A to B route. Life understands that sometimes the shortest route in distance is filled with unfinished road surfaces, potholes, traffic jams, or even unforeseen road changes that lead to a dead end and not the desired destination at all. But of course, you might not understand any of that. All you see is that your path ahead has become nearly impossible to continue and you are being rerouted, perhaps apparently away from what you were seeking.

What I came to understand through my own experience of crisis, of which my health was really only one (love and career were the other two, in case you were wondering), was that sometimes the quickest route from A to B is via C or even D. My relationship to my body had to heal for me to discover many things – not just a healthier way to create wellbeing, but a voice I didn't even really know I had within me. What I thought was a childhood fantasy of singing, surprisingly translated into an adult talent. I didn't expect it at all and it's one of the most beautiful things that has ever happened to me. I would have missed out on that, and been rather miserable with debilitating fatigue-induced unwellness, if my health crisis hadn't shown up in my life and forced me to make different choices. I didn't want it. But now I am glad for it.

BUT WHY DOES IT HAVE TO HURT SO MUCH?

You may wonder why you need a crisis as a sign for change in your life. Surely sometimes great changes can happen without such pain? Of course, that is possible. Signs come to us all the time. What we do with a sign is like the difference between the carrot and the stick for the donkey. The donkey can be inspired to move forward by desire for the carrot dangling on the end of a stick, or pushed by a smack to the behind with a stick. My wish for all living beings, donkeys included, is that the urge for forward movement happens in as pleasant a way as possible. I think life wants that for us too.

The problem usually is that we of the modern world are frequently too tired, distracted, overstretched or externally focused to pay attention to the initial signs, or perhaps rather more like the donkey that won't move forward even for a delicious carrot, perhaps just not hungry enough for something new. Perhaps you do sense the signs when they are smaller, such as a feeling of how nice it would be to have a rest that afternoon, but you ignore it because it's just a nice feeling and nothing more (or so you think). Or perhaps you notice a little twinge in your back that lets you know it's time to move your body with some yoga or exercise, or get a massage, but you ignore it until that niggle has turned into a pain that has you unable to move for three days!

Most people have a tendency to disregard the subtleties thinking that they aren't very important. This is something endemic in our culture that is so externally oriented. We think that unless it's a physical thing, we can ignore it and hope it will go away. Many people treat their emotions the same way. And yet when we learn to pay attention to the subtleties and treat them as helpful signs that we can do something now before we need to have a crisis to get our attention as things escalate later on, life does indeed seem to become kinder to us. It is because we are becoming kinder to ourselves. This doesn't necessarily mean that a crisis will never happen again in our lives, but it absolutely will reduce the need for them for us to grow and heal.

There is a saying I mentioned before – 'When we embark upon our correct path, the heavens become gentle'. It's sort of like driving a car. When you are paying attention, you respond to the little bumps in the road by correcting your hold on the wheel slightly. It's so subtle you do it without really thinking most of the time. It's only if you drift off and stop paying attention that you might suddenly veer off course and have to violently swing the wheel back into alignment – and give yourself an almighty fright – to put yourself back onto your side of the road and out of the way of an oncoming truck!

Subtle signs – which we can easily feel when we are present and paying attention to ourselves (and not talking ourselves out of what we feel and sense if we cannot see physical evidence for it as yet) – can keep us relatively on course in our lives and move us forward. Crisis is a helping hand from life to move us out of the way of something that would be dangerous, even though at the time, it really can cause us to feel jolted or frightened. It's just so much better than the alternative!

Things are changing, fortunately enough, because we are changing. We are becoming more mature in our understanding that reality is not only comprised of what you can touch and taste and already see. Through turning to nature – where much of the important seeding takes place in a way we cannot see – we begin to understand that there is a lot happening beyond what we consciously recognise at any given time. For this maturity to continue, we have to learn to trust in what we feel, even if appearances indicate something to the contrary.

An example of this was at the time when I was coming out of my exercise obsession. I was beginning to sway and feel quite faint when on certain machines at the gym. Common sense, looking back, said that I was utterly exhausted. However, I took myself off to a doctor to make sure there wasn't anything more happening. The doctor cheerfully assured me that there was nothing wrong and I would outlive him, probably to at least a hundred years of age given that I was so healthy. This was an externally-oriented assessment. He was looking to see what had already happened, what had already shown up as disease in my body. But nothing had – yet. If I had continued, it would have eventually. But I was feeling symptoms that were real enough to me. How many people go to the doctor because they feel something isn't quite right only to be told that they are imagining it or worse still, being a hysterical woman? That a doctor wasn't clobbered to death in cold bloody-mindedness by a woman with PMT at some point in the history of the modern medical profession, when explaining to his patient that 'she was imagining it', is a miracle indeed.

Anyway, having got little help from the doctor, I took myself off to a highly recommended acupuncturist in the beach side suburb of Cronulla, not too far from where I lived at the time. Daniel, who ran a very busy and effective practice at the time, was a friendly and astute Chinese medicine practitioner, who had studied in China and moved to Australia to practise his art and science. He was a healer with a genuine gift.

He felt my pulse for some seconds and looked at my tongue. I hadn't said a word yet. He then told me what my symptoms were and what was going on in my energy field. I was astounded! I knew it was possible to do what he had just done, but he was just so much more accurate, even than other acupuncture practitioners I had visited in the past. His acupuncture sessions were very helpful to my body. I floated out of his healings feeling absolutely wonderful. I still had to do my part in changing my lifestyle and learning a different way to live, but he helped me feel well again for the first time in years. He also enjoyed my sessions because I was able to feel the movement of the chi (or energy) in the body when he placed needles in certain places. Sometimes he would place a needle in my foot, and I'd feel the effect elsewhere. He would explain that I was feeling the energy lines or meridians, as he called them, that moved through my body. I didn't know where those lines were – it was rather complicated – but I did feel energy; and for Daniel, to have a person who could explain the feeling and flow of energy he had studied from ancient texts was quite a thrill. We both enjoyed our time together for different reasons.

Now, does this mean that doctors cannot help us with health issues? Of course not! There is a time and place for different kinds of help. However, the difference between Daniel and the doctor was that Daniel worked at a more subtle level than the Western-trained doctor. They were both trained to deal with disease, but whilst Daniel worked with injuries and disease that had already shown up at a physical level, he also was able to work at a level where problems had not yet become so obvious and chronic or acute that they would show up in physical tests a Western-trained doctor could conduct.

In time, just like the seed would grow into a plant, the subtle cues that Daniel and I could sense would become externally visible and show up in tests a Western-trained doctor would identify as a health problem and then treat according to Western methods. However, I wanted to deal with the issue before it got that bad – sort of like spotting and removing a weed rather than letting it go and allowing it to take over the whole garden before then trying to eradicate it. That would just be a much more difficult and unpleasant a job! So I trusted my feeling that something wasn't quite right, and I was lucky enough to find a healer who was skilful enough to take my generalised intuition and know how to respond to it with specific and effective healing techniques. Although I am a person with a highly developed intuition, I believe that you and I know our own bodies best. We can sense when something isn't right. We just have to learn to trust ourselves and if a medical practitioner cannot trust us enough to look into what is there, or doesn't have the training or skill to be able to do so, then we keep looking until we find the answers we need. We take the threat of a crisis to be enough of a crisis to get us moving!

Sometimes we get inner nudges that a path isn't quite right for us – continuing on a particular course of destructive action in our lifestyles, or our jobs or relationships aren't quite right – but for as long as we can sort of cope, we try to stick it out rather than go through the tumult of change. We can be like the doctor and say, "Ah well, maybe something is wrong, but it hasn't become as bad as it can be yet, so I'll just wait and see what happens!" Or perhaps things aren't great, and we know deep within that they need to change, but we don't feel like we have hit rock bottom yet, and so we try to stick it out until we really and truly know we don't have any choice but to change. Eventually, if we continue on that path, crisis will come along and force our hands. Or we can be more like Daniel, and treat the feelings we have as real, and deal with the situation earlier on, perhaps even avoiding the need for a bigger crisis later on altogether. In that way, change can be less painful or difficult than what it might become if matters get rather more out of hand.

In the spiritual teaching traditions of Zen, this is called the difference between the carrot and the stick, which I mentioned briefly before. Assuming you are the donkey (Zen doesn't worry about offending your ego), then you can either be led along your path of life by a nice juicy carrot dangling in front of you, or by having a stick smacked onto your backside forcing you along. Generally, we are going to prefer the prospect of something we want urging us to take risks to live a happier life. Sometimes we refuse to budge (donkeys being known for their stubbornness at times) and so the only way to get us to move is with a less pleasant alternative of a crisis.

This doesn't mean that if a crisis has happened in your life, you always should have seen it coming and avoided it. Sometimes you cannot. It might be about a matter completely beyond your control, destined to shake you up and move you on no matter how careful and aware you have been in your life. It would be taking things a little far to say that if you had paid more attention to your emotional life, you wouldn't have been affected by a tsunami that hit your home town, for example. Sometimes stuff just happens.

However, more often than not, there will be smaller signs that can all add up along the path heading towards crisis. Often these signs are not so small as to be hard to see. We often know all too well that something has to change. This is good. This gives us empowerment. Once we learn how to listen to our intuition (which you'll do in the workbook section), you'll have more confidence that life is not going to need to throw you into one crisis after another, because you'll be more proactive in walking towards the carrot (thereby avoiding the need for the stick!).

Once a young man came to see me for a spiritual guidance session. As I sat with him I felt a strangely overpowering urge to say something a bit abrupt and shocking. It had nothing to do with what we were talking about at the time, but it felt so sudden and clear that I just had to mention it. I said to him, "Your choices in your sex life are causing you emotional suffering and putting you in potential physical danger too. You need to be more careful with yourself." I didn't really know what he was doing that was so potentially harmful, but I did know that the instinct to say those words to him was a true and good one. I also wondered how he would respond to my sudden outburst! He just sighed quietly and said, "I know."

The story then unfolded that he had been engaging in unprotected sexual encounters in semi-public places with numerous strangers, and had been feeling depression, anger and increasing negativity within himself through that process. He was self-aware enough to realise that what he was doing was not good for him. He was wise enough to know that he needed to stop it. When I gave him some 'homework' in the form of some mantras to repeat (ancient affirmations and prayers) to help him step onto the new path – and avoid the need for life to 'force his hand' with a crisis down the track – he was open to it. The carrot for him was not feeling the negativity he was feeling and loving himself enough to stop doing things that were harmful to his body and mind, not to mention his self-esteem and sense of self-love.

Then about a week later I got an email from him. He said that he had researched the homework I had given him and found information on the internet that suggested it was very powerful and brought about spiritual growth and change in ways that one couldn't necessarily control. He didn't like that idea and he was frightened. He couldn't trust that the change that would happen would be loving and helpful. I understood. I also knew he needed a strong prayer and mantra to deal with the darkness he was pulling in to himself through his choices. What he was really scared of was change.

Sometimes it's hard to trust, especially if our trust hasn't been 'rewarded' in the past because our instincts were damaged and we placed our trust in less than worthy people or situations. Whilst I don't believe that life has to be a constant struggle, I certainly do acknowledge that it is an advanced school for personal growth and it can come with some hard knocks. So yes, it can be hard to trust in change when change has been difficult in the past, or we are yet to see the benefit of it (because it sometimes is not until many years later that we understand why or how a situation we once rejected became a helping hand in our lives). Whether that young man took a chance and trusted in change or had change forced upon him through a crisis, I do not know. What I do know, is that life will be helping him in the best way for wherever he is at on his journey.

I think of it like this. Say there is a mother and very young child playing in a beautiful parkland. The child is discovering his taste for freedom and adventure. The mother watches indulgently as the child comes to her, then runs away, then comes back again and so on, until the child moves to the edge of a lake. The child cannot swim. The child has never seen anything like that lake and leans over to get a closer look. The mother sees the child about to fall into the lake and screams at him to step back, knowing that a gentler rebuke would have been ineffective in combating the fascinating lure of that unknown lake. The child, startled and hurt by his mother's anger, cries, but steps back. He is safe from that unknown danger. He doesn't necessarily understand it, but the mother does. She wants to protect her child from harm. Freedom and adventure, yes. Drowning, because of the child's ignorance and the mother's neglect, no.

So he experienced a crisis – a feeling of being denied the warm love of his mother. Was he denied that love in reality? No. He was given the benefit of its fierce wisdom and protection. What he makes of that experience is up to him. He might become distrusting of this mother's love or he might give her the benefit of the doubt and continue on his adventures, perhaps learning how to swim when the time is right and then being able to explore that lake when he is better prepared later on.

This is how we can understand that no matter what meaning we attribute to a crisis, in truth, it's about getting off a path that can lead to no good, at least at that time, and onto one that is better for us. It is said that we know when we are truly progressing spiritually when we are able to be as grateful during a famine as we are during a feast. This is much more possible if you remember that you have the equivalent of an attentive and loving mother on the lookout for you. This mother is Life and she is – no matter what your immediate reaction to appearances may be – always acting in your best interests.

"Any kind of crisis can be good. It wakes you up." – Ryan Reynolds

CHOICE

What crisis is meant to lead to is choice – choice in attitude, choice in response, choice in beliefs. Will we see this as a sign of defeat, of despair, of depression and give up? That is the choice to contract, to pull away, to regress. Sometimes we might do this for a little while before making a different choice. But to try and live that way is not living at all. It is becoming afraid and refusing to grow. It is curling up into a little ball so that we only live in what we know and try to avoid being hurt by the guiding hand of life (sometimes gently at our backs, sometimes giving us a sharp slap to wake us up and move us out of danger).

But perhaps we make a different choice, a choice to look for the silver lining in that cloud, no matter how hidden it might be at first, and consider it a shake-up specially delivered by the universe to put us back on the best course possible for our lives. We can choose to believe we are being moved from the wrong place and the wrong time, into the right place and the right time, to be ready for great things heading our way. We will explore alternatives, seek out other options, ask for help – from people and from life – and be open to what else there could be. We will dare to dream and act with positive belief in why it is all happening. That is a different choice. That is the choice of courage. In the workbook section, you'll be guided to find your own choice to deal with any crisis, big or small. Sometimes you just don't realise how incredibly brave you are, until you put your courage to the test.

I often hear people say, "I don't have a choice!" But we always do. We cannot control the external events in our lives, but we can choose how to respond to them. And in choosing wisely, we can turn proverbial lemons into lemonade. But you have to give yourself the benefit of looking at something with an optimist's view. Instead of seeing a big obstacle in front of you as a blocked door, consider it as something to climb up onto to increase your viewpoint and make even better decisions for your future. Or imagine there are many more doors that will show up in your life, and one will open easily for you. That would be the *right one* for you. But you have to choose to keep on trying to open those doors so that you can strike it lucky – through your own efforts and life's guiding hand – at the right time.

CHAPTER 4

Confusion

· ·

CHOOSING YOUR BREAKFAST

I am completely obsessed with Jane Austen novels as well as film versions of the books. I know I am not alone in this. I have often thought about what the appeal is with period cinema. There are many reasons no doubt, although one that really nourishes me is the relief from modernity. Whilst I enjoy many aspects of modern life, including freedom as a woman to do pretty much whatever I want and the joy of hot showers, flushing toilets and electricity, there is something that seems quieter, simpler, less distracted and more present in those period dramas. Of course if we were focusing on life in the slums of London, there would be rather less refinement of manners and rather more chaos, but in those society drawing rooms of Jane Austen's heroes and heroines, there is a simple focus on people and feelings. It is a smaller world, more detail-oriented, more subtle. There is a mental relief from the speed, diversity, expansiveness and complexity of modern living. This brings me a sense of pleasing calm when I dive into that world for a time, before returning to my own time zone with renewed zest.

I don't know many people who would want to give up the benefits of modern living, but I do know rather a lot who would like to overcome the sense of overwhelm that leaves us feeling confused. Sometimes I notice people in the supermarket looking utterly bewildered by the amount of product available. So much choice! What does this do, what does that do … what do the children want to eat? What is toxic for health? What is actually healthy despite all the claims printed on cereal boxes? Do I even want to eat processed cereals?

Bewilderment can become overload fairly easily. When that happens a person can feel unable to make a decision. That sort of paralysis in small ways can erode our sense of self-confidence over time. And that's just with choosing a breakfast cereal or brand of washing detergent. Imagine then dealing with matters of love, work, where to live, financial questions and lifestyle. Well, you don't have to imagine. You more than likely already do need to deal with those things.

There is so much incoming data in the modern world, with some researchers suggesting that a small child has already taken in more information than what some of our predecessors would have needed to 'compute' in their entire lifetime. I can well believe it. There is so much incoming data that we could choose – if we were particularly inclined that way – to constantly receive communications twenty-four hours a day. I suspect that most of us are not even aware of the extent to which we are bombarded with messages from social media, magazines, television, radio, email, the internet and the like. When something becomes commonplace, it is easily labelled as normal or even acceptable, even if the effects of it are not healthy – a bit like the state of highly processed and treated foods that are damaging to our health, but eaten by so many that we figure 'it must be all right'. But just because a lot of people say something, that doesn't mean it is true. History has shown us over and over again that the people who seemed to be heretics, claiming that the earth wasn't flat or at the centre of the solar system, were actually just seeing beyond what the mass of humanity could fathom at the time.

We have ancient bodies, designed to live in natural ways in a modern world. Our bodies and minds do their best to adapt to increasing demands – but sometimes that adaptation fails. I don't think this is a bad thing at all. In fact, I believe it is a hidden blessing. Sometimes failing to adapt to a system is the only way we'll be ready, willing and able to opt out of that system and find a better way to live.

SYSTEM OVERLOAD

If we overload the body with toxins, and don't give it time and support to release them, eventually it reaches a point at which it cannot clear those toxins effectively anymore. The toxic load becomes too great and the response is that you start to feel tired, fuzzy-headed, irritable and generally unhappy, unwell. It would eventually happen even if you were eating healthy food, but just too much of it. If you don't give your body a chance to digest and eliminate what has gone in, you won't feel very good. Allowing for elimination is important for the body.

A beautiful and extremely fluffy orange cat was my precious soul animal and feline companion for over a decade and he taught me a lot during that time. He never seemed to be happier than when he had left something smelly in his litter tray. He positively frolicked with joy afterwards.

Elimination is important for the body and for our wellbeing. It is the same with the mind. If flooded with incoming data and not able to process and either discard or apply the information received, the mind will feel overwhelmed and begin to shut down, just like the body. That overwhelm is a system overload, similar to that which happens on a physical level. There is too much going in and not enough coming out. The result for the mind is the same sort of cloudy thinking, doing-a-lot-and-not-seeming-to-get-anywhere-good confusion that signals a system overload leading to a system breakdown. That might show up as a constant sense of anxiety, as depression, as a lack of productivity or clear sense of direction. Or it might seem as if 'everyone wants a piece of you', or as feeling cranky like you are going to 'snap' at any moment!

If you haven't worked it out yet, I am a radical optimist, so I do see that even breakdowns can become breakthroughs if you know how to work with them. My preference for all of us, however, is that we learn to deal with situations before they have to become so severe. Confusion can turn to a sense of paralysis and depression if we don't nip it in the bud, so to speak. To do this requires that we offload what has become too great, giving ourselves a chance to clear out what has been to make sense of where we are headed. I'll guide you through this process in the exercise in Chapter 9 called 'Crystal Clear'. You can use it anytime you feel overwhelmed and confused, inefficient, tired or in need of refreshment.

CLEARING THE CLUTTER

Recently, I travelled to a country town to run a spiritual workshop. In the two days before and after the workshop, I conducted personal sessions for the participants. In one of those sessions I met a kind-hearted and sensitive woman in her forties. She was struggling with where she lived. It was, in her view of things, too small. Having just heard from another client that she struggled with her kitchen which was, for her liking, just too large, I wondered if the next client would be a golden-haired woman who would tell me that her house was 'just right'. That didn't happen, which just goes to show that although life can be utterly beautiful, it isn't meant to be a fairytale!

Anyway, as this client told me of her home that was too small, something just didn't seem to sit right with me. I listened carefully for the truth in what she wasn't saying. I soon realised that she was absolutely overwhelmed with clutter. Her house might have been small, but what made it too small, what was causing her distress, was not the size of the house, but the amount of stuff crammed into it.

I talked about taking small steps and tackling one box at a time, but the response to any suggestion, no matter how unthreatening I believed it to be, was that she didn't have any room to do so. She did have room to do things she wanted to do however, so I realised that space was less an issue than she believed it to be. The real issue was fear.

Clutter is an expression of confusion – just at a physical level. A bit of mess can show a creative mind, but if that mess is becoming overwhelming, then there is something else going on and it's not creativity. It's fear of space, of openness, of choice, of the future and what could be. It's a fear of being empty because one hasn't been sufficiently mothered enough to know how to receive, to trust that if we open our arms, we will actually receive. Instead, people who struggle with this state fear that if they let go they'll end up with nothing and that will be the end of it. They don't trust enough that the nothing can then become something (better) if they are willing to run the risk of it. They are – like most of the population these days – afraid, and not certain how to deal with that fear. It is just that for people with a weight issue or with hoarding, fear shows up in a more physically obvious and less socially acceptable way. Fear that shows up as fear of eating and nurturing the body, or fear of possessions and ownership (and the commitment that entails) tends to be more socially palatable. Yet it is just fear in a slightly different outfit.

Clutter that becomes hoarding can quickly turn into overwhelm and confusion. Although you might think that person lazy, or dirty, or disorganised, it is actually an expression of a genuine psychological and emotional distress that can be very painful to confront and difficult to deal with. The woman I mentioned above was building a prison of possessions around her. I believe that she felt suffocated and was in danger of collapsing under the weight of what she was holding on to. She didn't want to give something away in case she needed it in the future. Her own body was very overweight too. I believe her body and her apartment were showing her that she had to learn to let go, to trust a little more that life would give her what she needed, when she needed it, and that it was okay to not have to hold on to the future possibilities (with furnishings for a place she was yet to find or own) or the past quite so much. I empathised with her, having been through both of those situations myself, though on a less dramatic scale to how they were showing up in her life. I had enough familiarity with the sense of panic, dread and fear that existed beneath the excess weight of the body and excess accumulation of possessions, that I truly did feel compassion for her. But, I knew how freeing it was to let go, and to learn to balance being able to receive with feeling empty sometimes (and being okay with that feeling), and to learn to trust in the rise and fall of our lives in various ways, just like we learn to feel comfortable with the seasons of nature (though we may prefer some seasons to others).

It's my sense that we live in a time of being overfed and undernourished on so many levels. Clutter is a plague of modern humanity – whether it is obvious in the body that needs a detox from the chemical-laden lifestyle that even the most health-conscious amongst us finds tricky to avoid in the modern world, or the home that has more space dedicated to storage than living areas, or the mind that is overwhelmed with so many thoughts it cannot focus on what is really important. No wonder we are so often confused. To recognise that is to be honest. And that honesty – or truth, as the expression goes – can be what sets us free.

THE MATRIX

Most of us don't realise that we live within systems at all. We think that what we believe about ourselves and the world is real, that some things are not to be questioned, and although what we choose to believe may greatly curtail our personal freedoms, for many people, a sense of certainty brings comfort – until, it doesn't. Then, as Anaïs Nin is often quoted as having said, "And the day came when the risk to remain tight in a bud was more painful than the risk it took to blossom."

The popular movie *The Matrix* features a storyline based on the idea of breaking out of one reality to discover that it wasn't reality at all. In that film, a group of rebellious free-thinkers fight against the powers that be to free humanity from being exploited and used for purposes that have nothing to do with their wellbeing and everything to do with serving hidden agendas and powerbrokering. The liberation from the dream world isn't simply a matter of one day being asleep and the next day being awake however. The process of escaping from the dream world is difficult, with the powers that be doing all they can to undermine the process of liberation for the film's heroes. This process of struggle causes one of the rebels to want to return to the dream world, where it all seems more comfortable and easy, even though he knows it is fundamentally a dark and destructive way to live. Despite the many challenges, the story ends on an uplifting turn where the heroes eventually do break through into a more loving and free world.

The system, or matrix, as it is called in the film, is not so far from the truth of how we live. Our belief systems are just that – systems. They can change. The current way we know how to live is not the only way. It's just one way. One system of beliefs, that could – if circumstances change – become another system of beliefs. We might choose to believe that what we know is all there is to know, or all that there is that is worth knowing. This helps us feel secure in what might otherwise seem like a paralysing uncertainty.

Yet the beliefs about ourselves and the world – perhaps that anyone who comes from a different town, culture, religion or economic background is untrustworthy, for example – do not only contain us and help us to feel safe, they can also limit us and prevent us from growing and experiencing all that life has to offer.

Our belief systems are something like a child's playpen. They are necessary during formative stages, but regressive if we don't learn to venture out into the garden as we become ready, then into the world of schooling, and then the world of work, and so on. Even when our beliefs seem more open-minded and make us curious about others and the world, if we hold on to anything too tightly, without a willingness to let go of what we have known, so life can keep leading us to our fullness, to all that we can be, then we'll get stuck in our own matrix. That matrix is not only about the quality of the belief systems we have – are they fear-based or more open and loving? It is also about understanding that no matter what we believe there is a reality that exists just as it is, no matter what our opinions of it may be. Believing that life is something to be feared doesn't make it so. It does tend to colour our interpretation of experiences and make it harder for us to live our lives happily and with peace though. Overcoming the matrix is about realising we get to choose our belief systems, that they are things we choose to create, not reality to remain unquestioned.

Belief systems are essentially a somewhat organised group of beliefs we have about ourselves and life. They are based on our interpretation of experiences, what we inherit from our parents and our particular culture, country of origin and even birth experience (whether that was an easy thing or a more challenging experience for mother and baby), and our particular temperament that tends to shape the way we experience life and view the world. Those factors combine and we end up with our 'story' about ourselves, life and the world. These beliefs, or opinions, interpretations and stories clump together, creating partial realities which we usually take as being the whole story or the 'real truth' (at least for a while).

You could consider a partial reality, or belief system, as something like the trailer for a movie. You'll get snippets of the story, but not the whole picture. Have you ever seen a film where your expectations based on the trailer were so different to the actual film that you wondered if it really was for the same movie? This is what our partial realities are like, especially if they become rigid, fixed and resistant to change. They become distorted and misleading, not really telling us truthfully about the bigger story of our lives. We might fixate on one or two events that took place, interpret them in a certain way, and they become the 'evidence' to support our belief systems. We are in a partial reality that keeps us trapped, a prison of our own creation, and it can stop us from living a happier and healthier life until we learn how to kick it to bits – or life does it for us – and then realise something startling, confronting, terrifying and wonderful.

The stories we use to create our beliefs about the world are just stories. Our beliefs are not necessarily truths, they are more likely just opinions. Our views of the world and life are realities we choose to engage in, not something that is fixed and 'has to be' a particular way. As you realise this, you learn that you can choose to live in realities that are more loving and less fearful. You aren't in denial, you aren't in a dream world, you are experiencing this world in a particular way. Just like when people look at the same glass, and some will see it as half empty and be afraid, and others will see it as half full and feel genuinely lucky and grateful.

Fortunately, you can choose to drop a story, a belief system, at any time, and learn to adopt a new one. You are absolutely allowed to do this, anytime you choose. Becoming happier in life is just as much about unlearning what we have come to 'know', as much as it is about learning new things. In the workbook section, I'll guide you through a process to crumble and reconstruct your life systems, and to support you if confusion has already started that process for you.

You can think about it like this: imagine there are three people, all blindfolded, and an elephant (and none of them walked into a bar!).

One person stands at the (very calm and patient) elephant's tail and touches it. "The elephant is thin and wiry!" he declares.

The second person stands at the elephant's ears, feeling their flat and velvety softness. "The elephant is soft and paper-thin!" she declares.

Finally, the third person touches the round belly of the elephant and declares, "The elephant is round and large!"

They are all partially right but none wholly so. If they'd remove their blindfolds and were willing to see the whole elephant instead of only the bit right in front of them, they'd have more understanding of that beautiful creature. Instead they grasp only the slightest and most partial 'truth' and end up so very far away from the reality of the creature standing practically under their noses.

This is what our systems are like. They are our grasping at life with a blindfold on because we are either not willing or not yet able to see all of it right before us. If we did, it would be far more strange and beautiful and inexplicable than we could imagine. I mean, if you really could look at an elephant objectively, as though seeing it for the first time, wouldn't you call it strange and beautiful? They are completely odd and gorgeous animals! Perhaps we are not quite ready or capable to let go of needing the elephant to just be 'one way'. Perhaps we cannot quite take in the strange beauty of that creature as yet. It's a bit much for our narrow view on what constitutes beauty, perhaps.

Our personal beliefs and viewpoints can helps us understand life and experience it in a limited way. At some point, perhaps when the elephant is getting impatient with all this tomfoolery, and starts to stride off towards more interesting life experiences, we are going to need to remove our blindfolds and get out of the way lest we end up trampled under the part of the elephant we managed to filter out of our partial realities!

IGNORANCE UNDER THREAT

You'll know when a belief system or partial reality is under threat of exposure, or when – to use the example above – that elephant is getting twitchy and ready to move on, because you'll have a strong reaction to whatever could challenge it. It might be another religious or political point of view, a person, an event or even an image in the media. You may feel your grip on your world, and what you once believed to be true, right or the only way you should or could live, slipping away. Or you might fight with all your being, denouncing that other viewpoint as evil or stupid or ignorant, or whatever it is you can fathom, to push it away and keep your own belief system intact. Why? Because you are afraid of what you might find out.

When I was twelve years old and in the sixth class of primary school, we did an exercise on Remembrance Day, observed in Australia at 11.00 am on the eleventh day of the eleventh month. I think '11/11' really stuck in my mind because of the numbers, but being basically a peace-loving soul who found war a devastating concept to deal with as a child – and even now as an adult – I liked the idea that this moment was about remembering peace and the ending of war, as well as acknowledging those who died. I never really believed that death in itself was something to fear, because you would be returning to the love from which you first came, so that was okay. What frightened and disturbed me was the way we treated each other in war, the suffering and disturbance to body, mind and heart that this sort of experience could create.

In my sixth grade class, we drew pictures to honour Remembrance Day. Nearly thirty years later, I still recall what I drew because of how much it meant to me at the time. I drew a little cartoon of a Turkish soldier at Gallipoli, and an Australian soldier, a member of the Anzacs, laying down their weapons and shaking hands. They recognised each other as people, not as a Turk and an Aussie, not as enemies, but just as two people who were fighting in a terrible war. They were, in that moment, allowed to step outside of the horror of war and into their humanity and brotherhood. That meant a lot to me as a child, just as it does as an adult.

Why I wanted to share this recollection with you is to illustrate a point. The two soldiers in my cartoon were able to shake hands because they dropped their belief system that the other was the enemy and had to be killed. Peace could prevail. Common ground could be found. For that to happen, belief systems had to be dispensed with. Was a war really necessary for there to be so much suffering and devastation that finally, someone said "Enough!"? I would not like to think so. What I do know is that we don't have to allow things to get bad in our own minds and lives before we can choose to drop our belief systems and adopt something that serves us and the world better. Sometimes the best change in belief systems happens when we stop allowing our heads to interfere with what our hearts know to be true, when we stop thinking quite so much and start feeling much, much more.

"Sixty minutes of thinking of any kind is bound to lead
to confusion and unhappiness." – James Thurber

Changes in belief systems can feel like an incredible upheaval. Even if you don't want that particular belief anymore – that life has to be a constant struggle, or that you or someone else are not lovable nor acceptable – letting it go can open up a whole new, and even at first, confusing and unknown world. This might be exciting and welcomed. You might be so fed up with situations that don't seem to really be working in your life that you are ready and willing to rip off that blindfold. If you are afraid, however, then your response will possibly be less than excited. You might feel very afraid. If you find it hard to feel your fear and respond to it consciously, as many people do, then you'll mask it and express it as judgement, condemnation, hate or ridicule instead.

No matter whether your response is welcoming or resistant, once one of your systems is challenged, you are going to be in for a journey from one way of being towards new land. As the saying goes, 'the only way to get to new land is to lose sight of the shore'. That often brings with it a sense of the unfamiliar, and as you try to orient yourself to the new land you haven't quite set foot upon as yet, confusion is usually felt. This is why I don't see confusion as a bad thing at all. Provided we work with it – we let go and allow the new life that wants to happen, happen. Then confusion is a helpful sign that our cages have been rattled, and that means the doors are going to be easier to open to set us free.

Sometimes the belief systems in our lives need to change even if we don't want them to. The yoga-loving vegetarian might need to change their diet due to chronic malnutrition and become a yoga-loving carnivore. I know of people who were banished from their yoga communities for such behaviour. It was obviously a challenging transition for all involved, yet that is what life asked of them. Or, for example, the endurance runner might develop health problems and their belief systems – if allowed to continue – will lead them to having a stroke if they don't give up their sport and find a different way to approach their wellbeing.

The mother whose children leave the nest will need to find a broader sense of her role in the world beyond mothering her children if she is to move beyond a sense of loss and discover her next phase in life. Perhaps she is absolutely ready for it, slams the door shut, does a gleeful jig at the prospect of her newly-granted freedom, and turns one of the kids' bedrooms into an office and goes out to celebrate with her girlfriends. But perhaps that is not the case. What if all her energy, love, focus and devotion have been poured into her children for decades? The thought of having to live without that mantle could be utterly terrifying. Who will she be? What will she do now? Shifts in life that trigger changes in our belief systems can be joyful and exciting, but they can of course feel very testing.

There is a movie called *Raising Helen* featuring actress Kate Hudson in the lead role. Helen is a freedom-loving, dynamic young woman working in a demanding job in the fashion industry. Her life is stressful but also glamorous and successful. She leads a fairly self-centred life, focused only on work and her own little world, venturing into the more family-oriented world of her two older sisters and their families for special occasions, and that's about it. Then one day, her elder sister and brother-in-law die in a car accident, leaving their three children behind. At a surprise in the reading of the will, the children are not left in the custody of the other older sister, who is a very capable, motherly type and very much wants to adopt them, but in the care of the night-clubbing younger sister Helen. She rises to the challenge as best she can – with some very comedic moments as her old life becomes increasingly incompatible with her new role as parental figure (rather than the cool but somewhat irresponsible aunt). Her world and beliefs – about herself, her role, parenting, family, love and more – all get turned upside down.

What Helen finds is that the life she has loved needs to give way for the love that has found its way into her life. It's not always an easy journey for her, but she manages to take the steps that life has shown her, and the transition successfully happens with her claiming her unexpected role as a parent and a great bond of love and trust developing between her and the children. She is brave enough to take the journey that life has presented to her, and she eventually transforms quite considerably into a fuller, happier and more mature version of herself – for the greater good of the man who falls in love with her, and the children who become her own.

What is entertaining in a movie however, can be hard to accept in life. There will be certain belief systems you might not want to hold on to anymore, especially if those systems are based on ill-health, toxic habits, poverty, or just aren't working well for you. I have seen it in organisations going through transitions from one corporate culture towards another because of a change of ownership or management consultancy assessment, for example. People can become frightened because of the uncertainty. They may not feel in control in such a process – and in a way they really aren't. It probably seems a bit like you belong to one family with a set of rules you understand, and then suddenly the family starts to change, along with the rules, and you have to learn how to fit in with what will be acceptable and what will not be acceptable all over again. It is unfamiliar, and if they don't have a fundamentally trusting attitude towards life, they will likely feel very unsafe about not being in control. Apart from fear, a sense of being stuck in a situation that isn't enjoyable can give rise to competing needs: to stay and be safe, or to see something through because you feel it is worth the effort and risk to do so; or to jump ship and move on, to take this as a cue to look for something new. The conflict of competing desires can generate a lot of confusion as a person tries to ride the waves of change.

Some people will be the early adopters, so to speak, and grab on to the new way with a missionary-like zeal. Perhaps sometimes we need such extreme behaviour of clinging to a new truth as if it is the great saviour to our dilemmas – even if just for a time – because leaving an old system behind and trying to adopt a new way of living is a real challenge.

Change happens all around us, yet people who are actually capable of sustaining a transformation of self, of health, of attitude, are the people we often look to as role models because going through genuine change is hard. It is possible, absolutely, but we have to be willing to put in the work for it. That means not only being willing to learn something new, but to keep going until it becomes our new reality so we can leave the old life – and the old confusion – behind us. It means growth. Growth is natural but that doesn't make it easy all the time! It takes courage, confidence and creativity. You have these things within you, but like that bird that has to test its wings in order to fly, it's often the push of confusion that forces us to break free and open up to new possibilities, and discover that we are capable of more than we once believed (and therefore, get a new belief system too!).

IT'S YOUR TIME TO STEP UP

When faced with confusion you are being put to the test. It is life throwing down the gauntlet, so to speak, and asking if you will step into your power. You are being given a chance to break out of the belief systems you have known. What that means is that how you have lived will no longer be right for you at some level. It might be that a belief system has to change – your religion, your approach to nutrition and exercise, your beliefs about relationships, money, work or your body. It might be that an identity you have held on to becomes irrelevant – children leaving home, divorce, retirement or retrenchment, relocation, financial changes or health issues. Or perhaps you have just reached the edge of what you know – finished a course of study or gone as far as you can go with a certain job, feeling stifled in the town you live or your career and so on. At some level, your life wants to change and you need to change too. Enter confusion.

Confusion happens at the edge of what is known and is a sign that you are ready (or soon will be) for something else to happen in life. You probably won't really know what that new 'something else' could be. You may have no idea at all! Or you might imagine or envision something (although the reality may turn out to be rather different to what you anticipated). Confusion signifies that you have entered a transition zone and the world as you have known it is not going to make sense anymore.

That may seem very dramatic or even frightening, but actually unplugging from a belief system to find a better way of living is very liberating. It is naughtiness in a good way. Most genuinely powerful spiritual people from various religious and spiritual traditions have a rebellious streak. They don't rebel against the establishment for the sake of being a rebel, they simply know a better way to what most people know. They know that this other way is so wonderful, so healing, feels so good and makes them so much happier and able to help more people, that they are willing to be at peace, even if others don't always understand them, or maybe even think they are crazy.

Personally, I don't believe that any of us are really approaching true sanity until at least some of the people around us think we are at least a bit weird or different. Some people embrace their uniqueness as a badge of honour, others are learning not to be afraid that if they are different they will be rejected – rather than loved or admired – for their uniqueness. If you were raised in a family or culture that has issues about being different, then it might be harder for you to accept the uniqueness within you. But it is my experience that every person on the planet has things about them that are the same as every other person – particular needs for love and fulfilment, for example – and also that every person on the planet has something unique about them that no-one else has. We are all ordinary and extraordinary. I have never held the belief that if everyone is special, no-one is special. I feel that there is quirkiness in the heart of every human being, and that quirkiness, that difference, is the part of us willing to get confused sometimes in order to discover something more about ourselves, about life, about what can be.

"It is no measure of health to be well adjusted to a profoundly sick society."
– Krishnamurti

SPOILT FOR CHOICE

Once I worked with a very talented (though not very modest) young woman who was a gifted artist and excellent drummer too. She was also a dancer and could make clothes and undoubtedly had many more talents lurking underneath the surface. I commented on her multi-talentedness to which she replied that it was hard because there were so many things she could do well. It reminded me of a comment I overheard about myself during my university years where one of my friends said to another, "It's hard not to hate Alana sometimes because she's so good at everything she does." Obviously she was yet to see me try to sew or ride a bike, two things on a long list for which I claim no skill at whatsoever.

The truth of it is that this young musician and artist echoed something I had struggled with too. If there are many possible paths in your life, sometimes choosing one is overwhelming and confusing. I sometimes envied some of my friends in law school who were so passionate about law and knew that that was what they wanted to do from the time they were very young. Though that being said, most of them ended up doing something else eventually anyway. For me, my career – which has been such an incredible blessing and gift – was something I felt very confused about then. At that time I knew I loved being on stage, singing, writing and performing. I loved my absolute freedom to explore as much spiritual, New Age and self-help material as I could handle. I had no idea it could become a profession. Yet that is exactly what has happened, though confusion still strikes at times when I wonder, decades on, exactly how to sum all that up in a pithy job description when people ask me what I do for work.

Before I went through one of the most confusing journeys of my life – from law school, through a short-lived (and most ill-advised for my temperament) detour into retail work – then eventually working as a healer, I had no idea what I was going to do with my life. Fortunately enough, I didn't have to understand that in advance. For my life and career to work out, however, I did have to change the way I operated – rather dramatically.

In order to do well academically, I had learned to be incredibly organised and structured in my approach to a heavy workload. It served me well and I passed most of my exams with excellent results and even managed to be made dux of my high school. In university, I applied the same methodical approach but with rather less passion – I was a bit over schooling by that stage, to be honest. I found my studies boring and that lack of interest translated into a lot of my energy going into reading books on chakras and aromatherapy rather than contract law, and the only thing I found interesting in property law was a three-second reference to the property system in my beloved Jane Austen novels. Apart from those three seconds of curiosity, the rest of the course was so mind-numbingly boring, I actually nearly failed the course because I just couldn't bring myself to read the textbook. Despite this, I managed to gain my law degree and gain some good job offers. I didn't want those jobs, of course, but at least I had some offers! The approach I had developed had worked for me. I was used to operating in a very structured, organised and goal-oriented way.

So it was a bit difficult to suddenly step out of that career path and realise I couldn't chase goals with my new career as a sort of psychic, healer, spiritual guidance counsellor and so on, because I didn't know what that career was going to be. It sort of evolved over time. I started off doing tarot readings, which became healings, which became counselling and then psychotherapy, teaching workshops and on and on, until I was up on stage singing dance tunes with conscious themes to an audience aged seven to seventy plus, and even then, it still kept evolving. I believe that even though I rarely knew exactly how my work was going to turn out, life knew all along exactly what sort of 'plant' I was meant to grow into, whilst I had to wait and see, trusting and experiencing it just as it happened.

That meant giving up a lot of my planning, and learning to use my discipline and hard work not to try and build things before I knew what I was supposed to be building! It meant learning how to be more spontaneous and unscripted with my work, and trusting that things could work out even when I wasn't working according to a definite plan of career progression. Well, maybe life knew what that plan of career progression was, but I certainly didn't. I still accept that there will be surprises around most corners. Sometimes this evokes confusion as I grow into what is happening, letting go of what has been. Trying to figure things out is a constant process.

What is different now is that I understand there's nothing wrong with this. I don't always enjoy the confusion much, though I have learned to expect that when something is happening with my work that I don't understand, it means something interesting is happening, and when the time is right, I'll be able to see it and know it. Until then, I just take one step after the other and do my best with what I can do, make a commitment to what I can commit to, and keep going – just like everyone else who is willing to work towards their success in life and live from their heart.

Being willing to grow into what you want out of life will bring you much joy – if you are willing to allow life to guide you rather than trying to control everything that happens and resisting anything that seems a little risky or uncertain. If you choose to live that way, then you'll find that life is indeed very generous and willing to give you anything you ask for (although the way it comes to you and the form your desire takes may not be exactly what you expect!).

One of the 'costs' of receiving whatever you ask for is confusion. This is not meant to be a permanent state of being, but it is going to arise every time you are taken beyond what you know. It's natural. It's good. It's something that is a sign of moving ahead. And – perhaps the best news – it's temporary, at least until the next time it comes up again!

"Confusion is a word we have invented for an order which is not understood."
– Henry Miller

Sometimes you won't be able to understand where life is leading you or what is happening. People often say 'everything happens for a reason' and I do believe that too. It doesn't mean you'll always know what that reason is – sometimes life will actually seem very unreasonable indeed. Do you think the caterpillar turning to mush is finding that process reasonable? From his perspective, quite likely not. However, if mush is required for him to do what he is meant to do – change himself into a butterfly – then it's reasonable that he is given what he needs to be able to fulfil his potential.

So it is with us. Often life is most confusing when we are in the grittiness of turning into the best possible versions of ourselves. It isn't fun at the time. I have been through it many times and can speak with much experience on this topic – in particular, with a lot of authority on the subject of throwing tantrums at the universe before surrendering into what is. Yet in all honesty, once I get past my tantrums, I have only ever looked back at what I went through with gratitude and wonder, because of where it eventually led me.

"Gratitude unlocks the fullness of life. It turns what we have into enough, and more.
It turns denial into acceptance, chaos to order, confusion to clarity. It can turn a meal
into a feast, a house into a home, a stranger into a friend." – Melody Beattie

So even though it is uncomfortable for most of us, confusion isn't bad. It isn't a sign that you are doing something wrong, it's a sign that you are growing, that you are doing something *right*. As philosopher Søren Kierkegaard put it, "Life can only be understood backwards; but it must be lived forwards." Understanding can come in time, but if you want what you have asked for to come true, what you dream of to happen, then you'll have to be willing to have times in your life where you don't understand, where things don't always make sense, and where the only thing that really keeps you going is a sense of trust (and perhaps also a very good sense of humour).

The first time I ever did a supported headstand in yoga was when I was travelling and working in western Europe. There's something about travel that can give you permission to try new things, so when my teacher at the time asked if I would like to have a go at one, I agreed. I was fit and healthy and thought that if he thought I could do one, then I probably could, although if you had asked me some months earlier in Australia if I could have done that, I doubt I would have said yes. Then however, I was willing to give it a go, although I had no idea what I was supposed to do. How did one just suddenly end up in one of those weird-looking headstand poses without breaking something important, like one's neck?

I trusted my body and I trusted my yoga teacher. I listened to his instructions and as I flipped myself upside down, and followed his guidance about how to move my body in a slow, careful and controlled fashion into the correct posture, I felt disoriented by the unfamiliar sensation of my entire body being upside down with my legs straight up in the air. I said to him, "I feel as though I might fall backwards because I cannot get a sense of where my legs are."

He gently took hold of my feet and pulled them back an inch or so to rest them against his chest for a moment. "I am here, with you" he said. "You will not fall."

And so trusting that my safety net guide was there, I allowed my body to push straight up and learned what it felt like to be in a headstand. When I relaxed and just went with the process, I very much enjoyed the posture. He was there and I trusted I was safe. I experienced something new and gained some confidence in being able to overcome something I didn't think I would have been able to do. I was happy to take it 'one step at a time' and know that that was enough to get there.

In the workbook exercises, I'll guide you through a process that will help you let go of needing to understand everything now, to realise that you don't always have to feel in control to be safe, and to allow yourself to be led by whatever is happening, no matter how confusing that might seem at the time.

THE VOICE WITHIN

During the ten years I worked as a psychotherapist, helping people deal with all sorts of issues from the most everyday sorts of matters to deeply spiritual challenges, one thing I found with all my clients is that the things they said to themselves on a daily basis really mattered, in terms of their sense of confidence, in being able to deal with what life was handing to them.

Like most people, I have a mixture of negative and positive voices within me. I have learned to use the positive ones that have helped me get what I want out of life as often as I can. I inherited a belief from my mother that I could do anything I set my mind to, and I still firmly believe that the world is our oyster, so to speak. If we are willing to trust ourselves, work hard, be optimistic and keep going, all doors we want to walk through will eventually open for us – at the right time according to a bigger scheme of life, of course.

The negative voices have been a bit trickier to deal with. Mostly because I – like most people – didn't realise they were there at first. They are a bit like the bugs that come out into the kitchen at night-time when no-one is paying much attention. It took me a while to see that although I was a gentle and loving person in many ways, I had a way of treating myself that was very harsh. If something wasn't done successfully – even at first try – I would feel it was a failure, that I hadn't worked hard enough, and would lose confidence in myself. This was the dark side of believing I could do anything if I wanted to. I had to learn how to set some limits on this negative and critical voice to understand that things still needed time to grow and develop which would mean that sometimes I would have to be patient. This wasn't accepting failure; this was wisdom. So when I noticed myself speaking or thinking negatively towards myself, or anyone else for that matter, I would take a moment and 'turn my mental frown upside down' and look for how to change that voice into one that was encouraging rather than critical.

This wasn't about becoming weak or indulgent. It was about becoming even stronger as a person, to be able to retain courage and optimism even if I had to wait years, or decades in some cases, for certain dreams to come to life. It helped me keep trust when I was confused and uncertain and afraid, learning to let go of having to be in control and understand everything at the time it was happening, so that I could let life happen and grow happier as a result.

It took time, but eventually I found I was able to change the voice within so that it became more encouraging, loving and appreciative. As I did this, the anxiety I had struggled with as a young person eventually faded away. Whilst I still get impatient and restless to create something new or make some (positive) waves in the world at times, I am more patient and serene than I have ever been. If a negative voice comes up, I take my time to respond to it with reassurance and love. Negativity has less of a grip on me than it once did because of that approach. I have learned not to be afraid of confusion, and to use the voice within to help me endure it with more grace and happiness. I might not always love it, but I can be okay with it and just accept that that is how things are at that moment, and at some point, they'll change and my view will become clearer – for a while – until the whole process happens again!

My first spiritual teacher once said to me that the negative thoughts we think are the equivalent of throwing a piece of furniture around a room in the spirit worlds. We might think that a little negativity here and there doesn't matter much, but what she was teaching me was that a thought can have more power than we realise. Our words and thoughts are powerful. We just don't always realise exactly how much so until we start to change them. The way this happened for me, and the way it happens for anyone, is to become aware of how you speak to yourself, what you think about yourself. You cannot change something you aren't even aware of in the first place.

The trickiest part of working with the voice within is that the way we speak to ourselves is something that is most often unconscious at first. We tend to inherit it from our families, or whomever we spend the most time with as children. If you have ever heard words come out of your mouth and thought, *Oh my god, I sound like my mother!* then you've had a moment where the voice within became the voice without!

Sometimes we won't even realise what we believe until we hear ourselves say something and wonder who on earth is speaking. Sometimes this is one of those positive experiences where someone is struggling and you open your mouth and a stream of wise and helpful words come pouring out. Later you may well wonder where all that wisdom came from! It also happens in a more negative sense, where you might suddenly have a moment where you hear yourself and realise you sound like a whiny, grumpy pessimist for whom nothing in life goes right.

It's worth pulling yourself up and challenging yourself when you find yourself thinking or speaking as a person you don't particularly want to be. If you think and then say something enough, you'll start to believe it. We are, in effect, mentally and emotionally conditioning and programming ourselves on a daily basis. The words and beliefs we choose (remembering that partial realities are just one choice – there is always another way to look at something, another belief we could choose, in any given circumstance) are the substance of our daily emotional and psychological meals. Just as if you were to feed yourself nourishing instead of destructive food on a daily basis (with the occasional blip here and there), if you feed yourself good thoughts and feelings on a daily basis you'll feel better. You'll have more energy. You'll be able to live well. You do this by choosing to have gratitude for what you have and a positive expectation for what is coming (rather than anger for what has not yet been, or fear about what might not seem to be). You can choose either way, every day. It's not bad if you've been thinking negatively, it's just a habit that won't get the best out of you, and you might want to give it up in favour of a more positive attitude that *will* get the best out of you and your life. In the workbook section there are plenty of exercises to help you transition from grumpy to grateful.

As our words and beliefs are the basis for how we experience the world, do we dance in the rain and become willing to notice the rainbows, or do we grumble that our recently-washed car will get dirty? It is worth becoming more aware of our attitudes and thinking. You might not think of yourself as having a negative attitude until you start to catch your thoughts and notice how you speak most of the time.

If you do believe that your attitude could use an upgrade, and generally that is going to be the case (and therefore nothing to be ashamed of – but something to act on), then you are also going to need to be patient. If you have truly believed that you have to be in control, that life is something to be afraid of, that you always get the 'leftovers' rather than first choice, or that you need to feel threatened rather than inspired and hopeful when someone else 'wins', then it might take you a little while to gain trust and start to believe and then feel differently towards life and what it wants for *you*.

If you believe, no matter how much money you have, in an imminent threat of poverty, then you will speak in words that tend towards limitation, scarcity, competition and survival. You might not realise you are doing it, but it will come across this way to others. This is the power of thought, and eventually it creates a sort of repulsion that does actually limit your opportunities for love and connection. Your thoughts can begin to create a reality that you'd rather not experience. You'll even change the way you stand as a result of such thinking.

Studies have been done on the likely victims of crimes, based on a simple test of showing criminal offenders pictures of people and asking who they would be likely to target. They chose pictures of people who seemed to be afraid based on their posture – closed up, hunched over, head down, broadcasting a fearful attitude. It is an instinct of predator towards prey perhaps. What matters is that you can change how you come across to others by changing what you believe. A defeated, frightened person breathes more shallowly and tends to hunch forward rather than walk confidently with an open posture and clear gaze, unafraid to make eye contact with others or even to smile.

Imagine you were an employer interviewing two candidates with the same credentials for a position. Are you going to give the job to the person who seems confident and happy, keen and interested to succeed, or the person who believes that they never get anything, and don't even know why they are there for the interview because they obviously won't get a break … and so on? Even just writing about that sort of attitude makes me feel drained! Though two people may have similar abilities, attitude is so important. It can attract – or repel – opportunities, people, situations. This is where we get the expression, 'what you speak about, you bring about'. What you think about enough, you start to bring about too.

In the workbook exercises, you'll be guided to break through beliefs and habitual responses that you don't feel are really beneficial to your life, and encouraged to enjoy ones that are more constructive and appealing – for you and for all those good opportunities and people you are ready to invite into your life.

You might accept all this and start to worry about negativity lurking inside of you. Don't. It's going to be fine. There is always a chance to start afresh, right now in fact. You don't have to worry about what's been. You can start to look forward to what is coming and be grateful for at least three things you can identify right now. Can you list them now, in your head or aloud? Done? Then you've already begun to break the pattern and build a new one. Well done, you.

WHO'S SEATED AT YOUR INNER TABLE?

Each one of us has more than one voice inside of our heads. It's not quite the same as being completely crazy and hearing voices, though it's not completely different to that either! If you have a voice that is urging you to be brave and take risks, and another one telling you that you should be afraid and to play it safe, you may end up feeling a bit crazy at times. Reassure yourself that most people have these sorts of internal conflicts about how to live running in their heads.

You could imagine that these different voices are spoken by imaginary personalities, such as the inner critic (the part of you that never thinks anything you do is good enough), the inner friend (the part of you that actually *likes* who you are), the inner cheerleader (the part of you that believes in yourself and is encouraging and optimistic), the inner child (the part of you that knows how to play and learn new things, and is most like *you*) and so on.

You could also imagine that they are all seated around a table within your mind and heart, with each one giving an opinion about what you should or should not do in your life. Some will have more value to offer than others, but at our inner table, just as in life, sometimes the loudest voices are not always the most intelligent.

If you allow the child within to have too little power, you'll lack joy, spontaneity and fun. If you allow that child too much power, you'll lack responsibility, maturity and commitment. It's all about balance. If, however, some voices have been fearmongering, making you feel like rubbish, or constantly questioning whether you are good enough or getting anywhere in your life, then it is possible that it's time to do some interior management consultancy and cut loose some of those internal figures. You are absolutely allowed to choose who gets the right to speak at your inner table, and you can choose to listen most to those that are most helpful. In the workbook exercises we'll explore this further.

As this process takes place you will feel happier within yourself, become more successful and productive in your life, and feel more confident to take on new challenges. You will become more conscious of the way you speak to yourself (and to others) and you'll start choosing your words with more awareness. Your spoken words will become more positive and you'll start to generate a field of optimism around you. You'll feel better and naturally attract more favours, help and benefit from those around you. Life may not always be a piece of cake – certainly we are here to learn and grow, and sometimes that can involve challenge – but you'll feel a lot more positive about it, and much of the struggle that negative thinking brought into your life will no longer be an issue. It might seem incredible that such an 'invisible' inner change can bring such visible outer transformation, but it does, and the best way for you to experience this is to try it.

WHAT IS IMPORTANT IS WHAT MATTERS TO YOU

There is a way to honour the good things trying to happen in your life through confusion, without getting stuck in it either. That is to make a commitment. When I feel confusion in my life, I instantly ask myself, "What do I need to commit to here?" You make a choice and you honour your commitment no matter what. That commitment will become your anchor, the point that you hold on to with effort and focus, which sees you through the passing storm of confusion. It is sort of like keeping your eye on the light of the lighthouse whilst the storm rages around you. You let life do its thing, and you do yours, and then things can work out, and unfold, just as they need to.

Commitment takes courage. It means you are willing to say yes to something, even if it seems like it could be an impossible dream. It means you are willing to give up your faith in doubt and impossibility and instead put your faith in love and optimism. In a world where there is plenty of fear, doubt, bitterness and even sometimes sadistic pleasure in another's failure, it takes a lot of guts to put your faith in happiness and joy, to believe in something you aren't sure is possible but really want nonetheless.

There's a reason why stories of people who seem to have attained the impossible resonate so deeply in the human heart. Inside your heart is a desire to live a dream that feels special to you. It might not be the same as my dream, or anyone else's dream, but that doesn't matter. What matters is what is important to you. If you are going to make a commitment to something, willing to sometimes put yourself through the stress and strain of hard work to keep believing when things don't seem to be working out for a while, then you'll need to make sure it matters to you.

Many people struggle to really take joy from their commitments because they are committing to something they think they should – based on what seems to matter to everyone else – rather than committing to what really matters to them. Perhaps they worry that it is selfish to take care of their own needs or doubt their own inner voice as having enough value to be taken seriously, believing that the voices of many must be more powerful than the single true voice of their own heart. Or perhaps they don't even think about it at all, just unconsciously going through the motions of living as they were taught, without questioning if there could be more to life.

Commitments that mean something to you actually give you energy and bring you joy, even when there is heartache in the process if things don't seem to be working out the way you hoped they would (or within the time frame you hoped). The reason the right sort of commitment (and by that I mean what genuinely has value for you) brings you energy and happiness is because it is what you are meant to be doing.

In both the Buddhist and Hindu traditions there is the teaching of 'dharma'. This is a word from the ancient Sanskrit language and has many meanings, one of which is 'right living' or 'right livelihood'. Put in the simplest of terms, this means living the life you are meant to live, including the work you are meant to do, and assuming your rightful place in the world. That might be a place within a family, being on a world stage in some form of leadership or other, a role as a performer, as a mother, as a guide for your friends, or as a person who is naturally a good communicator and is meant to help exchange information with others. Dharma is about living your truth – *your* truth – whatever that might be.

If you were born into a family of lawyers who want you to be a lawyer just like them, but you want to be a singer, and you dream of singing, you sing whenever you can, you love to sing and it fills you with joy, then your dharma is to break with family tradition and be a singer. You are not supposed to quash your heart and try to fit into the family way just for the sake of tradition. If anything is going to make you confused, that sort of conflict between head and heart is certainly going to be it.

The heart is the keeper of your dharma. It is your guide, your inner way-shower, and the light that helps you see through darkness. Sometimes you will only see just enough to take one step, then another, as your heart leads you, and sometimes you'll get a farther-reaching glimpse of where you are going. You can trust that no matter whether things appear to be clear or not, if it feels right, then you must keep going on that path. The heart is the most powerful tonic to clear confusion. When you listen to the heart you don't need to know all the answers in advance. You just need to know what feels true for you in this moment, for this day. Your heart is the compass that guides you to your true north, your rightful place, your right livelihood and lifestyle.

And you'll know what is in your heart because it will mean something to you. It will seem important to you. When you want to make a commitment to something, committing to live your dharma or right life can be scary because it really does matter to you. Doing things where you have less attachment to the outcome of something can be so much easier. Learning to live wholeheartedly and go for what matters to you can be downright terrifying at times because the prospect of stuffing it up and falling flat on your face means so much more to you too. Yet it is only in the heroism of the heart that we truly can find ecstasy, joy and freedom from confusion. It is only in what really matters to us – no matter how big or small it may seem to our minds – that the heart can become the light that sees us through even the darkest night, even if it does just shine enough light for one step at a time.

In the workbook section we will explore an exercise so you can be clear about your priorities and make a commitment to the people and things in life that will bring you greatest peace and happiness. I'll also share with you a beautiful and simple healing exercise for any time you are finding it hard to know what your heart is telling you. It is simple and easy and can be done in a few minutes.

You see, Life really wants to dance with you. She's the most responsive dance partner that there ever was, and she'll respond to your every step forward. But if you don't take a step, you are leaving your most radiant dance partner to become a wallflower and missing your opportunity for the dance.

My prayer and blessing for you is that any confusion in your life pushes you to commit to what really matters to you, that you take the chance that life is handing you, even when it is disguised in a challenge. That is the way life can rally around you and lift you, guide you, push you and embrace you, into the beautiful destiny calling you.

CHAPTER 5

The Other 3 Cs

· ·

Once you realise that chaos, crisis and confusion are signs of a new life calling, and that there are ways you can work with those signs – getting creative, making a choice and a commitment – you are ready to put that understanding into action. The workbook section later on will give you practical tools to do just that.

Before we get to the practical exercises, I want us to get a bit spiritual together first. I am not talking about religion – whether you have a religious path or not is totally up to you and not particularly relevant to this chapter. The spiritual approach I want to mention here is a way for you to do two things. Firstly, this chapter will help you get your mind in a good place to be able to do the practical exercises more easily – and take on board all the information from the first four chapters. Secondly, it will help you realise you have a spiritual side, no matter whether you have thought of yourself in that way or not previously, and it can really help you live your life with more meaning and happiness, even if you don't have a religious path to follow as well.

What I have dubbed as 'the other 3 Cs' will help you respond constructively, positively, intelligently to even the biggest, baddest, most intimidating challenges in your life. These 'other 3 Cs' can help you handle anything you meet on your life journey. Anything. They are the basic three-point coping strategy you can come back to again and again. You can use them when your life is flowing easily and you can use them when things seem to be falling apart. They will always support you and help you find the strength you need to hang in there whilst you find your way.

All the exercises in the workbook, and all information we have covered so far, are based on these three principles. I call them 'the 3 Cs to avoid going crazy'. The more you rely on these other 3 Cs and get used to thinking about them on a daily basis, the easier and more graceful your life will be. They won't remove the challenges completely – because as we have seen so far, challenges are actually meant to help you in a positive way – but they will help you manage those challenges with more peace in your mind and happiness in your heart. They will support you in getting creative in chaos, in making a choice when you are in a crisis and in making a commitment when confusion threatens to overwhelm you. They will help you take on the chaos, crisis and confusion in your life to transform them into fuel to move you into your new life phase.

You can consider it like this – for many people, work is a necessity in order to earn an income and put food on the table. You might not be able to avoid working, but you do get to choose whether you enjoy your day's work or not. These other 3 Cs will help you enjoy the inner work of your day much more, even on those shocking days that I call 'doona days' where you would much rather just stay under the doona all day than face whatever gauntlet life has thrown on your path.

So let's meet these other 3 Cs that are going to become your three-point support system to take the messages of this book and apply them to heal and transform you – and your life – from the inside out.

CONSECRATION

To consecrate something means to make it sacred. Consecration might sound religious or something only 'very spiritual' people do, but that's not the case. Consecration is easy and it's helpful for every person. It's an attitude. It's about being able to see through the eye in your heart, rather than just the eyes in your head. When you look through the eyes in your head, all you see is what appears to be the surface of things, rather than the bigger picture. When you look through the eye of your heart, you remain open to possibilities, to a different perspective. You trust what you feel rather than what appearances dictate. The heart understands that, as the expression goes, 'you should never judge a book by its cover because appearances can (and often do) deceive'.

There's a story from the Chinese Taoist tradition that shows the ability of the heart to see things differently to how the eyes in our heads would see things.

In this story, an old man lives in a village. One day his only horse runs away. The villagers say, "This is terrible!" and try to comfort him, but the old man says, "Good or bad, I cannot say. It just is."

The next day, the errant horse returns, bringing with him two additional wild horses. The villagers rejoice at the man's unexpected good fortune. "You must be so happy!" they say.

"Good or bad, I cannot say," replies the old wise man. "It just is."

And so the old man uses two of his three horses, whilst his son rides off on the third. The son falls off and injures himself so that he can no longer ride.

"How terrible!" cry the villagers, to which the old man says, "Good or bad, I cannot say. It just is."

The next day, the Chinese military ride through the village looking for able-bodied young men to be conscripted into the army. All but the old man's injured son are taken away, to which the villagers respond, "Oh, but this is good … " and you know the old man's reply of course, is that he cannot say if it is good or bad. It just is.

The eyes in our heads are quick to decide if something is good or bad based on very limited circumstances. In my own life, there have been times when I have not been given what I wanted at a particular time, and not long afterwards, my sorrow turned to joy when I realised what a disaster it would have been had I 'got my way' after all, and how much better the solution that eventually came my way was.

The heart is much more willing to refrain from snap judgements and just trust in what is happening, knowing it cannot always know why or how, but that doesn't mean there isn't some higher plan unfolding for the betterment of all. You cannot always understand it, but you can – if you learn to look through the eye in your heart – trust in it and feel more at peace. After all, life is going to do exactly as it does whether you allow yourself to be tossed about on oceans of emotion that label some things as bad and others as good, or whether you aim to see from the eye within your heart instead, and be at peace with what is, knowing that sometimes you just won't understand why life is doing what it is doing, but that there must be some higher purpose to it at another level.

As you learn to see with the eye within, which I'll guide you to do in the workbook section, then you'll start to realise you need to control things so much less than you once believed. This can frighten you at first, but fairly soon it will become a tremendous relief. If there is one C you have to give up once chaos, crisis and confusion enter your life, control will be it. You'll see that this is okay and not a cause for concern. You don't need it. Life has a habit of working things out. We need to do our part, but it is so much less and so much more than we once thought. The 'less' is about needing to control how things work out and when. The 'more' is about showing up each day to whatever life brings us with an open and trusting heart, knowing that far from being naive or silly, this is courageous and constructive. It is also about conditioning our states of mind and our attitudes to a more positive inclination. This isn't about putting a false gloss on things, it's about genuine belief in an underlying helpfulness in life that is actually, no matter what, trying to nurture you so you grow into yourself. Growth isn't always easy, but it is always a good thing.

When you can see in this way, you become able to consecrate your daily life, to see it as something more than just 'going through the motions' of existing. Most of us hunger for more sacredness in life without really knowing what it is, or thinking that it belongs in the realm only of religion or mysterious spiritual workshops and rituals. But everyone needs some sacredness in life, something that seems special, valuable, worthy of respect and reverence. Even if you aren't religious or don't consider yourself to be overly spiritual, perhaps especially then, to be able to see your life as more than just a marathon to get through, or a meaningless struggle, but as something that is meaningful and has a deeper purpose gives you courage to look beyond what doesn't appear to be working, to find the bigger plan that is working out perfectly every day.

When you consecrate something, you give it meaning. So instead of just being ill or just suffering a break-up, it becomes a struggle you are going through to get to a better life, to let go of what is no longer rightfully yours or an old identity in your life, and to prepare yourself for something new. Context can help us bear a struggle that is painful and sometimes make it less painful because we no longer see it as a sign we are doing something wrong. We see it as a rite of passage, as an initiation, as part of how we become a wiser and better person, as part of our personal development and spiritual growth.

Spiritual initiation exists in many tribal societies. Rites of passage are not just about age, but about gaining maturity and stepping into positions of leadership and respect within a community. We miss out on many meaningful initiations in modern culture. Getting drunk the moment you turn eighteen or twenty-one (depending on where you live in the world), hiring strippers the night before you get married, or going out for drinks with your girlfriends when your divorce finally comes through are examples of our modern attempts at rituals to acknowledge a rite of passage. They don't always hit the mark, really helping the person to process the change in their lives, which is what a ritual for a rite of passage is really meant to help you do.

It is healthy and completely normal to feel some anticipation at a change in your life – whether it be turning forty or fifty or sixty, or suddenly becoming a parent (or grandparent) or being in a relationship where you were single for a long time, or the reverse, where you are suddenly single after being in a relationship for a long time. Changing careers, retiring, being made redundant, starting or finishing school … these are all rites of passage, and they need to be consecrated, to be recognised as meaning something (other than a now legal opportunity to drink alcohol, for example). When you learn to see the sacred in your daily life, you'll find that even ordinary life becomes more special, more meaningful.

Perhaps this is why we can place so much emphasis on approval from others or on external signs of progression, such as through gaining a promotion, for example. When we are denied our rituals of initiation, our acknowledgement of maturity and progress in life in communal ways, we can look for that natural need of acknowledgement in other ways. They aren't always the best substitutes, but if you are hungry and all that is available is junk food, then that's probably what you are going to eat!

Praise is an important part of consecration. One of the first things I tend to hear from the spirit world when doing a session with someone is a word or two of encouragement, of acknowledging how far they have come, as well as a sense of encouragement for where they are going. Too much praise – when it is not in proportion to what has been achieved – can have a negative effect.

I have met people who have developed a sense of entitlement because they have had life easier than most, and perhaps believed this meant something about them was better than others who have had to struggle more. This can create a surprising laziness in some people, as though they should just get what they want without any effort or discipline on their part. A person falling into that sort of sense of entitlement has the psychological maturity of a spoilt child – even if they are in an adult body. What they may need more than praise is encouragement to apply themselves to a meaningful task.

I know of some parents that focus more on being strict with their children, rather than praising their efforts, for fear that they will become lazy. Yet not enough praise can leave a child feeling insecure and trying to win the approval of a parent, or of other people who might not be the best role models. Insufficient acknowledgement can leave a child feeling disempowered and stop them from internalising a validating voice. The validating voice is the one that tells us we are doing okay and to keep up the good work, especially if we are having a challenging day or trying to break out of something that has been difficult for us to change.

We need to balance the voices of encouragement to continue to improve with the voices of acknowledgement and approval for what has already been accomplished. We need this balance in ourselves and in how we relate to others, especially children. If you raise a child that doesn't know how to self-validate, they are going to seek the approval of others to fill the gap where their own self-approval and self-encouragement would have been.

Sometimes the desire for the approval of others can come at too great a cost, inviting exploitative people into one's life who are willing to take advantage of a lack of self-esteem for their own selfish ends. We don't want to raise a culture of children so lacking in inner power and internal validation that they grow into adults who don't know their own worth, their own truths, and hand their personal power over to others in desperation for some sense of approval, because they cannot give this to themselves. We don't want to become adults like that either!

We need to give ourselves permission to continually improve our efforts, but also to appreciate all we have done up until this point. This is how we bring the sacred into our daily lives. Even the smallest steps or 'wins' we have gained need to be honoured as something important. They might not be the final result or all that there is to do, but they are important. They are steps, and as we know, every journey is made up of many steps. Without them, we wouldn't get anywhere. If you are more of a 'big picture' person, you might forget how important the day-to-day choices and steps are, but without those smaller choices, there are no big successes. We have to honour the small – to make it sacred and special and appreciate it – and to truly have the energy to keep going until all those small steps add up to a big leap on our life paths.

Finding a healthy balance between praise and discipline helps someone feel they are a capable person. They can perhaps do more, but because they have done well so far, they have the confidence to continue, to develop, to grow. Genuine praise, that doesn't puff up a person but acknowledges where they are going well, can be the difference between giving up and keeping on going. Without acknowledgement, life can seem rather long and the mountains we feel we need to climb loom simply ever higher, no matter how many steps we take. We need check-in points along our journeys, times when we feel like we are getting a sign and hopefully even more often than not, a thumbs up from something that is watching us, loving us, guiding us, through life.

Consecration is a reminder that life is the great initiator, that it is giving us tests and challenges to help us grow, but also to mark having passed through a rite of passage. So when you are letting someone or something go out of your life, or welcoming someone or something in, you take a moment and acknowledge what this is like for you. How do you feel? What does it mean about your life? Are you starting a new chapter? Are you taking a risk in letting someone or something out of your life, or inviting someone or something new in? Are you trusting more, even when you might feel vulnerable or uncertain? Is this a sign you are growing bolder and listening more to your heart rather than putting faith in your fears? Can you acknowledge this – maybe light a candle, or just say aloud that you are proud of yourself?

This is a way to acknowledge the initiations of life – those doorways we go through, thresholds we cross every time we move house, start a new job, leave a relationship behind, start school, graduate from a course or complete a project, get married, start writing (or finish) a book, make a major purchase, see a child go through a new phase in their life (like diagnosis of an illness, or making a recovery), learn to drive, visit somewhere new, conquer a personal fear, or do something that we normally wouldn't do. Some days are so challenging they feel like an ordeal, a type of initiation, and it's hard just to get through the day. Other initiations are much more pleasant. Perhaps your child has his first child and you become a grandparent, or you own your first car and you have a taste of independence.

Whatever life presents to us, when we consecrate it, the ordinary can become an initiation, and we have a sense of deeper meaning and purpose, just because we are willing and able to recognise it. Consecrating life, seeing anything – but especially the challenges – as an initiation of sorts, an invitation to step up into a new cycle of life, can help us trust in what is happening. It gives us a framework for optimism, even when the going gets tough.

You'll know when life is offering you an initiation in a challenging way because it will feel like chaos, crisis and confusion in a very intense form, often all at once. It is a bit like being squeezed or pressed by life so your good juiciness can be released. Being squeezed like an orange by the big, strong hand of life doesn't feel very good at the time, but it is a productive action nonetheless. If we see it as a chance for something better to be evoked from us – sort of like a challenging teacher that gives praise but also sets harder tasks for homework when they realise we are capable of more than the average task – then we can take pride in our struggles and encourage ourselves, knowing we are outgrowing something. And remember that outgrowing means growing into something new. Those two things cannot be separated.

The eye in the heart sees this, though sometimes the eyes in our heads only focus on what we are losing and the pain of that. Consecration helps us remember that whatever we are being asked to give up, to let go of, is actually an offering of sorts on the altar of life. It is handing over something to life and saying, "I give this to you, so you shall return to me what is truly needed, according to a greater wisdom and power than my own limited self can understand."

You let Nature take her wise course with you, but it is not from a place of weakness, but from understanding that life is sacred and meant to be trusted. And when things get *really* challenging, you remember that although our culture doesn't have many formal initiations in place to mark our transition through various phases of life (perhaps with the exception of getting drunk when you come of age or before you get married), there are initiations given to us when we are ready for them (whether we *feel* quite ready or not is another matter, of course). Those initiations are the things that bring up chaos, crisis and confusion, given to us as a sign that Life is saying, "Hey there, I see you. You're ready for something more – here's your chance to grow into it!"

So you don't need to turn seagull poop on your car into a holy revelation necessarily, but you can look at your life events – even the twists and turns – as being evidence of a loving and guiding hand of life, helping you to grow. This is consecration. It's not foolish or whimsical (though a bit of whimsy now and then is good for the soul). Consecration gives meaning to the mundane and helps you feel that the spiritual aspect of yourself is alive and well (it is, you just have to remember it). Having the spiritual side of you awakened isn't about a belief system, a religion, or having to shave your head and go meditate in a cave for twenty years, though if you want to do those things, that's just fine, of course. But awakening the spiritual part of you means learning to look beyond what appears to be at first glance. It means having some trust and faith in what's happening, even when you don't understand it. It means assuming an attitude that you are loved, and meant to grow into the best possible version of yourself, and that even if you have absolutely no idea what that best version could be, life knows and will guide you into it. That's your life purpose, to become that best self, and everything happening in your life is leading you there. That is what consecration brings you – a reminder of a bigger scheme unfolding in your life, for your benefit.

When you feel that your spiritual connection is more real, that life is helping you to grow, then you'll realise that spirituality isn't something that happens in other worlds. It's actually meant to help you in the physical world, right in the here and now. People have often said to me, looking surprised at the time, that I am very down to earth, as though being spiritual is not about having your feet on the ground, but floating off with pixies in la-la land. Yet I find spirituality to be extremely practical. It is *meant* to help us live a better life. When you consecrate your life you are accepting this – you actively seek to use your spirituality to help you live your daily life, which is what it is meant to do! I'll help you find ways to do this through the workbook section of this book.

CAPITULATE

To capitulate means to surrender, but giving up and giving in are not the same. Giving up means turning away, deciding not to care anymore, to walk away. I don't believe we ever need to give up on life. What we *do* need to do, especially in the face of chaos, crisis and confusion, is to learn how to give *in*. Giving in is about recognising that a wisdom greater than our own is steering our course. To surrender into that is wise indeed! This is not the same thing as being weak or lacking in willpower. Not trusting our strength of will is what happens when we give up altogether. Giving in, however, means we become braver, and smarter. It is – as the expression goes – 'being willing to lose the battle in order to win the war'.

Giving in means you recognise when a bigger force than your own will is at work in your life, whether you believe that bigger force to be life itself, or the universe, or the hand of God, or whatever your belief system entails. Giving in means you learn not to feel humiliated by this, but humbled by it. With humiliation, we feel defeated, as if we have failed, done something wrong and are being punished by not getting what we want. With humility, we become able to recognise that we don't always have all the answers. Rather than rushing in to judge something happening in our lives, we might instead say, "Maybe there's a bigger picture here I just can't see yet."

Being humble in the face of life itself is very intelligent. It is based on the principle that life may have something to teach us that we don't quite know yet. Do you think you know everything in the world there is to know? Of course you don't. Sometimes there is a hidden arrogance in pitting ourselves against life. We think – without realising it – that we know better than life, or the universe, or God (again, depending on your personal beliefs). But in your heart, you probably know there's always something new to learn and it's quite possible you don't have all the information yet. So something that appears to be unwanted in your life right now, with a little more information and understanding that will come in due course, might end up being the very thing you consider to be a saving grace.

This is giving in. It is learning how to work with the happenings in life, sort of like deciding to surf a wave in the ocean rather than getting cross when it doesn't go in the direction you'd wish. Giving in is flexibility. Sometimes people confuse this with weakness of purpose that allows one to be swayed by external forces, tossed about by the erratic push and pull of life with no 'staying power' to stand true and firm in one's position or viewpoint.

Many people have been taught that remaining firm and stoic in one's belief, no matter what, is a sign of strength. It is good to have a firm sense of inner truth, but if you are not willing to bend when a greater force would otherwise break you, allowing your strength to give you flexibility, then that is not clever. You might miss out on a wonderful opportunity to evolve your belief systems and become wiser and happier.

The world is changing at a pace that seems to be ever quickening. This is exciting and holds great potential for change and healing in ourselves and our lives, at a much faster rate than we might have believed was possible. You could say that spiritually speaking, the earth is in a very fertile phase for human development. I cannot help but wonder if that is because of the amount of utter crap that's perpetuated in modern media (which we can use as rich fertiliser if we are clever about it), not taking anything we are told or sold at face value, and questioning everything instead.

Given this available speed for development, it makes sense to look to nature for some guidance on fast growing plants that truly flourish. Bamboo is one such example. Bamboo is one of the fastest growing plants, typically growing centimetres per day, and reaching fullness in one season. That's very impressive! It is extremely strong and very flexible, bending with the wind and storms, resuming its upright position after the onslaught has passed. It is not diminished through its flexibility, it is not changed. If anything, it is more powerful because of it, more able to thrive. Bamboo simply continues to flourish, and rapidly at that. With a myriad of practical uses that supports humanity as a source of food, clothing, shelter, homewares and medicine, bamboo is an extraordinary gift to humanity on a physical level, but spiritually and symbolically, it offers us guidance too –

on how flexibility can allow one to reach fullness more quickly.

Giving in means waving the white flag and allowing whatever is going to happen next to happen, with a sense of trust that it will be for the best, no matter what things look like at that moment. Yes, there will be times when you think a certain situation *couldn't possibly* be for the best at all – it being the exact opposite of what you think you need and want. Yet in time, those things can become the very things you become *most appreciative of and grateful for*, almost like some type of divine intervention in your life – with the wisdom of hindsight, of course.

In my early twenties, I was at a crossroads in my life. I didn't want to continue on with law as a career – although I had decided I would at least finish my degree and complete the work experience offers that came my way. A friend of mine at the time pushed me, quite relentlessly, to go and see a spiritual healer. I'd never seen such a person before and although the worlds of spirit and healing, energy and alternative medicine, had fascinated me for a long time (having grown up in a household with a mother far ahead of her time and 'into' all sorts of natural and alternative healing), I really hadn't given it much thought beyond that. Eventually I booked in to see this healer, mostly to quiet my friend's constant nagging, although I was curious too. It was towards the end of my degree and I was really feeling most desperate to know *what* I was going to do with my life. Finding work that was going to be suitable seemed to be a most difficult task. I just couldn't work it out.

On the day of my reading, I waited outside her shop at the Hurstville shopping centre. I noticed it was locked up, even though I had arrived on time for my session. I had driven to an area I didn't know, a reasonable distance away from my university and I had classes to get back to. I hated feeling that my time was being wasted and I was quite cranky because of all that. Then I noticed a lovely-looking blonde swanning down the street in a flowing dress. She walked straight past me, leaned down to pull up the security grill, and opened the front door before sashaying into the store.

I was still a bit cranky but mostly now, just intrigued. I followed her into the store – and was hit with a scent of sweet-smelling incense and a plethora of books on all things healing and New Age. I felt rather at home. It reminded me of my own study, where my legal text books were crammed on a large desk and my actual bookshelves were loaded up with books on topics far more to do with spiritual laws than the more mundane human variety of law. Eventually, she called me upstairs to a quiet little alcove with two chairs, a table and some peaceful music playing.

"I saw you outside," she said, and I as I waited for her to apologise to me for having to wait outside for her to turn up, she took a sip of tea, and then continued by saying, "walking around old temples." And then I realised she was talking about a past life and not about my grumpiness at her lack of punctuality. I was fascinated. She spoke of various matters, some more earthly, some more spiritual. She talked of healing and of my work direction.

My mother, bless her, had tried every sort of possible method to help me find the work that would suit me. She sent me to careers advisers to be tested for aptitude in certain areas because what was offered in school in terms of assistance to find one's career path didn't seem particularly helpful. What came back to me from multiple sources was writing, communication and creativity. The key that would pull all that together into a vocational direction – spirituality – was missing. I guess no-one really thought of that as a viable career path in those days, though I suspect these days, working in the metaphysical or self-help field would be somewhat more mainstream than it was then, though maybe not much more mainstream!

During this reading, however, I listened to the woman speaking and I was instantly hooked. I just knew I was meant to be doing something like what she was doing with me in that moment, that I could fall in love with that work and that it was my next step in life. I had the unusual feeling of having 'known this all along' and yet it seemed – at least to part of me – entirely new information too. She would become my first spiritual teacher for the following two years.

That guidance came to me when I was at my most confused, in the most chaos, in a deep crisis within myself and really needed help. I had certainly given in. I didn't know what I was doing or where I was going, and the answer came to me in that rather unexpected way.

One thing my teacher said to me at the time, that resonated very deeply, was to pray. Now, she wasn't a religious woman by any means. When she spoke of prayer, she meant talking to the universe. I have always believed in a higher power. I saw the various forms of that in different religions as being different faces of the one love that exists beneath everything. That is just my personal belief and I have held it even as a little girl.

I grew up in an open-minded family, in a very multicultural city, and at school my best friends hailed from many religious traditions – Buddhists, Sikhs, Hindus, Greek Orthodox and Anglicans, as well as those who shared my own original Catholic background. When I got to university, my circle of friends, and my exposure to various religious traditions, expanded to include people devoted to the nature-based religion of Wicca, the Baha'i faith, as well as Islam. I never felt nervous or threatened by this diversity because it didn't conflict with my own beliefs. I saw religious paths as ways for various individuals to find what works for them. I didn't think one was better or worse, I just thought they were different paths for different people to find their way through life, depending on what suited them best and would help them the most.

So when my teacher told me to pray, I didn't feel it had to be in a certain way or to a certain form of god or goddess. It just felt like talking to the universe, to life – which I still do on a daily basis. To me it's like having a conversation in your heart with your oldest friend. Anyway, in prayer, my teacher told me that we shouldn't pray for our troubles to be taken away from us. We should pray to become brave enough to deal with them. This was a very good piece of advice that I agreed with at the time and still do, decades later.

"When you face the perils of weariness, carelessness, and confusion, don't pray for an easier life. Pray instead to be a stronger man or woman of God." – Luis Palau

It is my sense that prayer is what makes the difference between giving in and giving up. When you pray – whether you feel you are speaking to life, or to your own inner wise guide (yes, he or she is in there, I promise you, even if you think that guide is sitting on the sidelines and not saying very much at times) – you are taking steps towards handing something over. Of course you can use your prayers to say, "I want this and I want that," and it's okay, it's not like you are going to offend the universe by expressing yourself. But there are certainly ways to pray *well* that are less about trying to have life meet your expectations, and more about you rising up to grow (perhaps even gracefully – dare to dream!) through whatever has found its way to your door. You put in your best efforts, but ultimately you choose to believe that life is working according to a higher plan, and allow yourself to hand over your concerns to something greater and wiser than your own personal opinion.

This works. Even if you don't know what you believe in, or if you are praying 'just in case' there is someone or something out there listening. None of that matters as much as simply stating your prayers. If you don't like the religious connotations of the word 'prayer', then you can reframe this as 'having a conversation with life'. It will work just as well whether you think about it that way or as praying. What matters is that you have the conversation.

In Chapter 10, I will guide you on how to pray well, or to have a good conversation with life that brings the most benefit to you and your wellbeing, and helps you capitulate, to give in rather than give up.

I will also guide you through an exercise called 'Safe to Let Go'. Many of us know that trying to control life is not going to get us very far. We might not even realise we are doing it half the time, and the other half of the time we might not *want* to be doing it, yet we cannot seem to stop ourselves. Trying to control life is not bad. It is not a sin. It is not a flaw in your personality, but it is something that is ultimately impossible and therefore not going to create much confidence, peace of mind, or happiness within you.

Giving up on control requires that we trust. But it also requires we understand there is not only one extreme (trying to control everything) or the other (flopping onto the lounge and putting no effort into anything at all) from which to choose. Giving up control means giving up trying to direct an outcome. It doesn't mean you refuse to put in any effort, discipline or work towards what you would like to have happen in your life. Of course, do everything you can, but don't try to control what happens once you have done everything within your power. That is the time when you let go. You trust. You say to Life, "Okay, I am doing all I can here at my end of things. Now I'll look forward to your response!" It becomes a conversation, not you trying to dictate how life should behave.

There's a film called *Bruce Almighty* in which Jim Carrey stars as a man who feels that God isn't living up to his end of things. An unusual 'gift' is given to Bruce in response to his complaints when God (played charmingly by Morgan Freeman) hands over his almighty powers to Bruce, so that he can see what it is like to run the world for a while.

Bruce learns something about power and what happens when you use it wisely to assist others and when you use it unthinkingly for your own immediate purpose. In one scene, he tries to seduce his girlfriend into an amorous mood. He sneakily uses his divine power to pull the moon closer to the bedroom window. His girlfriend looks up to see a very large moon and is mesmerised by it. But he has unknowingly caused destructive tidal irregularities in other parts of the world, reported in the news the following morning. He didn't think about the possible repercussions of demanding that things just be as he wanted them in that moment. He wasn't really thinking at all. Well not with his brain, anyway.

When we dictate to life how it should be from our own limited perspectives, we don't always realise the full implications and consequences of what we are asking. What seems to be harmless enough for us to demand, might actually be downright harmful in effect for someone else. We might want the moon to shine just for us to create a romantic evening, yet there might be a better way for our love lives to blossom if we let go and allow it to happen. And that better way can benefit others too, rather than making some people win and others lose. Life has a wonderful ability to create win-win situations for all when allowed to do so. But we have to give up our selfishness and be willing to let life happen in order to receive, rather than trying to take without thought of the consequences.

In the film, Bruce eventually learns to stop trying to control his girlfriend through seduction and manipulation. One night, he hears her prayers through the God-given powers he has received. In a poignant moment, he listens to her sadness as she prays that she can find a way to stop loving him because of the pain the relationship causes her.

Bruce starts to grow up, spiritually speaking, realising that when he tries to control other people or situations to make life turn out the way he wants it, he is actually not creating happiness for himself or the people he cares about. His perspective becomes less self-centred. What he wants – a beautiful relationship and successful career – doesn't actually change, but he is no longer willing to do anything, including hurting the people he loves, to try and force those things to happen. He wants what he wants, but he learns to let go.

What happens during that process is that he actually gets everything he wanted all along – a fantastic career, and a truly connected loving relationship with his girlfriend – without any manipulation or selfishness on his part. He uses the other gifts he had (even before God made him almighty!), such as his quick mind and highly developed sense of humour, and learns to soften his attitude of 'life won't give to me so I have to take it for myself' into simply living as well as he can from his heart. No longer does he try to force God to give him what he wants in the way he thinks he wants it. He learns to trust in life instead. The result is that he receives all he ever wanted – and more – and that can happen because he learns to give in. He learns to surrender into life and to grow. He allows life to give to him rather than complaining and demanding.

Does this mean we aren't allowed to have a temper tantrum on occasion when things really don't seem to be working out? Of course, you are allowed to do whatever you like. Sometimes a little tantrum is a way to get some frustration out of your system. But can you move beyond it? Can you come to a place of trust in life and feel positive expectation about what is coming for you, even if only because it feels like a pleasanter and happier way to live in the meantime? This is how you capitulate, how you give in, without giving up. You trust that life has everything handled and you only need to do your part in that process, no more and no less.

In the workbook section I'll help you with practical exercises to learn how to give in, without giving up (and perhaps also, without a tantrum).

CONTAIN

If you try to cook something without a container, you'd end up with a lot of mess and not much of a meal either. Containers hold things in place. Whether it's whisking up a salad dressing or stirring cake batter in a bowl, or placing furnishings and people in the larger and more symbolic container of a house to create your home, containers are something you will have already used in your day-to-day life.

Containers also exist on psychological levels. They are similar to the purpose of a bowl in the kitchen. In that container, things can get mixed and instead of ending up splattered all over the place, they blend together into a meal to nourish your body. The psychological container is something less visible but just as important. It is the strength of mind that allows you to 'keep your act together' whilst there is chaos, crisis or confusion in your 'inner kitchen'. When you don't know what's happening, or how to get through what is going on in your life, the psychological container you have within becomes very important. It will be the difference between being able to get through the process and turning it into something useful and nourishing for your soul, or falling apart completely and finding the whole process of change too frightening to accept.

You'll perhaps have met people who fall into that latter category. They live in the past. They tell the same stories over and over again. Although life goes on, nothing in them really changes or grows. They become rigid as they age rather than vibrant and cheeky and sassy, wise and empowered (which are things age can bring because you stop caring quite so much about what others think of you, and that freedom can allow you to be yourself more than ever before). People who lack a strong enough psychological container cannot allow life to get in their kitchen and cook up something delicious. They don't have the ability to let that process happen. So they stick to beans on toast for every meal, day in, day out. But life can be a great feast. It is a shame if we don't try new tastes just because we don't know how or don't feel brave enough to try.

This section – and the exercises in the workbook chapters – will help you strengthen the container you already have within you, the part of you that can handle chaos, crisis and confusion. It's as though life is a great cook taking over your kitchen for a great meal – you can stand the thought of clearing up the mess because you know the meal will be so worth it!

If you feel you don't really have that container yet, that you tend to lose your head in a crisis and become depressed in chaos or overwhelmed by confusion, then there is no need to worry. We all build our inner containers, our ability to bear change, one step at a time. The workbook exercises will help you build your own container, but so will just reading this book. You'll find you'll be increasingly able to tolerate things that in the past might have been too much for you. Your inner strength, or container, will grow and you'll be strong enough to be flexible like bamboo, to bend without breaking – not like steel that refuses to bend and adapt. You'll find the middle way where you can experience change, but not lose yourself completely in the process (though sometimes of course, your identity will go through so much change you might feel you've lost your old self for a while, but with a strong enough container psychologically, you'll be able to hold yourself through that and trust that a new you is just around the corner).

The word 'containment' or 'container', in the sense we are using it here, comes from the weird and wonderful world of psychotherapy. I worked as a psychotherapist for over a decade and learned a lot about how difficult life can be if you don't have a strong enough container to handle life's inevitable bumps and bruises. I also learned that people build their psychological containers in different ways. What works for one person might not work so well for another. I'll go over some possible ways to build your container a little later on, and you can decide for yourself what works for you.

When your inner container is strong enough, it will just 'kick in' when you need it. In the same way, when you are mixing up a salad dressing, you don't just pour the olive oil and mustard onto the floor, you grab a bowl first and then add the ingredients. Your psychological container is also something you instinctively 'grab on to', without thinking, when you need it.

One time we really need a strong psychological container is in an identity crisis, when the way we think of ourselves and our place in the world doesn't seem so rock solid anymore. There are many examples of this: a mother suddenly finds her children have 'flown the coop' and no longer feels needed in the same way; a person who has been a powerful athlete through injury can no longer perform their beloved sport; or a man who has placed a great deal of emphasis upon his career is unexpectedly retrenched. It could be the ending of a relationship through any number of reasons, or a shocking moment where we realise something or someone we counted on in life is not at all what we once believed. Whatever the reason, when a crisis, or chaos or confusion (or all three) hits us, without our inner sense of containment, it can feel like we are completely lost at sea, and that can be a devastating feeling indeed.

When we are contained, we are able to get through a crisis in a constructive way. It allows us to do that old clever trick of turning lemons into lemonade. It doesn't necessarily make the crisis less challenging, but it does give us a sense that we are going to be able to work through it – somehow!

Containment is something like a psychological and emotional version of a temporary compression garment around a sprained limb. It gives support and a feeling of holding whilst there is an issue that needs healing. It's sort of like how it might be easier to really cry your grief out when a kind arm is around your shoulders, giving you a sense of comfort and support. When we have a strong enough inner container, we can give ourselves that sense of comfort. It's still nice to receive it from those around you, but if for some reason you have a challenge the people around you might not understand (even if they love you), then it's good to know you can rely on yourself. Maybe you are the head of a family going through crisis and you need to be the one upon whom others can rely. You need a strong container to be able to bear that additional pressure rather than feeling you are going to lose the plot completely!

Life is surprisingly good at providing us with helping hands when we need them – often through unexpected sources. Now and then, however, you might go through an experience of needing to be emotionally self-sufficient to learn how to rely upon your own inner strength to see you through a challenge. Building a strong inner container helps you naturally to be able to do this.

Without enough containment, we can become too afraid to allow ourselves to be impacted upon by whatever is happening in our lives. This is more like denial. It is the man who has terminal cancer and persists in acting as though everything is just as it always has been, whilst his grieving wife cannot begin to discuss the truth of what is happening with him. He doesn't have enough psychological containment to be able to have a truthful conversation with himself, let alone his wife. Containment is what is needed when you believe you have to remain stoically held together and not give an inch (whilst inside a veritable dam of tears builds up, waiting to burst out of you in a most inopportune moment, perhaps when the 'song' that reminds you of a loved one lost inconveniently plays over the sound system in the middle of a very public supermarket aisle!).

A container doesn't hold things in, it just holds things together so they can become something else. Your tears of sadness might turn into cleansing of your soul, forgiveness and moving on. But for that to happen, they have to be allowed to flow. And for that to happen, you need a strong enough inner container to realise that you won't be washed away with your tears; you'll just be cleansing yourself from the inside out, ready for new life. A strong container will allow you to feel strong enough to surrender into that process, and strong enough to rise up out of it when it is time to do so. Containment is what enables us to be like bamboo – to bend without breaking – and to rise upright again once the storm has passed.

BUILDING A CONTAINER

Apart from the exercises in the workbook section, there are other ways you can begin to build a container, not just to handle a crisis, but also to feel more secure within yourself more generally.

For some years I mostly enjoyed a friendship with a woman around ten years my junior. We bonded over a love of dancing, fitness and fashion (and an appreciation for beautiful men!). Whilst I believe we both loved and cared for each other, there were times when I felt an undercurrent of something that didn't quite feel so nurturing or loving. It added a complicated element to our friendship which I didn't understand at first. Speaking with my therapist and mentor at the time, I described a situation where my friend's behaviour towards me was less than positive, and it was puzzling because I couldn't see a reason for it. I was trying to bring some clarity to whatever it was hiding in the darker side of our friendship.

My therapist made a remark that I found startling. I also felt it held a kernel of truth. She said that sometimes people can be jealous of another's sense of self-possession. If they don't feel they have enough of it themselves – perhaps because through guilt or shame they have handed their power over to others, or given others the right to approve of them (or not) rather than trusting in their own inner validation of themselves as people – then they may feel resentful towards those who are more secure within themselves.

Those who are yet to develop that sort of inner security might wonder why they have to go through the dramas of trying to please others or pretend to be someone they are not. (I call this 'pretzelling ourselves' because we are trying to twist ourselves into what we are not!) Why should they have to do it, if I don't? The answer to this is that none of us has to do that *if* we are willing to build a strong enough inner container. It is a place where you can be inside of yourself just as you are, acceptable as you are, whether others understand your choices, flaws and fabulousness or not. It is how you become secure within yourself. It is the place where you get to know who you are and realise your inner qualities – like strength and compassion and a good sense of humour – which can help you realise your value as a person and your ability to manage the storms in life.

As your container grows stronger, you'll find the things that once perhaps really bothered or offended you, won't affect you nearly so much. What once may have really caused you anguish, might feel like a small irritation that is more easily dealt with. It is a little like a blend of developing a stronger skin, a more effective digestive system and a more powerful immune system, not just physically, but in terms of how you are affected by life events on psychological and emotional levels too. You'll still get rattled by events now and then, but you'll recover faster and with less suffering.

If you tend to be a more creative, sensitive, passionate or emotional person – and therefore, more likely to be profoundly affected by your environment and circumstances than other more detached personality types – then growing your container will actually feel stabilising, without shutting you off from feeling open to inspiration. You'll just have a sense that you can cast off unwanted influences more easily, whilst remaining receptive to creative inspiration. For those that would like to feel more creative, aware or inspired, building a container will help you do this because you'll feel secure enough in yourself to know yourself enough as a person, to be able to open up to new worlds of experience and inspiration without being afraid you'll get lost or forget who you are.

Some people turn to drugs to open up to other realms of information and experience beyond what they already know, but this is not typically a safe or balanced practice, with the exception of trained shamans who are guided in the practical use of plants by those who have tread the path of working with that substance before.

The problem with most drug use in a modern context is that it forces an openness in the mind and body when there is no container to hold whatever enters, and no development of a filtering system of mind, body and emotions that matches the temporary and artificially expanded level of openness induced by drugs. It is akin to putting a child in a situation that only an adult would be able to functionally deal with at an emotional and psychological level. If you build the container first, you can be open to more information *and the ability to use it wisely, to understand it and gain benefit from it*. You are prepared for whatever happens and can put even a challenge to good use in your life.

The more open you are, the more you need to be able to effectively process (discerning, using and releasing) whatever information comes to you. Being open is, overall, a good thing. It is a sign of growth and of life. Contracting inwards, hunching over physically (and mentally and emotionally), blocks the flow of life and energy. Although separating ourselves from the world and stimulation is a necessary and healthy part of living well some of the time, to hold that as an attitude to life overall is going to age you faster and make you less of a person than you would otherwise be. It's also kind of boring!

This is one of the tricky parts of the amazing phenomenon of the internet. There are many plus sides to the internet, but the sheer volume of data – not only available, but increasingly pushed into our minds through cleverly placed ads on webpages, not to mention random comments you cannot control seeing on social media – opens us up to more information very quickly. Depression, overwhelm, anxiety and fear are all normal (though unpleasant) reactions to too much incoming data, but unless we do our work on building a container to cope with all that, we will have insufficient containment to process it all. It's like trying to make a meal for ten people in a bowl that is the right size for a meal for one. It's crowded, crammed, messy and quite possibly stressful.

You may think that only 'sensitive' types are affected by this sort of thing, but it actually affects everybody. Sensitive types are more conscious of it happening earlier on, but the negative effect still takes root – perhaps even more so over the longer term – in those that don't notice it straight away. The things we struggle with in the modern world on a daily basis – like apathy, fatigue, a lack of purpose or meaning in life, a sense of despair, anxiety or depression that seems to sneak up in the middle of the night seemingly out of nowhere – are all normal and appropriate symptoms of overwhelm, of too much coming in and not enough being processed and released. If it continues for a long time, like an inner cup being filled drop by drop, it will overflow, eventually causing leaks, damp and mould. Suddenly it is apparent there is a problem to deal with, though sensitive types would have felt that sense of discomforting overfullness within earlier on.

Whether the issue is discovered early on or later in life by one of the side effects such as depression however, the solution is the same. No doubt eventually, how to do this will be taught in schools, but there has to be several generations that learn it first, realise its importance and then teach others. There are pioneers in every new way of being, and for learning how to work *with* rather than *against* life with a strong enough container is something you and I are learning and can then share with others. As enough of us learn how to do this, humanity will be in much more harmony with nature and each other, and the world will be an overall happier place. We can get there, but we all have to do our part in the here and now, one step at a time.

Having an effective container is vital as life becomes more complex and filled with interesting experiences. If you want to be one of those people who doesn't just decide to stop growing and keep telling the same stories over and over again, becoming (heaven forbid!) boring (!), then you'll need a container. It is what will give you the strength to adapt, to learn new ways of being, even as you get older, and to be able to let go of what no longer is meant to be in your life. There is no necessity whatsoever for old age meaning you become set in your ways. If anything, growing older can be liberating because you have had a chance to learn more from your life experience, and realise what matters to you, and what doesn't.

The world we live in is changing very quickly and we are meant to be a part of that. This doesn't have to be a source of insecurity or fear. We can be curious about what new gifts life wants to send to us, how our quality of life can improve through moving with whatever comes our way. It can be very freeing to imagine a different set of circumstances in our lives, and believe that a change could be for the better. It allows us to believe that sometimes we have the lollipop yanked out of our hand by life, because there is actually a seven-course feast waiting for us instead. Short-term tough love is sometimes a part of long-term kindness. Having a strong enough container allows us to accept this, process the messages in our life experiences, and move ahead feeling stronger for our experiences.

BRICK BY BRICK

Building a container is a bit like saving money. Small but consistent contributions will add up over time. You don't have to spend hours a day in building your container, but choosing to do activities you enjoy and gain benefit from for a little time each day – anywhere from five to twenty-five minutes – will create great gains for you. Even five minutes – perhaps doing one of the exercises in the workbook section of this book, and/or some of the following suggestions – will build up your container in a matter of weeks. Over months of your daily practice (or at least several times a week), you'll find you'll gain a lot of strength and resilience without feeling as though you have to become 'hard' or 'defensive'.

There are many ways to build a container and although it might sound like an idea that is hard to 'pin down', the methods of creating it are very simple and practical. You'll know when your container is really starting to grow because you'll feel the positive effect of your inner container when life serves you up a tricky situation to deal with. When you have that sense of being able to handle matters that once would have thrown you 'off your game', you will have your proof. It doesn't stop life with its inevitable ups and downs from happening, but it gives you an ability to process what takes place in a healthier and quicker way.

A good container is like the lattice a clinging vine plant uses to grow upon. A lattice gives support and allows for the beautiful fullness of the plant to develop. You are the plant, and the container you choose to build for yourself is the strength and size of the lattice supporting you. Even if you don't 'see' it, you'll feel the positive and empowering effect of it within a matter of weeks of regular practice.

So apart from the exercises later on in the book, what are other practical ways to build your container?

There are certain elements that if combined, will build an excellent container, no matter if you use quite different activities to bring that about.

Some ways to build your container could be: walking, doing yoga, meditating, visiting the seaside or a place in nature you love, listening to music, writing in a journal, dancing in your lounge room, playing with your pet, creating a feeling of a sanctuary by lighting candles and burning a lovely-smelling incense, doing exercise you enjoy (that you don't 'zone out' of), completing the exercises in this book, doing a relaxation technique by focusing on your breath flowing in and out, gardening, going to an art class, going to a counselling session, curling up with an inspiring book that uplifts or stimulates you, visiting an art gallery, or sitting quietly in a church or in nature and praying. You could use a combination of these things, or even something else altogether.

These are suggestions that will work, but it's not only what you do that matters. What will transform a random activity into a container-building success is how you do it and how often. The key elements needed to transform any activity into a brick-by-brick building process of your container is that the practice is regular, preferably several times a week or daily if possible. It might be for five minutes or more than an hour. A longer time is not more important than regular application. Less time overall but done more regularly is more effective than a lot of time infrequently.

What also matters is that the activity you choose feels like something you are doing for yourself. It needs to feel good – even with a discipline like exercise where you might have to overcome some inertia or resistance to make yourself just 'do it', you still need to feel that in doing so, you are doing something good for yourself. For a container to be built by an activity, you need to feel that it is part of your routine for your own wellbeing, that you take some enjoyment in it, that it is something for *you*. This means that building a container is usually a less social activity and more about quality 'you' time. Some people feel more comfortable with this than others, but if you can't learn to love, appreciate and enjoy your own company, you'll never feel truly secure within yourself. You don't have to give up socialising, you just need to find some time for your own inner work. Five minutes a day is not too much to ask of yourself for this. And if it is, then I suggest you would benefit from rearranging some of your priorities to make room for your own needs.

You may change the way you build your container over time. It will go from being something that might seem a little 'out there' to something that starts to feel very real and comforting all the time, and becomes a soft place to land when life seems a bit tough. You might go through a phase of dancing for several months, which might change to meditation, or expand to include journalling. Then dancing might come back into your life again. It is okay to change your methods, but give them enough time to work too. Don't expect that if you don't immediately feel more secure and safe that your practice isn't working! Give yourself time to let this soul medicine work.

For at least the first few weeks or, even better, the first three to six months, choose one or two things you can commit to regularly. Simple activities like a walk in the daytime and a few minutes 'talking to the universe', or praying at evening time before bed, are a simple and effective practice.

When you walk, feel connected with yourself, with your feet, your body, *you*, out and walking, for your own wellbeing. Take it as time for you. It is not just something you have to fit into your day, another thing to cram into your schedule. Time to build your container needs to feel like sacred time, time that is important and a priority and somewhat apart from just another thing to stuff into your full schedule. You have to make it a priority. If you are too busy thinking of all the things you have to do, remember that if you are too tired and worn out you won't be productive. Give yourself some time to replenish and feel good, then you'll have more energy for your other tasks and you'll be more productive overall.

To switch off the mind from 'getting things done' mode into 'taking a break and doing something good for yourself' mode can be quite hard to do, especially if you are the sort of person who finds it hard to take a break unless things are finished. Considering most lifestyles these days mean there is always something else to do on the list, you'll really need to break that habit!

Taking time to build your container has to become a part of your regular (hopefully daily) life if it is going to work. Once you get used to it as part of your day, you will enjoy what it brings eventually, and you'll build on that. But for most people, it's just a matter of getting started – and then to keep giving ourselves permission to just keep going with it.

CHAPTER 6

What Do You Really Want?

SPOILER ALERT

Once upon a time, I had to move house, leave the man I loved behind, and start a new life for myself, in a completely new and unfamiliar area. I became single after many years of being in a loving but basically emotionally unhealthy relationship, and feeling like I was on my own for the first time in years. Mostly due to the heartbreak, but the other factors certainly contributed, I felt like my world was ending. In a way, it was. I prayed to the universe and asked, "Is everything going to be okay?" and even before I had fully asked the question, I felt the answer fly into my heart as a soft, kind, but very powerful voice. It simply said, "Yes."

But that one word spoke volumes and brought me a sense of hope and trust. Although I could hardly see how that could have been the case at the time, that answer was true. Everything was okay. It did all work out. Yes, my world was ending. That much was true. But so was the fact that a new world was beginning at the same time. I just couldn't see that yet.

When you read film reviews on the internet, critics often put 'spoiler alert' when they are about to discuss what happens in a plot so if you haven't yet seen the film, and don't want the surprise ending to be not as surprising, you'll stop reading.

So here's your spoiler alert …

Firstly, everything's going to be okay. Yes, everything is going to work out just fine. Trust yourself and trust life. Relax a little more. You'll enjoy the journey more and be able to laugh more often at the twists and turns that show up in your life.

Secondly, the universe wants what you want for yourself too. Life is not trying to thwart you at every turn and make the pursuit of your dreams impossible. It's actually helping you get what you want. All your wishes and thoughts are answered. All of them. However, a plant doesn't go from seed to tree overnight – not even the fast-growing bamboo! You need to trust in the process of those dreams and wishes coming to life. They *will*, but you need to let the idea of a garden actually become a garden. That means going through the seasons to let growth happen and dealing with bugs and weeds along the way. It will all be worth it when you see your beautiful garden flourish with life, because after all, no matter how beautiful a dream or how pretty a picture, nothing beats the real thing!

WIZARDS AND HARRY POTTER

The mass appeal of the Harry Potter stories by J K Rowling was a surprise to some people (included in that were likely the three publishers who rejected her work before it was picked up by a smaller publishing house). Yet the young boy who goes to wizard school and learns how to work magic, create potions and speak magical words of power (with some interesting and varied results) captured the imagination and hearts of millions.

There is inside each one of us something of a wizard capable of transforming one thing into another, to take a challenge and create an opportunity out of it. I call this part of us the 'inner alchemist'. Have you heard of alchemists – the wizard-like, science geek dreamers who lived in the Middle Ages? They were considered a bit weird by some people, and fascinating and powerful by others. They are alive and well today in our modern world, practising their alchemy and magic in a different way – using the intelligence within that just knows how to transform a potential breakdown into a breakthrough using invisible but powerful inner resources such as attitude.

When you are building your psychological container, which we spoke of in the last chapter, you are creating an inner room in which your inner alchemist can do his or her best work. That invisible and incredible part of you exists, whether you know it consciously or not. Trusting yourself and life is what allows the magician-alchemist-wizard within you to turn apparent disaster into deliciousness. Guided from within, and using the exercises in this book, you'll take the raw materials of chaos, crisis and confusion and respond with some magic in your soul. Instead of reacting, you'll start to think more creatively. Instead of collapsing in defeat, you'll make choices and commitments that change what is happening, transforming lead into gold, mountains into molehills and adversity into opportunity.

GET OUT OF YOUR OWN WAY

So even when you don't quite see it at the time, your life is still working itself out in the best way, every day. From the little things that seem to go wrong, that later help ensure the things that really need to go right, actually do go right, and at the right time too (otherwise the right thing wouldn't be so right at all!), life is doing its job.

You might wonder if you are supposed to just let life do all the work for you, if there is really anything left for *you* to do, since life is so good at working things out. Life happens around you, sometimes it feels like it is happening to you, and you don't have much of a choice, but in truth, life is not separate from you. It thrives inside of you, causing you to grow and change from within.

When you desire or dream of something, it's life speaking through your heart, whispering signs of what you are meant to be. Those inner dreams and desires, no matter how unlikely or impossible they might seem, are the seeds life plants in your heart. They are the beginnings of the beautiful plant you are meant to become in the great garden of life. You are meant to grow and work with life to become that unique creature you are – in some ways, the same as everyone else, and yet also absolutely one of a kind. You are growing along with the rest of the natural world. Those inner dreams and desires deep within are not just fantasies. They are nudges from life to become all you are meant to be.

Your job is not to work out *how* you are supposed to grow into your destiny, or even exactly what it is supposed to look like, or even to know what plant you are going to be in *advance*. You don't have to know any of that. A lot of people worry that if they don't know where they are going, and exactly how they are going to get there, then they won't end up getting anywhere. I can tell you from experience that there's no point having a bunch of answers if they are the wrong answers for you. If you don't know your big purpose or destiny in life, that's absolutely okay. Even if you think you do, what you want might come together in a very different way to how you imagine. More often than not, it is better to not get too attached to the details of how, when, why, where, what, and just get on with living your life, and keep learning to trust and grow.

Most of the time we don't really know what will make us happy. We just get an idea stuck in our minds and want it, without even stopping to think if it is really going to be good for us. I have been approached by too many people wanting me to tell them how to make a particular person love them, rather than focusing on how they could attract the right loving relationship into their lives (even if they don't know who that loving partner is as yet). Rather than trusting that if someone is being taken out of their lives, there could be a wonderful reason for it, even though the pain of loss is hard to get through, they want to control who, what, when and where. This is the sort of attitude that blocks life from helping us. If we get fixated upon our happiness as only being able to happen in one particular way, or through one particular person, we start getting in our own way. Getting out of our own way means that we let life guide us, like a Sherpa on a great mountain climb.

Life will lead you in exactly the right direction, with exactly the best timing. It's kind of like those 'trust' games you might have played on school camps where you are blindfolded and have to learn to let another person give you instructions, step by step, to walk a simple path from one point to the next. You can't see, so you need to trust them to be your 'eyes' for you, and guide you. You have to choose if you are going to trust, listen and respond to your guiding friend, or not.

I remember during those blindfold games being so anxious I might fall over, or that my partner guiding me might suddenly just forget to tell me about a step or pothole beneath my feet, and I would fall and feel hurt and humiliated. None of those things happened though. What happened was at the end of the short trust exercise, I removed my blindfold and was amazed at how simple and basic the path had been, without any difficulties really, except for the nightmare of fear I had created because I couldn't see where I was going. In my head, the journey was really difficult! I had made the whole experience much harder for myself because I had let the fears of my mind get in the way of just trusting it would all work out. That exact same journey could have been quicker, easier and more fun if I hadn't been so afraid, if I had found it easier to trust.

Life is very much like one great big blindfolded trust exercise. The loving hand of life is at our sides every step of the way, giving us a gentle nudge here or guiding us through the voice of our hearts to go in a certain direction. Sometimes you get yanked up and it hurts for a moment, but you would have otherwise slipped and fallen into something far more painful. Yes, life is there, even whilst we are blindfolded without a clue as to what we are doing in the bigger scheme of things, and the magic of that is that trusting it, and just taking the journey, means you get to where you need to be anyway.

Now maybe you think, *Well, if I am going there anyway, why can't I just be in control and get there by myself without that damn blindfold and that big game of trust?* And of course, you can, if you like. You can choose to try and get through your life by only making choices where you feel completely in control of the process, the outcome, the destination, never veering from the path others have been upon, trying not to take risks and therefore having a need really to trust.

The trouble with this approach is that it's hard. It might seem easier and less complicated at first, with less chance of pain and struggle, but you'll see soon enough that it's quite the opposite, and less fun, interesting and energising.

It would be like you were going surfing in a bathtub, where you could quite likely control the waves, or lack thereof. Is that going to be as exciting as surfing in the ocean? True, you'll not fall off your board, or get dumped by a wave and end up with sand in your hair or salt water up your nose (not the most pleasant thing, but quite a good way to clear out your sinuses, coincidentally), but whilst you will avoid those things, you'll also miss out on the thrill of the wave, the companionship of other surfers, the fresh, salty air and the healing power of the ocean. You only get all that good stuff when you are open to life. You can't surf in the same way if you want to do it in an environment controlled by you, at home, in your bathtub.

Life is like this. If you want to really live it, and take the journey, you are going to have to learn to trust it, even when you don't know what is going to happen next. Otherwise, you'll become a person so defensive towards life you'll end up keeping the good stuff away from you just as much as the stuff you think you don't want (even though that is often what you later realise you really needed at the time).

Apart from the journey itself being less fun, the destination actually changes. When you choose to trust in life, your destiny opens up in surprising ways. When you are open to life, opportunities can happen more readily. When your arms are open to receive, you can receive. If they are crossed over your chest, it's just harder for you to get the help you need.

And for what? Life is already hard enough – it is strange, beautiful, wild and sometimes utterly devastating, and other times a truly exhilarating and inspiring experience. If learning to trust helps us, and helps everyone else too (because happy people who are helped by life want to help others too), then why not do it? Because you might get hurt? That will happen more so if you shut yourself off from life, feeding the fear in your mind. It's sort of like settling for crumbs on the floor because you choose not to climb up to the table and partake of the feast. That is the difference between a life lived from a place of fear and a life lived from a place of trust. They both take you to a version of your destiny, but will you be the thriving, vibrant plant of your full self, bursting with life, or a spindly little plant that has barely survived?

You get to choose which version of your destiny you are going to experience by how much you are willing to trust. Will it be either a pure, undiluted perfume version, or weaker eau de toilette version? Or if you prefer a more technological comparison: a full colour high definition picture instead of slightly blurry black and white! You get to choose. Life delivers what we are willing to receive. If you want the best version of your destiny, then you are going to have to give up the control and learn to trust instead, to let life really guide you into all you can be.

Some people believe that if you want to create something in your life, you must visualise every aspect of it in great detail. Apart from the fact that many people are not able to visualise clearly, I don't believe it is necessary for us to visualise in order to create. I am not saying that visualising details doesn't work. It *does*, but it also limits us to what we can currently perceive. Time and time again, I have created things in my life only to realise that, if I had asked for guidance and trusted, I would have been happier if I had let go and allowed what was happening beneath my conscious awareness at the time to take root and grow own its own, through me, but not directed consciously by my efforts. I call this 'getting out of your own way'.

When we get out of our own way, we stop being one of those interfering people that just make life more difficult even though they are 'trying to help'. We stop telling life what it should be doing and instead, have a conversation with it. We talk about what we want and we listen by responding to what is happening in our lives. We no longer need to climb every mountain just because it's there. Sometimes, if we do end up climbing the wrong mountain, or at least one that takes a lot of effort and doesn't bring us much joy, we learn from the experience and listen more to our hearts (and less to our minds) next time we see another mountain to climb. Getting out of our own way means doing only our part and not complicating matters unnecessarily through mistaken beliefs that if we don't sort life out, it won't know how to happen without our guiding hand. We trust what we feel and stop allowing the fears of our minds make life seem scarier or more difficult than it needs to be.

WHAT DO YOU REALLY WANT?

So if life wants for you what you want for you, some of you may ask, "Does this mean life wants me to have a Ferrari?" Maybe. Maybe life doesn't care too much for the car per se, but wants you to experience what it is like to manifest your dream, to create something – perhaps even something you didn't feel was possible. There can be great value in that, even more than the cost of a Ferrari!

Sometimes we can place moral judgements on what we want to create. Some things we want might seem more selfish and some things might seem more about helping others or community-oriented. Mature hearts do tend to want to look out for more than only their own immediate interests, but that is not a moral issue, that is just something that comes with inner development and spiritual growth.

There may be people who say they want to help another person, but what they are really interested in is what they can get out of it. Then there are others that just want to be happy, and their happiness really does help others. So let's not assume that certain desires are better than others, nor that as you grow, you won't have any desires anymore. They may change in quality, becoming about what you can share with the world rather than only what you can take from it for yourself, but it's likely you'll have desires of various sorts throughout your life journey and that's fine. There's no need to feel guilty or ashamed of this, especially if you are thinking about self-development and maybe wondering if you shouldn't be more 'spiritual' somehow.

What is more helpful is to ask yourself – without judgement – what you *really* want. What would you like to live in this lifetime of yours? What would feel like just the best thing ever for you? You might not have a specific vision of that, and as we know, that is just fine. But I bet you can get a sense of how you'd like to feel – happy, healthy, fulfilled, in love, passionate, satisfied, peaceful, excited, inspired … and so on. Those feelings are what you want – the way they come into your life is not your concern. Those feelings can become your prayers, your conversation with the universe, and you 'putting it out there' so what you want can come back to you, which it will.

I once dated a man for about six months, in a 'rebound relationship' after I split with my first long-term boyfriend. I liked this new man and was quite overwhelmed (in a nice way) by our passionate connection with each other, but I ended the relationship because I wasn't emotionally or psychologically ready to commit to a serious relationship at the time. My new man was asking me about my thoughts on marriage and I didn't even know if I was ready to commit to dating him for another few months, let alone spending the rest of our lives together. We weren't in alignment with each other and I knew it wasn't fair to either of us. So we broke off contact and did our best to get on with our lives.

About five years later, that man stood in his backyard, looked up at the sky and declared to the universe he was ready to have a relationship again, " … with someone really cool, like Alana," to use his exact words.

Around the same time, out of the blue, I suddenly felt compelled to find him again and make contact. I didn't have his number anymore or any way of contacting him, until it just occurred to me to search for him on a professional networking and job-hunting website I hardly ever used. Of course, he had a profile there, so I emailed him. He emailed back. He told me an ex-girlfriend had just randomly decided he should have his profile up on that professional networking website and had put it up a few weeks earlier. We met up, he told me his 'backyard prayer' story. I was astounded.

We fell back in love very easily and lived together in a passionate relationship for another five or so years. It was difficult to walk away from him when the time came to do so. We lacked the basic compatibility that would make the marriage to each other we both dreamed of a successful one. This was a painful experience, and yet I loved him very deeply and I couldn't regret the time we had together. I just felt grateful I was able to love him for those years together because he was very special to me. We lived out what was meant to be our destiny together. As Dr. Seuss reminds us, "Don't cry because it's over, smile because it happened."

Ironically enough, perhaps, it's often the things we don't really obsess about or worry about that seem to be created most swiftly and easily. Remaining detached and allowing life to have a chance to respond to you is very beneficial in terms of your success.

You could imagine it like this. Say you have a favour to ask of someone who wants to help you. You ask them, explaining why you need help and what you would like. They want to help, but they need time to think about how they can best assist you, what would need to happen for them to be able to help you, and how to create a plan to do so. You can either give them time and space to sort all that out, or you could pester them, calling them every few minutes, asking again and again if they will help you! Whilst they may still be able to help you, the whole process will be more time-consuming and convoluted. It can happen quicker and easier if you trust and let them sort things out in their own way and time.

So it is with the universe. Once you ask for something, the right situations and circumstances are set in motion. I have seen this at work at various times in my life and it is truly breathtaking in its scope, foresight and intelligence. It is so incredible, that I believe the universe knows what we want before we even know it! It is like life is already actively leading us in the right direction because it knows our hearts even better than we do at times. We can ask for what we want, but to really receive it most readily, we also need to learn how to receive. Guidance, for example, is the hand of life giving us a nudge in certain directions.

There was a time in my life when I really wanted to write my first oracle deck. Oracle decks are a beautiful and easy way to receive spiritual guidance. They usually consist of a series of numbered cards with beautiful artwork and an accompanying guidebook with messages. So you ask a question, pull a card, enjoy the artwork, and read the corresponding message in the guidebook. Presto! There is your guidance for that day or on that issue. A lovely idea!

I had just self-published my first series of meditation CDs. Self-publishing was a rather expensive prospect at the time, from time spent in the recording studio to lay down the background music, to the meditations being recorded, then time spent mixing and mastering the two different tracks. Then there was the cost of the graphic design and artwork, getting the printing done and the CDs pressed. That was only the first step! Then there was distribution and the like. Well, it was a big job, much bigger than I had realised when I first set out to self-publish.

Some years later, when I realised I didn't have the time, inclination or, I believed, the skill necessary to really distribute my work to a larger audience, I sought a publisher who had a distribution network already established. I knew that to get an oracle deck published, which would be an even more expensive and legally complex matter to create (given that rights and royalties would have to be paid to the artist as well as the author), I'd want some help.

My wonderful publisher, Blue Angel Publishing, found me through a series of circumstances I had no knowledge of at the time. Suddenly they were just 'there'. After we had been creating meditation CDs together for a little while, I had the idea pop into my head to forward to them the manuscript of a book I had written. My publisher was surprised because in his words, he 'didn't know I could write too' – something I obviously forgot to mention to him!

A year or so later, my publisher asked if I would be interested in writing an oracle deck based on the Buddhist Goddess Kuan Yin. He said that seeing my manuscript had got him thinking in that direction and although he had originally considered asking a more established writer to do that project, he kept feeling he should ask me to do it. I felt so overwhelmed with excitement and gratitude. When I promptly agreed, he said he would email me the artwork he had already secured for the project.

I waited for the email and when it arrived and I opened up the artwork files, I nearly fell off my chair. Before me were forty-four images of artwork I had loved and collected for many years previously. I had been printing it off the internet, just to have it around me because I was so touched by its beauty. I had no idea who the artist was, or that all the images were even by the same artist, and yet here they were, those very same images that had captured my heart years earlier, before I had even met my publisher. I felt as though this project had been waiting for me to get to it, the manifestation of a heart's desire before I even knew what it was.

This sort of thing is what I mean when I say that the universe knows, even before we do, what we truly want and need and is leading us into it, and why life sometimes seems like a joke – in the best and kindest way – where we are perhaps last at times to get to the punch line.

This doesn't mean we aren't 'supposed' to ask for what we want, and instead just sit back and wait for life to happen. Destiny needs a helping hand sometimes. She has a lot to do! We are here to learn, grow and experience too. It's just that we don't have to demand from life like a screaming toddler throwing a tantrum, though perhaps some days you will do so (or is that just me?). What it means is that life is your companion, your partner, in the process of manifesting your inner desires. We can help our destiny along with our efforts, but don't need to whip it into submission either. It's about learning who we are and what we are destined to be as we grow, trusting the innate design within us that knows what it is meant to be.

The desires in your heart are the breadcrumbs of life, trying to lead you along your life path. So certainly, do ask for what is in your heart. Just remember that taking the journey, the process of creation, is your 'payment' for the desires. This doesn't necessarily mean it will be a hard journey or even a long one, though it may be at times, and either way, it's okay. It's just the journey, neither better nor worse for however long it takes or however much the road twists and turns. If you feel like your life journey has a lot of bends, twists and turns, and seems to be taking a while, you can take that as a compliment. Just consider that the universe thinks you are far too capable to just have a simple, quick little straight line of a life, and you'd become bored if you weren't challenged to your level of ability!

To really engage with life and communicate your desires, I suggest you focus on two things: gratitude for what you already have (as there is no more powerful fertiliser to receive more), and the *feeling* in general rather than specific detail (unless you want to try that out as an experiment or two first) of what you want to experience. This will be the opposite of what many self-help and creative visualisation texts teach and I acknowledge this. I don't dismiss the other teachings at all, I just suggest that if you want to allow life to guide you into something more wonderful than what you can currently envision, then it makes sense that you would have to trust and remain open to what you don't know yet!

WHAT YOU WANT, WANTS YOU

In case I haven't made it quite clear yet, what you want, wants you. Or another way of putting it: life is leading you towards what will fulfil you, bring you the most joy and happiness, and is helping you live a life that will bring out the best in you. That doesn't mean it will always appear to be the easiest path, but avoiding what life is handing you, to try and make your life easier in the short-term, leads to more struggle and suffering in the long-term (even, actually, in the short-term too, often enough).

Resistance is the real issue here, based on lack of trust. It isn't about your life having to be more difficult in order to be happy or some such idea. So the tricky part is trusting even when that doesn't seem to be happening. It is often only in looking back that we see the silver lining shining through what once seemed to be the darkest clouds in our lives. The good news is that the more we trust, the more we can find our way through life without always needing to have to wait for rainbows to come from a thunderstorm. Sometimes they can happen with just a quick little sunshower too. Trusting life doesn't always mean we have to push through challenge. Sometimes it will mean that an unexpected and much easier path for us opens up too.

There is a saying that 'life wasn't meant to be easy'. Whilst I believe we are all here to take a journey, and that journey involves challenging growth opportunities at times, I also believe our attitudes can transform much of our suffering into peace and happiness. We can see the proverbial rain shower as good for the garden and a chance to feel cosy and grateful that we have roofs over our heads and beautiful open windows through which to smell the rain and enjoy the coolness; or, we can get stroppy and depressed because we can't go to the beach that day and lie in the sunshine. One attitude creates happiness and a sense of wellbeing, and gratitude. One creates mental unhappiness and a feeling of deprivation. Yet it is the same incident that triggers both. The choice is up to us. Our happiness in life is often less about what is actually happening, and more about what we choose to make of it.

BIRDS OF A FEATHER

There are two expressions that sum up a philosophy known as 'the law of attraction'. The law of attraction works for better or worse. So on the downside, 'if you lie down with dogs, you'll wake up with fleas', but on the upside, 'birds of a feather flock together'! What the law of attraction teaches us is that we can have a big influence on our life experiences through cultivating the sort of attitude we want to feel. We could keep focusing on what we feel is not working, on what seems to be wrong and talk ourselves into an unhappy, grumpy, depressed and miserable state of mind. But if we want more happiness in our lives, then we focus on even the smallest thing we can be grateful for – and feel happy about – now. From that, more happiness grows. The law of attraction teaches us that what we put out into the world is amplified and returned to us, that 'like attracts like' and it all starts with our attitude.

In cultivating a positive attitude, and choosing to 'let your smile change the world rather than the world change your smile', you'll start to notice the law of attraction working in your life. When you help others, others will want to help you. When you feel good, others around you will feel good too. This is how we become a positive influence in the world. It's not by trying to change other people or taking control of what is happening in the world, it's by working on ourselves, choosing how we respond to life, and being kind enough to ourselves to put some time into building our inner containers through self-caring practices on a regular basis. Then, no matter what is going on, we can always choose to just shrug our shoulders, figure that life is plotting some genius twist of fate and trust in that, whilst choosing to feel as good as we can in that moment where we have no clue what is going on anyway.

Metaphysical writer, Florence Scovel Shinn, born in 1871, was a woman ahead of her time. She, like me, was very keen on the power of words to generate a particular sort of life experience. Complaining, gossiping and speaking negatively tends to attract misery. Hence the saying, 'misery loves company'. Florence Scovel Shinn used the example of talking on the phone to a friend who would complain and whinge about all the things she didn't like and didn't want. Her friend would call it a 'good old-fashioned chat'. Florence Scovel Shinn didn't think it was so good at all. In fact she described it as a draining and tiring experience, as you can perhaps well imagine.

So one day, Florence decided to tell her friend she didn't want to have any more of those good old-fashioned chats. She wanted to only have new conversations, about what they loved and what they wanted. Their conversations turned into a source of energy, excitement and positivity rather than negativity and fatigue.

We can do this too. Sometimes people mistakenly believe that being positive is inauthentic or fake, that it is putting a false gloss on things. Acknowledging all our feelings is important – even those some might consider negative like sadness, fear or anger. Anger might be letting us know we need to redefine a boundary in a relationship where a person consistently takes advantage of your good nature, as an example, exploiting you and not treating you with respect. Of course that would make you angry! That is a sign to change how you are behaving in the relationship and what you are willing to accept from others. You don't have to carry on being angry once you have received the message the emotion brings and act on it. Nor does 'acting on it' mean you have to dump your anger on the other person. That's not so helpful. What it does mean is you get creative about other ways to behave in the relationship (perhaps like Florence Scovel Shinn did) and choose which new way you'd like to behave and make a commitment to act on it. Then your anger passes because you don't need it anymore, and you can choose to connect with a more positive state of mind once again.

These are the ways we can tweak the law of attraction into our favour, so the birds we flock with are uplifting ones that help us feel an increasing sense of wellbeing, love and happiness, rather than flea-ridden dogs that leave us feeling irritated, used and unwell. You might not think you have much choice about whom you spend time with – certainly there's that old saying that 'you can choose your friends, but not your family'. I believe that at a deeper level everyone in our lives is there for a purpose – even the people you don't think you are choosing, like family members. Life gives us what we need to grow. So growth through learning how to relate to your family members in constructive ways, or even at times, if needs be, to take a stand and go your own way for a while, is allowed. It isn't about you rejecting anyone, it's about you doing what you need to do to become happy. When you feel strong enough within yourself to be positive and create an attitude to the world that allows you to smile when you want to smile, no matter what, then you might be ready to reconnect with your family, or particular groups of friends, again. You might even have a positive effect on your friends and family with your new and improved attitude!

You might also have to get rid of the idea that being happy is nerdy and being dark and brooding is cool. Having loved and lived with a dark and brooding man for several years, and being utterly miserable with him, despite loving him dearly, I can personally say that the attractiveness of the brooding, intense personality that cannot surrender easily into spontaneity and joy is best admired from a distance, if you need to admire it at all. The coolest people I have met, and certainly the ones I enjoy spending time with, are the ones that are happiest within themselves and therefore have little or no need to try and force others around them to behave in ways they can control. When someone is happy within themselves, they tend to accept others as they are too. They have no need to try and force life to be other than what it is either. This is very freeing and enjoyable for all involved.

Choosing your company wisely makes more sense if you consider that people feed us or drain us with their energy. Like food – the energy other people bring to us can enhance health or deplete it. You'll know how healthy a person is for you if you feel good after being around them for a while, or if you feel awful, even if not five minutes before seeing them you felt great. If that someone is a close friend or family member, then you'll need to choose how to deal with the situation. That might mean limiting time in exposure whilst you work out how to remain feeling happy even whilst they may not be. It might involve having a 'Florence Scovel Shinn-type' intervention, like I shared with you above. It might involve learning that just because someone you love is unhappy that it doesn't mean you cannot be happy within yourself – and maybe even you'll end up inspiring them with your positive attitude.

When you choose to surround yourself with people who are good for you, who can receive and give love freely, and to whom you can be good for too – by being yourself – then you'll be creating positive energy for yourself and for them. You'll be working with the law of attraction by letting go of what you don't want in your life, to allow for more of what you do.

COOL, CALM, COLLECTED

You can become a master of the 3 Cs if you choose your attitude. You can become cool, calm and collected, even in a crisis, or in chaos or confusion, which is kind of when it matters the most.

The exercises in the workbook section, the last four chapters of this book, will help you in simple, practical ways. Don't underestimate the power of a simple guided exercise to help you see things in a new way, or have a sudden breakthrough that frees you from a persistent old pattern that has kept you stuck in struggle, doubt or fear. Change can happen in an instant. We might be working up to it for years, but when that moment is upon us to finally be freed from something – even if only moments earlier we believed 'that is just the way it is and some things can never change' – that change will happen, and that can be quick indeed.

As you journey through the exercises, and step by step, apply what you are learning through this book, remember the old saying that 'Rome wasn't built in a day'. Little steps all add up to a big journey. Do the work, but don't do it all right now. One step per day is good. One step every day is fantastic, actually. Even if those steps are small most of the time, as you gain confidence through that process, you'll eventually take leaps.

The Workbook

· ·

Introduction to the Workbook

These workbook Chapters 7 to 10 will give you guidance for simple and effective practical tips, tricks and techniques to walk this talk.

If you find you relate to chaos the most at this time in your life, then you might want to work on Chapter 7. If you relate to crisis the most right now, then move on to Chapter 8 if you prefer. Or if you feel so steeped in confusion that you don't know how to progress, then keep it simple and move straight into Chapter 9.

If you don't have a preference, then just work through the exercises as listed, perhaps one each day, every few days, or once a week, whenever you feel you need a boost.

If you are feeling very spontaneous, then you might want to simply trust your gut. Have a browse through the sections and choose what seems to 'jump out' at you and capture your attention, and work through that particular exercise.

You can also repeat an exercise as often as you like. Some exercises may well become part of your daily 'container-building, trust-making, sanity-creating' practice. Others you might just do sometimes, when you need a boost.

TRAINING WHEELS AND GRAVITY

Sometimes reading an idea is enough to set a chain reaction of new thinking in motion, and your behaviour begins to change in response to this without you really needing to do much more than allow it to happen. At other times, you'll need some support to take that idea and transform it into a reality in your life. The practical exercises in the rest of the book form the workbook section. These are the tools to turn the teachings into a reality. They help you get your mind in the right zone and feel the reality of what you are tuning into through the teachings of this book. They are simple, quick, and anyone can do them, even if you don't feel you can visualise easily.

If you have done guided meditations or healing exercises before, these will feel very easy for you indeed. If you are new to all this, it might seem easy or quite strange. Here's a reassuring tip: as long as you just go through the process, you can't get it wrong. Every time you do the exercises here, you'll improve. You'll add another layer of strength to that inner container I was talking about earlier on. You'll put more positive energy and love into your mind and body. You'll contribute to your inner spiritual bank account with some good energy, which will give you the strength to soar later on when an opportunity comes your way, or a challenge pushes you to find the courage within to believe in yourself and just go through it. In short, it's all good. Just do the exercises as best you can and you'll benefit from them.

As you start to think differently about what is happening in your life, you'll have times where life feels great, joyful, uplifting, and you'll find yourself smiling more (even without a particular reason – people may wonder what you have been up to!). That will happen more and more often. Yet there will be other times when you'll need reinforcement for the new way; you might be waiting to really see the benefit of trying out a more positive attitude or seeing the results of your efforts. Remember when we talked about the seasons of growth being like the seasons in nature? So you might be in a long, cold winter, wanting it to be spring, and wondering if it is ever going to happen for you. It will, but you have to be prepared for some moments where you might lose faith or distrust yourself or life, especially if that is what is more familiar to you at first.

This is the 'two steps forwards, one step back' phenomenon, which happens when you are learning a new habit of thinking or behaviour. In the world of therapy, we'd probably call it 'resistance'. It is the inertia, the regressive streak in all human beings that resists change, growth and healing, even if those things will ultimately bring more happiness. It might sound perverse, but it's not really. It's just part of life on this planet. You could compare it to gravity. It drags things down, but it helps to keep them on the ground too. Imagine trying to eat your lovely lunch without gravity. Getting it into your mouth would be a struggle, as would digesting it.

Without gravity in the physical sense – and in the emotional and psychological sense, where we pull back from change towards what we already know instead – there wouldn't be growth. There would be nothing to push against to lever ourselves up, no starting block from which to push off. We don't want to succumb to gravity so much that we cannot summon the strength required to evolve our mindsets or try new things (and therefore be open to a new and improved life experience). Yet without any tension or friction there's likely to be little motivation either. We need a bit of push-pull to get the inner fires burning, so to speak. Friction creates sparks and heat.

Ever wanted something more because you thought you couldn't have it? A person? A job? This is the friction or push-pull that can get us motivated to reach for something new.

I'll share a story with you from my own life to illustrate the point. It's a bit embarrassing though I can laugh about it too – I was such a naughty girl!

It was at a time when I was looking for part-time work. I was in law school and the costs of legal textbooks (and my even faster growing collection of spiritual, self-help and New Age books) was increasing rapidly. I applied for many jobs, one of which was (I laugh to think of it now) in marketing. I loathe the idea of trying to sell someone something. If you are good at it and love it, fine, but for me, ick. As soon as someone tries to manipulate me into buying something, I tend to get bored and shut down. I don't want to impose that on someone else and I never have.

So there I was, in a job interview, for a job I would undoubtedly hate, and didn't really want, with a young man – probably not much older than me at the time in his early twenties. The first part of the interview was in a group. We were all young go-getter types and as he talked about high levels of competition for the job, and the sort of positive, go-get-'em attitude they valued and how high achievers would thrive in this position, all my ego buttons were pushed and I wanted the job. Well, I thought I did for about five minutes. He made it seem as though it was a great favour we were even in that interview and whomever gained this position would be a winner. We all wanted to be winners! He was obviously not too shabby at marketing the marketing position to us all.

The group interview then ended and private interviews with individual applicants continued. In the interview room, I answered all his questions using my intuition to feel what he wanted to hear. (Shocking, I know. I have since learned to use my powers for far less evil purposes.) Then came the crunch moment where he was considering whether or not to offer me the job. I had a very strange realisation in that moment. I realised that no part of me – beyond that small part of my ego that wanted to 'win' the competition the interviewer had turned the interview into – really gave a hoot about this job and certainly, I didn't want it. I also knew I wanted to be the one to turn it down. So when the interviewer asked me if I would be interested in the job – which I knew meant he was about to offer it to me – I lied straight out. Not my finest moment! I told him, yes, I was very keen. He offered me the job.

I immediately, and I will be the first to admit, rather perversely, turned it down. He was shocked. I was appalled at myself, but that was the game he set up and I had decided to play it. I left that interview having lost several hours of my life which I'll never get back, and having learned that my ego was quite ready to go after something I knew I didn't even want, just because I thought I couldn't have it. I was appalled at myself, but it was a good wake-up call and I eventually did stop trying to climb mountains just because they were there, focusing my energy instead on what really mattered to me. So the experience was ultimately helpful.

I realised something about myself and about human nature more generally. If things are too easy, we often tend to minimise their value. We all want a free lunch now and then, and people love the idea of a 'free gift', but if you give away anything too freely, people can undervalue it. Add a bit of struggle to having to get there, and the perceived value seems to increase.

I have known people who have had so many amazing opportunities come their way, and they – perhaps because they have been spoilt for choice earlier on in life – have just let them go. I remember one friend telling me about various career opportunities she had been given that I would have grabbed a hold of instantly and *never* let pass me by, but she let them slip through her fingers. I actually felt a flash of anger when she told me her stories initially, which I later realised was a sense of jealousy and frustration. How could someone who didn't care – and didn't bother to pay due respect to the opportunities given to her by taking them up – be offered so many good things, and I, who had to struggle to even get a tiny amount of the opportunity that came to her, and was willing to work hard on everything that came my way, be given so little in comparison? It was like my grandmother used to say, 'God giving nuts to people who don't have the teeth to crack them'.

Eventually, I came to my senses and remembered that comparing your life to another person's is not very helpful. We all have our own paths to walk and what is useful for one person may well not be so for another. But we are all loved equally and given whatever we need to grow and become our fullest selves. No matter how much it may appear that some have an easier ride than others or get a bigger slice of the pie, we all get what we need to grow, what will support us best to become all we can become. Some of us might seem to get the bigger challenges in life, but that will be because we are big and bold enough to handle them and not become bitter, instead developing into quite incredible and inspiring people capable of love and compassion, wisdom and contagious joy!

So I got over my woe-is-me attitude and remembered that my friend needed to live her life in her own way – which would be perfect for whatever she was meant to experience and become this lifetime – just as I needed to trust in my own journey. Because I tended to say yes to everything, bordering on over-commitment far too often, and trying to make everything work, less opportunities were better suited for my temperament at that time. Until I learned some discernment (not climbing every single mountain in sight, as I mentioned before) then I could let things come and go more easily too. Funnily enough, the more I did that, the more opportunities began to come my way too – some of which weren't right for me, and many of which really were.

So whilst I don't believe that life *has* to be all struggle, there are certainly times when having to push to grow gives us benefit. There are some people that suffer from what is known as a 'sense of entitlement'. This is a tendency to just expect that people will do whatever they want, whenever they want it, and that life owes them just because they exist. It's very different to believing you are entitled to a decent life – or even a good, amazing, incredible life – and being willing to do whatever is required to experience that. The latter has a sense of personal responsibility and maturity involved in it. The former, the sense of entitlement, is immature, babyish and not pleasant to be around. What I find interesting about people who demonstrate this sense of entitlement, is that whilst they may often (but not necessarily always) have a lot of material comforts, they are deeply lacking in a sense of soul, of purpose, of meaning and depth in their lives.

Perhaps those things come from a deep need to give something to the world, to make a contribution in some way, whether that be to your family and friends or to a cause you believe in, or to prove to yourself you can succeed in your chosen field of work or overcome various personal challenges in other ways. It is the struggle that creates the soul in a person.

Soul and depth can be created through joy too. But without the sense of struggle, no real joy is possible either because joy exists in each of us, right in the depths of our being. We have to go deep to tap into those depths. It is often the struggle that opens us up deep enough to be able to tap into it. Some of the most joyful people I have met are those that have got through the struggle. And some of the most painful people to be around are those that live on the surface. Things seem happy and lucky at first glance, but it doesn't take long before a sense of a directionless, lost, and psychologically and emotionally crippled person becomes more real than the surface gloss.

Some of these people seem to end up on reality television shows where others watch them and either get jealous of their lifestyles or take sadistic delight in how their lives aren't perfect after all. I watched reality television for a brief period of time when I was with a man in a relationship with me as well as super-large televisions (he found my apparently tiny screen impossible to watch). He had a subscription to cable television and I fell into a temporary seduction with the entertainment channels. When I left the relationship – and its enormous television and cable subscription – behind me, I moved into a new home without television access. I took up my childhood passion of reading again, and watching movies sometimes instead.

Whilst I was actually much happier not immersing myself in the world of reality television (I used to feel a bit dirty after watching those shows!), I did think about what it was about the people on some of those shows that was so fascinating at first. They appeared to live – by Western cultural standards at least – wealthy and even glamorous lives. They looked so beautiful and by all accounts had so much to be grateful for, and yet their lives were so frequently plagued with drama and unhappiness. Sometimes all I could see underneath a beautiful face and clothes was the pain of a person who really didn't know themselves at all, and put more value on the surface than what was underneath. Whilst I am an appreciator of beauty, I know that having it on the surface without developing inner strength does not make for a pretty picture in the long run.

As I realised this, I suddenly found myself in a most unexpected moment of gratitude for all the decidedly unglamorous struggle I had gone through in my life that had taught me how to be strong. I realised whilst I didn't need or want to have a life that was only struggle, I could honour that the challenges which had come my way had helped me become a person I liked being. If I hadn't had those challenges, I very likely would have simply grown my ego, instead of my heart, and ended up just as superficially-oriented and unhappy within as some of the people I saw in those television shows.

I guess you could say that I came to see the evidence of tough love in the struggles of life, and that sometimes having a superficially easier life, with wealth and social status apparently in your favour, does not make for a happier or more joyful individual. Those that seem to be able to manage a life of material abundance with some happiness and peace of mind are those who learn to give of what they have received, and who have genuine and loving relationships with others, and often have had to work through great struggles first to get to where they are.

So if things aren't as easy as you think they should be, think again. You might just be getting a vote of confidence from life that you are going to become a truly awesome human being, and that this is part of your soul obstacle course to build inner strength and other qualities that will have you becoming a person you are happy and proud to be.

Part of this gravity in our emotional and psychological make-up is experienced as resistance, or even in severe cases where we perhaps take more than one step back, as regression, where we seem to fall back into a worse state than we were previously. This is okay and a sign that we are healing, provided we are willing to see it in context and realise it is not a failure, but a part of the growth process, *and then just keep going*. I have always felt that failure is not the stuff-up or falling over so to speak, but about whether or not we get back up and keep going.

This sort of gravity is how we build strength. In time, you won't need as much effort to hold your new attitude in place, or pick it up it when it slips a bit. You'll sustain the new behaviour or thinking much more easily and it will feel natural, like 'second nature' to you. Resistance will stop pulling you back. You will have overcome it – until you are ready to progress to a new level, when the process begins all over again. You'll get used to it after you've had a breakthrough or two, or three, and understand the process after a little while.

Getting to a breakthrough however, typically requires some training wheels, some support and some encouragement – especially when the thrill of the new wears off and it seems to be almost easier to slip back into negative thinking or fear or doubt for a time. Don't worry too much if this happens. It often does just before you are about to break through into a new level. It's sort of like an old lover who calls you after no contact for months, just at the time when you are finally letting go of the old relationship and becoming ready to move on with your life. Consider it a testament to your growth and just chalk it up to the 'wobbles of transition'.

These wobbles of transition are a bit like a tightrope-walker who loses a tiny bit of balance and has to wobble a little to regain a sense of centredness to then keep walking that tightrope successfully. These wobbles are signs that we are moving forward. Don't hold yourself up to an impossible standard of perfection. It isn't realistic or necessary to imagine that you read the book, do one exercise, and then have changed your thinking forever and never have a challenging moment or 'bad day' again. What you'll find is your life will improve and the challenges will become something you are able to embrace and turn to your advantage more often and more quickly. The 'bad days' will be far fewer and of shorter duration, but you will still be human, growing, and having your ups and downs as you experience this wonderful and unpredictable life of yours.

PUTTING IT INTO ACTION

I was not the sort of person to do the exercises in workbooks. I found them interesting. I would read them, and then go on to something else. So when I began writing my first project, my publisher suggested I write a short exercise in each section of the project I was working on. I wondered if anyone would really do them, let alone find them of benefit. However, I trusted his judgement and having created guided meditations for my students for many years previously, it was relatively quick and easy to create guided exercises in written form too. They just seemed to stream down from somewhere inspired, and pop right into my head! So I gave it a go. During the writing process I visualise and feel what it would be like to complete the exercise as if I was the person reading the book and doing the process. If I feel something 'click' then I know it will work and that's what I write.

When the feedback started flooding in that the exercises in many of my projects were so effective, and people were having amazing and sometimes most unusual successes with them (such as curing a previously lifelong phobia of the dentist whilst doing a self-confidence exercise!), I realised my publisher's excellent instincts were right. People did want to do these exercises. They found them helpful. So I have continued to use them in most of my work, including this book.

There is a power in your mind and body to change your world that you probably don't fully understand. I've been working in the human potential movement for decades and even I still don't fully understand it. I just know what works and that if you do the work, it will work for you – and that it doesn't always have to be work, it can be play too! So there's some fun stuff in this section as well. It's a bit like driving a car, as one of my chi gung teachers puts it. You don't have to know how the mechanics of the car works in order to drive it; you just drive it. It's the same with these exercises. You don't have to understand how they can possibly work; just know that if you do them, they work. That's it.

It's up to you if you choose to apply what we've explored so far through these exercises. My advice to you is to trust your heart and if you feel to try something, just try it. Don't know which exercise to try? Choose one randomly. I actually believe in synchronicity and everything happening for a reason, and what appears to be random to us, is just a higher order at work beyond our immediate comprehension; or in other words, there are no accidents, no mistakes, just life happening all the time.

So choose anything and start there. Have fun and enjoy your effective healing journey.

WHAT IF I CAN'T VISUALISE?

Finally, some people find it hard to 'see' in their minds. That's no problem at all. Doing these exercises will help you develop that ability, but it's not essential to have that gift to do the exercises effectively. Some people are more visual, some are 'feelers', and some don't really connect with either of those qualities.

You'll notice I use the word 'pretend' in the exercises. This is for those people who cannot easily feel or visualise. It doesn't mean that the exercise is less powerful or won't work. It just gives your mind a way to access it. So pretend away and let the exercises work on you just as they are meant to!

CHAPTER 7

Workbook Exercises for Chaos

· ·

PRACTICAL EXERCISES FOR FINDING YOUR WAY THROUGH CHAOS INTO CREATIVITY

EXERCISE 1: TRAIN YOUR BRAIN – POSITIVE REINFORCEMENT TO DERAIL NEGATIVE MOMENTUM

Why you want to do this exercise:

Our mental habits are not something we tend to pay much regard to, and yet the things we repeatedly think affect the chemistry of our bodies. You can think your way into certain states of health and happiness – or ill health and unhappiness if you so choose – even without anything much changing in your external life at first. It *is* possible to change the way you think about life and your life will change as a result. Since you'll create attitudes, habits and behaviours, as well as body chemistry, with your thoughts, you want to make sure you derail negative train of thought quickly and effectively.

This exercise will help you disrupt the momentum of negative thinking. Negative thought patterns can be triggered even with just a small disappointment or perceived criticism, failure or setback. I have had experiences in my life where I have been disheartened over something that I thought had happened, and it *hadn't*. I only found that out later! I suffered absolutely without reason. I had created the whole thing in my head! This sort of crazy mental negativity is pretty common. We react to what we *think* rather than what is *actually happening*.

This exercise will help you get your thoughts to be constructive rather than destructive, helpful rather than hindering. It is a habit breaker and a new habit maker. You can use it as a quick fix whenever you feel yourself falling into a negative pattern of behaviour or thinking, or as a deeper exercise when you really just want to *feel good* and attract more of that good feeling into your life, kicking the law of attraction into positive effect.

Getting ready:

Find a place where you can sit or lie quietly and not be disturbed. This will likely mean closing your email program, switching the mobile phone onto silent, non-vibrate or off completely, and closing a door if needs be. If you need to put a 'do not disturb for twenty minutes' sign on the door, go right ahead.

You only need your guidebook with you to read through the simple instructions, but you can also have peaceful music playing or a candle burning if you have time to set that up and want to make this exercise feel that little bit more like dipping into a sanctuary.

Sit quietly and breathe in and out for at least five breaths, until you feel you are beginning to relax. If you have been unconsciously holding your breath, or breathing shallowly in the top of your chest (a natural response to stress), then take a moment to place one hand on your belly and see if you can gently raise your hand by breathing deep into the belly. Your hand will lower on your belly naturally as you exhale. If you need more than five breaths to do this please give yourself that time. The more relaxed you are, the more powerful the exercise will be.

The exercise:

Repeat these words aloud, or 'in your mind' if you prefer. If you are able to speak aloud though, it can be most powerful to do so, even if you speak in a quiet voice.

"I am open to goodness, peace and love. I am allowed to feel happy, to feel good. This helps me and makes the world a better place for others too. Even when there is a struggle, I deal with it, and return to feeling happy again."

You are now going to visualise, or imagine, or feel or pretend (whichever one of these feels easiest for you) that there is a train running along some tracks.

It might be going slowly, like a chugging steam train, or very fast, like a high-speed Japanese train. It doesn't matter which. Let your train be whatever feels right at this moment for you. It might have a colour, it might have black smoke pumping out the top of it or you might hear the sound of the train as it follows the tracks. Your image might be very detailed and clear, or fuzzy. Whatever it is, is just fine!

You are on that train.

You notice it's going through a place you don't want to spend much time in. It is a place that feels just the way you feel when you are most stressed or depressed. You might see, sense or feel a landscape or the weather as you pass through that place. Don't worry. It won't last long.

You hear or imagine, or pretend to hear, the hiss and screech of the brakes as the train slows down, approaching a junction so it can change tracks. You know you are going to leave this unappealing place behind you now. Such a relief! Imagine, visualise, feel or pretend that any negative thoughts or feelings are being left behind in that place now. You can toss them out the train window, or put them in some bags and throw them out the window. Do you feel more free, light and happy as you do this?

The train now switches onto the new track.

Imagine, see, feel or pretend that you can physically feel the pull of the train onto the new track in a very different direction. You are heading out of darkness, towards the light. It is gathering speed now, and rising up a little bit, along the new track.

This track feels different. You feel happy about being on the train, and on that track. You like where you are going, even if you aren't exactly sure about all the details because you haven't been there before. You feel optimistic. You feel relaxed and you are enjoying the journey.

Imagine, visualise, feel or pretend that you can feel the soft warmth of sunlight through the windows on your skin, the gentle rocking of the train as it smoothly and powerfully glides along the tracks, a sense of happiness that you are going somewhere good. You may feel excited about this destination. You know good things are waiting for you there.

Close your eyes and relax into that feeling for at least several breaths in and out.

If you fall asleep, have a little nap. Enjoy your journey.

When you are ready, open your eyes. Place one hand over your upper chest, near your heart. Imagine, feel, visualise or pretend that there is a soft, good-feeling glow in your heart that spreads through your chest, and rises gently up to your head and all the way down to your feet.

You feel good, relaxed, on the right train, heading in the right direction.

When you feel ready, you have finished this guided exercise.

EXERCISE 2: A BETTER KIND OF MENTAL HEALTH DAY

Why you want to do this exercise:
During a particularly difficult time in my life, in which I was torn between my feelings of deep love for my partner at the time, and the fact that our relationship brought me a great deal of unhappiness, I had an unusually dark moment. I was driving home and a thought popped into my head about what would happen if my car hit a pole and I died. Instantly, an answer to my thought filtered through my mind: *Oh, but I am not ready for this life to be over yet, I am having so much fun!*

I don't know what shocked me more – the darkness of the initial thought, or the joy of the response, because during that difficult time in my life *fun* was not a word I related to very much. This unexpected moment pushed me to question exactly how my life could be considered fun when I was in emotional pain (when I wasn't the sort of person who enjoyed pain and suffering!).

I acknowledged that I was struggling. I realised if I chose to spend the rest of my life with the man I loved, I would undoubtedly be miserable, which was so difficult for me to bear that it took me years to really accept it as truth. However, at a deeper level, there was a part of me gaining strength and empowerment as I learned to care for myself enough to leave an unhappy relationship, no matter how deeply I loved the man in question. I loved him more than I had loved any man before, so this was a big emotional challenge.

I had the sense of my spirit, the inner part of me relishing that challenge. It was surfing my emotional ups and downs like waves. It was excited about how my eventual decision to leave – and to rebuild a new life based on more love and kindness for myself than I had ever been able to summon before – would affect me and empower me to be a more loving and helpful presence in the world. It knew that new life would flower from the old life I was leaving behind. And it knew I was being asked to give up the one thing – in this case, the one person – I thought I would never have to leave. When I finally did leave, that very painful separation was not only a goodbye to my life as I had once known it, but a hello to a very new and different, and eventually much happier, life too.

This taught me two things. Firstly, there is *always a positive perspective* available to us, no matter how despairing or dark something may seem to be at the time. To access that, we need to be willing to do so. Sometimes we can hold on to misery like it is our best friend! We don't want to let it go. Perhaps it is familiar. In this exercise, you'll learn what my spirit taught me in that moment. You can be suffering deeply, and you can feel the happiness of your spirit urging you to grow through whatever is going on, and can see the good places this dark time is actually leading you towards – even if you can't quite see the light at the end of the tunnel as yet.

The second thing I learned through the process of leaving that relationship is that the best kind of mental health day comes from expanding your comfort zone. When I was in that relationship, and not quite ready to leave it, I spent a lot of time unconsciously holding myself back from growing. I knew at a deep level that when I was ready to grow, I would be ready to let go. But I didn't want to let go! The edge of my comfort zone was the edge of the relationship. It wasn't particularly a pleasant sort of comfort, given the dark emotional content of our relationship, but it was at least familiar.

Until I was ready to give myself real mental health (which is peace of mind) by doing what I knew I needed to do, I settled for a toxic version of true mental health, which was escapism. I watched loads of television. The fact that my television hasn't been hooked up to a cable in the years since I left is something of a sign about how out of character this was for me, and how much of a sign that I was trying to switch off. I was trying to find peace in my mind by dissociating from what was happening. Of course this only prolonged the inevitable, and it made me miserable because watching all that junk on television was a fairly misery-making mental diet anyway. When I was ready to grow my comfort zone, I could let go of my anguish (and my excessive television-watching addiction), embrace my destiny and gain peace of mind.

This exercise will help you get ready to take a step. You might already know what your next step is meant to be and be preparing yourself to take it, or be in the midst of taking it right now. Or you might have no idea how you could expand your comfort zone as yet. As you go through this exercise you'll be given the energy you need to be open to your next step, to expand your comfort zone and experience the best kind of mental health day, which is the peace of mind that comes when you know you are living your life in the best way possible. It's not about perfection. It's about progress. It's about being willing to outgrow what you have known – as scary as that can seem – and embrace what is trying to happen in your life with trust.

Even if you don't clearly understand what your next step is as you do this, that is just fine. It isn't about showing you what you are supposed to do right at this moment, although that may come to you as an understanding through doing the exercise. Consider that the icing on the cake, so to speak. What this exercise is meant to do is help you understand that it is safe and actually in many ways *enjoyable* to expand your comfort zone, and help you feel this as a positive rather than frightening experience. It puts your mind in the right place to be open to the next steps on your life journey, whenever they happen to reveal themselves to you, whether that be this day, or in a month or a year from now.

If you find you tend to live in your head – and as a writer who works at a desk for a good portion of the day, or is always dreaming up new ideas for books and the like, I understand how easy that is – then this exercise will also help you 'ground', and come into your body. Just doing that can be enough to give you more energy and help you feel safer and more at home in your life. You can use this exercise anytime you feel stuck in your head, or need to expand your comfort zone to take on a new challenge that life has decided you are ready to take.

Getting ready:

If you have a small handheld mirror and you wish to make this exercise a powerful one, then you can use that. However it isn't essential, and I have a version included in the instructions in which you don't require a mirror to do the exercise effectively if you prefer not to use one.

You'll need to find a place with some privacy, where you won't be interrupted and where you can feel safe to relax without worrying that someone is going to burst in and interrupt you. If that means locking yourself in the bathroom or the car for ten minutes or so, then go right ahead and do that. Turn off your phone or put it on silent and give yourself some precious minutes of 'me time'.

The exercise:

Start by saying: "I have the courage within to live my best life. Life wants me to find happiness and fulfilment. I trust myself and I trust life."

If you need to repeat this statement two or three (or more) times until you can feel relaxed whilst saying it, that is just fine. Take several minutes if needs be. There's no rush here and your exercise is not a long one. It's fine to take your time with each step.

In a moment, you are going to close your eyes and relax for several breaths. Stress, being in your head, or simply a fast-paced day, can lead you to unconsciously hold your breath or breathe shallowly.

Place a hand on your belly if needs be, and take some gentle, deep and slow breaths. Really let go on the exhalation. It feels good! Breathe in and out as though there is a gentle wave flowing, a wave of your breath.

Keep your eyes closed and do this relaxed breathing for at least more than three breaths, and for however long feels right for you.

When you are ready, open your eyes.

Then you will say the next affirmation. If you can, try to say this statement in a relaxed tone of voice. If you need to say it more than once before you start to feel it – even a little – that is just fine. If you don't feel like you really believe it, that is okay too! You are taking a step towards it and that is what matters here – taking the next step, not where you are or think you ought to be on your journey.

"Life is helping me grow into my happiness. My comfort zone gets a little bigger each day. I trust where life is leading me. I am happy to try new things and think in new ways. I embrace my progress and personal growth, step by step. Life loves me and helps me each day. I believe in myself and I believe in life. It is safe for me to live and grow according to life's plan for me. I am very grateful for my life."

Now it's time to pick up your handheld mirror, if you have one. If you don't have a mirror then you can skip this section. Just skim over the next few paragraphs and continue on from there.

If you have the mirror, allow yourself to gaze at your face reflected back at you. This special, unique face expresses *you*. If you can, have a little smile on your lips whilst you look at yourself. You might even be able to say, "I like you!" and "I love you. You are doing a great job! I believe in you!" If that seems too confronting, then just smile at yourself and say, "Hi!"

Really feel that you are seeing and acknowledging yourself. It can feel very strange to really look at yourself in a mirror rather than assessing yourself, which is what we typically use mirrors for. Use this chance to really imagine that you can see into your own eyes, deep into your eyes. Can you see yourself deep within your own eyes? What do you see there? The strength that has got you through so many events in your life? The beauty and promise that is within you? The love? Also perhaps, the pain of the past?

See it all and judge none of it. You are an amazing being and you have already grown so much. Just see that, deep in your eyes.

Gaze at your mirror for a little longer than what feels easy or comfortable. You don't have to make it confronting, but do allow yourself to go into a deeper place of seeing and recognising yourself than you have been before, even if it is just a little bit more.

Put down your mirror and when you are ready, you are going to relax a little more by taking two or three slow, deep breaths in and out.

Then you are going to 'hold your hands' together. Look at your hands. Notice their colour and shape. These hands allow you to do so many things. Can you acknowledge some of them? Cooking, hugging, grooming, loving, driving, gardening, shopping? Patting your pet? Wiping a tear from a child's face? Touching your friend's shoulder or your lover's body?

Feel the warmth or coolness of your hands. No judgement, just notice.

Then place them on your heart. Feel the connection of your hands with your heart. Then notice the warmth, the beating or the feeling of your heart beneath your hands. See if you can really feel your heart. Relax like this for several breaths.

To complete this exercise, say the following in a relaxed tone, repeating it if you feel you need that 'nudge' to accept what you are saying a little more.

"I am worthy. I am loved. My life is unfolding to a greater plan. I accept the steps I need to take and I trust myself. I grow naturally and I am brave. I take the steps I need to take at the right time and in the right way for me. Life loves me and is guiding me forward. I feel peace of mind and peace in my heart. Every day I am growing into all I can be."

Close your eyes and relax for as long as feels good. If you need something to imagine, sense or feel, so you stay relaxed, you can picture or pretend that there is a soft, steady glow of a candle in your heart or your mind, or both. It's almost like you can see it from behind your closed eyes – still, gentle and warm.

When you are ready, just open your eyes and you have completed this exercise.

EXERCISE 3: DREAM A BEAUTIFUL DREAM

Why you want to do this exercise:
Trusting life and where it is leading you doesn't mean you don't have a say in what happens in your life anymore! Life is your partner, your cheerleader, your teacher. It will help you manifest your destiny. It will respond to your wishes and dreams.

Taking practical steps to live the life you would like to live is essential, and it's so much more exciting to do this when you feel *inspired*. Taking action and working for something you have some feeling for, some passion for, some love or interest in, is a bit like making love with a person you adore and cannot get enough of, as opposed to someone you neither barely know nor are even particularly interested in! The former is much more invigorating and stimulating! Daring to go after what you love and what has meaning will inspire you with so much more energy and courage, and fulfilment, than working hard for that which you care about less.

To dream a beautiful dream, something you will be willing to become your own hero for, something that moves you from within, gives you the passion you'll need so when life responds with a challenge to help you get to where you want to go, you are willing and able to rise up to meet it. If your dreams don't really inspire you, why would you bother putting in any effort to overcome an obstacle? You wouldn't. We need love and passion to get us to move.

So in this exercise, we'll work with love, with what would feel amazing to you. Don't worry if you think your dream is silly or impossible or unusual and something that no-one else would understand. Those are the best sort of dreams! Those are the ones that really speak to you. Working for another person's dream – no matter how much respect or love is behind the notion – is not going to fulfil you. Your dreams may well help others reach their destiny, but your dream needs to come from your own heart. Whether your dream is to live a quiet and happy life; to be wildly and passionately in love with life, with your work, with a partner, with your own being, with the universe; whether your dream is to write or sing, to be a dancer or an artist; to be a great parent; to discover your unique purpose in life; whether to have a successful career or to get an education, or travel the world; or to build a foundation or charitable organisation, or a thriving business; to have a loving family; or become spiritually enlightened; or just find the time to exercise each day and feel healthy … whatever you dream, trust it. It is not too big, nor is it too small. If you feel love for your dream, then it is just right for you.

The way you'll be guided to dream your beautiful dream in this exercise is by learning to feel the essence of what you want rather than getting stuck on details. An example of that is to focus on how good it feels to be in love, for example, rather than picturing your love life having to involve a particular person you have in mind. Or you focus on how confident and satisfied you feel with your career being established rather than getting caught up in having to win a certain proposal or job offer for you to be a success. If your dream is about your children making great lives for themselves, you focus on how happy, proud and relaxed you feel about your child making their way in the world, rather than trying to cajole or force them onto a particular career path, for example. Or if your dream is to be a millionaire and retired at forty-four, then you focus on the feelings that idea has for you – perhaps a sense of a life well lived, but also plenty of time before you to live, travel, explore and be in the world with a sense of security and freedom.

How does that feel? Probably quite relaxing and exhilarating. So you focus on those feelings for this exercise, not on the details you think need to take place.

When you decide to give up the idea that things have to go a particular way, you don't have to feel depressed or defeated if life seems to deviate from the course you have set. You also give life many more opportunities to deliver situations that match the feelings you are generating. Remember the law of attraction? Like attracts like. You'll attract what you want more easily, and even more swiftly, when you focus on the feeling and allow life to respond, rather than getting intense and pushing for things to turn out the way you think they should, when and how you think they should, and how you think they should. You are not giving up on a dream, but you are giving in to life's wisdom about what the final 'version' may appear to be and how it can best unfold. Life may have a far better idea of how you can attain your dreams in the best way (in fact, it does).

You'll be guided in this exercise to generate the most positive, magnetic energy to invite what you yearn for into your life in the best possible way with the best possible timing. It's much easier than you think. Forcing a dream will just give you a headache! It's better to enjoy the process. It makes it not only more pleasurable, something that will give you a nice tingle for the rest of your day, but also more effective.

You can do this exercise when you want to call something wonderful into your life, and even just when you want to get yourself out of a bad mood and into a good mood.

Getting ready:
For this exercise, you'll need a place where you won't be interrupted. If you can lie down or be seated in a very relaxed position, all the better. If you can be somewhere in nature or have a beautiful piece of music playing, and perhaps a candle lit, that might help you

relax and feel you can really give yourself some 'me time'.

Those suggested 'extras' are not essential to do the exercise, but relaxation is; so if you have a pot on the stove or a telephone call due, then do what you need to do before you settle down to complete this exercise. It won't take you long – only around fifteen minutes or so – but you might find it harder to truly relax and get the most out of this exercise if you spend most of those minutes hoping you won't miss your phone call or that the pot on the stove won't bubble over!

Do you see what I am saying here? Set aside some time for yourself and this exercise will be more powerful and effective for you.

The exercise:

Start by saying this statement: "My dreams and desires are messages from my heart. I trust my heart. I trust life. I trust myself. My dreams and desires become clearer and more alive every day. My dreams feel really good! Those dreams and desires are gifts bringing happiness into my life and the lives of others too."

If you need to repeat this statement three or even four times, to really feel it, then please do so. You can say it in a relaxed tone. There is no need to be intense or 'strong' in how you express it. The more relaxed you are, and the more you enjoy feeling the truth of this statement, the more powerful it will be.

You are now going to imagine, feel or pretend that you are in a peaceful, dark, open space that feels very safe and comforting. It is a happy place to be.

See, sense, feel or pretend that the good-feeling dark space extends as far before you as the eye can see, as far behind you as the eye can see, as far to either side of you as the eye can see, and as far above and below you as the eye can see. You are safe and feel surrounded in a nice way, like a loving hug, and very relaxed in this space.

Imagine, feel or pretend that there is a faint echo of a strong and healthy heartbeat – slow, regular, soothing. You can feel, visualise, hear or pretend that it helps your own heartbeat follow suit, becoming stronger, slower and more regular. It helps you relax even more and feels very good.

You can close your eyes and just be in this open, dark, relaxing space, with this deep, strong heartbeat that feels good, for as long as you wish.

When you are ready, it is time to visualise, imagine, feel or pretend that there is a shimmering silver mesh that supports you gently but firmly in this same place. Visualise, imagine, feel or pretend that you can bounce up and down on this net. It's fun! Then rest and relax.

As you relax, the net you are resting on becomes more noticeable. It seems to have a cool electricity moving through it.

When you feel something, this net amplifies it and makes it bigger. Your feelings don't just remain with you, they reach far and wide, travelling along this net, like an energetic broadcast. They invisibly attract people, situations and opportunities, gifts and assistance that *match* the feeling you are sending out through this net. You don't need to see how or who or when. You just know it happens.

Sink into this net with a good, relaxed feeling. Take your time and imagine, visualise, sense, feel or pretend that you are feeling the best sort of good feeling and happiness possible.

If you need to also visualise, feel or pretend that you are in a particular situation for that to happen, without getting too caught up in details, that is fine. You might be relaxing on a tropical island, or snuggled up in front of a fire, feeling cosy and loved, or feeling the thrill and happiness of successfully attaining a goal.

If you find it hard to feel that, simply imagine there is a smile in your heart. Imagine you can smile at your heart, and your heart can smile at you. There is simple love and kindness there. You may like to place a hand on your heart if this makes it easier.

Relax for a few breaths, and when you feel good, imagine, visualise, feel or pretend that the good feeling being carried through the net, far and wide, is attracting all sorts of good things into your life. You don't need to see or focus on this in great detail. Just know, believe or pretend it is happening. All you need to do is relax and feel good.

If you feel a negative thought or bad mood coming over you, you can easily come back to simply smiling at your heart and allowing your heart to smile at you. When you are in a place that feels more loving, then continue again. You want to amplify the goodness, not the grumpiness!

If there is a particular dream you have, you might like to spend the last moments of your time imagining, feeling or pretending that your dream has already come true. If you don't have a particular dream in mind, then just imagine, feel or pretend that you are as happy in your life as you could possibly be.

Take your time and get used to feeling that way. Does it feel very different to how you usually feel? Can you get used to feeling that new way? Can you imagine even more happiness? Maybe you can imagine feeling so much happiness in your heart that it flows all around you and touches the hearts of other people too.

When you are ready, open your eyes and say: "I feel really good about my future. I live a good life. I feel happy for so much in my life. I am so happy that more good things are coming my way. I love to share that happiness with others through my smile."

If you need to say this – gently and in a relaxed way – more than once to really feel it, that's fine. Go right ahead.

You have completed your exercise.

Don't worry if you don't feel a strong reaction to this exercise. You will feel happier after completing it, but it may take you several attempts before you learn how to put yourself into a good mood. It can be tricky to learn to let go of feeling bad about something. You have to want to do it.

If you are worried that someone will get away with something unless you remain angry at them or suffer and are unhappy, forget it. The only person you are hurting is yourself. Be willing to feel good. You deserve it! That willingness is essential if you are going to be able to dream your beautiful dreams.

If you are surprised by how hard it can be to give up a bad mood or negative feeling, don't worry too much. If it was easy, there would be many more happy people in the world!

Give yourself a chance by doing this exercise regularly – perhaps every week – until you get the hang of it. It does get easier with practice and you don't have to force it.

You are learning here not to push or force, but how to let go. You can do it. It's just a new habit to get used to, and you will do so with a little patient and practice.

EXERCISE 4: CLEARING THE CLOUDS

Why you want to do this exercise:
Your mind can be your best friend or worst enemy. It can help you remain open to life and its many possibilities, with a positive viewpoint that gives you fuel to get to where you want to go. It can also convince you that nothing will come to any good, that it's all just going to end badly, and in doing so, rob you of the strength you need to refuse to give up until you get what you want.

Your mind is like the sky. The sun can be shining, but if the sky is so filled with clouds (like the fear, worry, concern or doubt in your mind) then you won't see the sun or feel its warmth nearly as much as you would if the sky was clearer.

Learning to let your thoughts come and go, like clouds passing across the sky, without getting caught up in them is an art. It's a type of meditation. It amazes me that most people think that meditation is so easy they should be able to do it straight away, and if they can't, then something is wrong with them. My first 'meditation' was me thinking the entire time that I didn't know what I was doing and wondering if everyone else in the group was having a far better time than I was – not exactly a calm and peaceful experience!

For most people, learning to let thoughts come and go, without them grabbing your attention and making you worried or afraid or distracted, is difficult at first. It does, like most things, become easier with practice. So if you get caught up in your thoughts, you do the same thing that every meditation student and every meditation master does – you notice them and, without judging yourself for it, simply let the thoughts go and come back to your task. Do this again and again, as often as needs be.

The more you do this, the more you'll start to feel the sky behind the passing clouds rather than focus on the clouds and worry what they might mean (rain, a coming storm, no beach that day, the end of the world), even though the clouds pass and nothing much happens after all!

This exercise helps your mind become more clear and peaceful. Then it will be so much easier to understand what you need to do, or not do, as the case may be.

It also helps you change your relationship to fear – seeing it as something that comes and goes rather than a force you have to allow to run your life. You will begin to see things for how they are, instead of believing in the distorted viewpoint that fear creates.

Believing in fear is like believing the sun doesn't exist anymore because the clouds have covered it up. It is true that it might not feel as warm with all that cloudiness, but it is still there, and once the clouds pass, you will feel it again. It hasn't gone anywhere. It's just been hidden for a short time. This exercise helps you understand this, and feel more peaceful and less afraid.

Getting ready:

If you can be outdoors during the day, or somewhere where you can see the sky, that would be a lovely way to do this exercise. But you can also complete it indoors without seeing the sky, if that is more practical for you.

What is most important is you have some solitude if possible, so you won't be disturbed or distracted. That will probably also mean you'll need to turn off your mobile phone.

The exercise:

Get comfortable by sitting, or lying down if you prefer. You are going to relax by focusing on your breath flowing in and out. You may softly close your eyes for several moments whilst you do this. If you can imagine your body relaxing too, that is good.

When you have started to relax, you can visualise, imagine or pretend that you can see the sky. Or you might prefer to open your eyes and look at the actual sky if you can see it.

Notice the colour of the sky. Is it clear? Are there clouds? Are there birds or planes moving through the sky? Or can you see the moon or stars at night? Just notice it and relax as you look at the sky with your eyes open, or see it from within you with your eyes closed.

If your mind wanders off into various thoughts, that is okay. When you 'catch yourself thinking', just come back to observing the sky in a relaxed way.

Imagine, visualise, feel or pretend now that your sky has become filled with clouds that pass across it. If you need to close your eyes to do this, do so now.

Your clouds might be wispy, white and fast-moving, or big, full and dark, rolling in thick waves. Let your sky become as cloudy as it needs to be.

You may have an emotional response to your sky filled with clouds. You might not feel comfortable with it. You might feel fear, or you might become watchful, as though a storm could be building up. Whatever your response to your cloudy sky, just let it be. It is okay to feel whatever you feel.

You now notice something very beautiful. A graceful white bird appears from behind the clouds with powerful wings outstretched. It is sure and strong, as if appearing in slow motion.

This white bird is fearless and it loves you. As its wings continue to move through the air, the clouds begin to dissipate. They are pushed aside, bit by bit, until your sky – no matter how dark it seems to be – becomes clear, bright and still.

You see the bird in the air, white with a golden halo created by the sunlight behind it now.

Visualise, imagine, feel or pretend to see the bird in your clear blue sky, with the golden sun glowing around it now. Your mind and your heart relax. Your breath slows and deepens.

You are loved.

You are seen.

You are safe.

You are at peace.

Everything is going to work out.

Be with this for as long as feels good for you. Relax.

When you are ready, open your eyes and you have completed this exercise.

You can repeat this daily for at least two weeks if you wish to learn how to soothe and clear your mind more easily. If you make a commitment to doing this exercise regularly, you'll notice it becomes easier for you to feel trusting, happy and optimistic. Your mind will start to relax and you won't feel so alone or afraid. You can come back to this exercise at any time you need to feel safe and secure, to let go of anxiety, fear or doubt.

EXERCISE 5: EVERYTHING YOU WANT IS ON THE OTHER SIDE OF FEAR, SO RISE!

Why you want to do this exercise:

It is said that fear has two possible consequences: to cause us to forget everything and run, or to face everything and rise. The choice is always ours. Fear is not something we have to deny or be ashamed to feel. It is not a 'bad' emotion. It is a sign we are being pushed to go beyond our comfort zones, into something new and exciting. When we remember this, instead of pulling away from life when we feel fear, we can actually *feel good about feeling fear* because we realise we are growing. Our fear is letting us know there is a big step before us now, to leave the past behind and open up to new life. So when feeling afraid, rather than pulling back and hiding ourselves away, we can take a big breath (and remember to exhale!) and step up to face whatever challenge is before us.

With this excellent attitude, you can become curious about your fear and investigate what is on the other side of it. This exercise will guide you through a simple process to do just that.

There are real threats to our wellbeing from time to time – a dangerous driver being one example – but does that mean every time we feel afraid it is because there is a genuine threat to our safety? Absolutely not! Real threats are the things that just happen instantly and your fear is more of an instinct than emotion. It gets you to move out of the way of a swerving car on the road, for example, or urges you not to park in a particular alleyway if it just doesn't feel right.

In the past, our ancestors had the same instincts too, though it was more likely to be about running from a hungry lion rather than avoiding a speeding car swerving onto the pavement. Despite what most journalists, advertisers and politicians would have you think (undoubtedly for their own ends to secure columns, sales and votes), genuine threats to our safety are far less common than we've been conditioned to believe.

So why do so many people feel so afraid? Some people believe that fear is pushed into the masses like a drug, to keep most people enslaved in ways of living that ultimately supports a few at the expense of many. Many conspiracy theories exist with varying degrees of credibility. Others believe we learn fear when we are children as part of our social conditioning. What matters to me however, is not why people are afraid, but the fact that if they are willing to let go of their fear, they live better lives, are happier and create a better world for the rest of us too. So whilst I could write a book on how fear is instilled in us – including through what we learn as children, what we get fed through media and advertising, and how some exploit the fear in others for their own selfish ends – what matters most to me is that you are freed from it. This exercise will help you free yourself from your fear.

The best way to free yourself from fear is to learn to trust a little more. If you don't trust in life and the natural growth that happens during your life, you will be afraid of change itself. Considering that change is how more happiness and fulfilment is brought to you, that's a bit of a problem! If you don't also trust in your capacity to adapt and evolve through change, you will feel more afraid of life than if you learned to trust yourself. You have already got through so much in your life. You need to give yourself some credit for what you've survived already. So what if you haven't been perfect and if you've made mistakes? It's the same for everyone. You learn from the mistakes as best as you can, and you become smarter and stronger because of it, which is very clever of you!

If you don't take this trusting (and forgiving) attitude towards yourself, you'll let fear get the better of you. I see this happen to people more often than I would like. They try to drown out the voice of their fear not by facing it head on and saying, "Who cares. I am going to live my best life and take risks anyway!" but by becoming obsessed with gadgets, games, addictions, and holding on to routines not because they are healthful or helpful, but because they are *known* (even though sometimes the devil you know is actually not better than the devil you don't!).

The tragedy with this sort of fear is you are not in any real danger of anything other than becoming uncomfortable for a while as you move towards greater fulfilment, wellbeing and happiness. If we see change as a threat to our sense of self, identity and world view, we really are biting the hand that feeds us because change is the hand of life reaching out to invite us on an adventure. If we are stuck in fear, we won't see that. We'll see the grim reaper at our front door instead. You can imagine in such cases, you may well rather forget everything and run.

Change can be scary to the part of us that wants to feel in control or always appear to be perfect (which is rather hard to do when you are trying something new, haven't mastered it yet, and probably feel a bit clumsy or unskilled at it for a while). Yet going through change brings you to a different life. Whatever is not working can be left behind as you go through change. Whatever you want that you don't yet have can be found as you go through change. Change is not the enemy. Change is your best friend.

This exercise will help you stop slamming the door when change comes a-knocking. Instead, you'll be able to open up that door to run outside to greet that dear friend, and be ready for some fun and new beginnings in life.

To support you in feeling more trust in yourself and life, to not be so afraid of change, this exercise will help you release unresolved trauma from your body and mind. Pretty much everyone carries some degree of unresolved trauma from the past. Most of the time we don't realise our opinions are little more than expressions of past wounds we haven't got over yet. Instead of realising that if we let go of unresolved pain, we can begin to experience far more constructive, helpful, positive opinions about ourselves and the world, or else we think that our opinions, based on past pain, are real. We might believe that life is hard, that certain people are dishonest and cannot be trusted, that you only succeed if you are lucky, or that some people will always lose in life no matter how hard they try. These things are not true, but if you don't release the pain that supports that belief, you'll act as if it is true, reinforcing the belief through how you interpret the world (for example, your glass will always seem half empty), and you'll strengthen your belief in your own negativity and view the world through fear-tinted glasses.

Life *will* feel like it becomes harder for you, but it is by your own creation. And it doesn't have to be that way. That is why we want to release unresolved trauma. It helps you let go of certain beliefs based on the wounding (because you never can forgive that person who betrayed you and so you tar every person who reminds you of them with the same brush, for example). When you let go of the wounding, and the beliefs created because of it, you are more free to accept the hand of life and live in a way that feels better, brings you happiness, and the good things you deserve that you can experience when you are more open to life and what it has to offer.

You might think you don't have any unresolved trauma. The more you feel that is the case, the more likely it is that you *do*, and the more you will benefit from the clearing in this exercise.

The easiest way to identify unresolved trauma is to look for the symptoms of it. These include emotions that erupt for no apparent reason, or are out of proportion to what is actually happening in the moment. So if a person cuts you off on the road whilst driving and you feel so much rage pass through you that you want to kill him, then you can be sure that something deeper is unresolved in you. It is quite likely that the person driving either didn't see you, or is just an unskilful or selfish driver, and being murdered for their incapacity on the road is a tad extreme. Don't judge your reaction in such a case, but do notice that if it is unreasonable in terms of intensity considering what is happening, then it is coming from another place, and is about another story, at a deeper level within you. The feeling might have been triggered by what happened on the road, but it's not really about that. It's about an unresolved issue you are probably not aware of at a conscious level.

Another sign of unresolved trauma is recurring illness or pain in the body, especially when you cannot seem to find a medical reason for it. You aren't imagining those symptoms. They are your body speaking to you, trying to release blockages from the past that are clogging up your system and getting in the way of a free flow of energy (sort of like a hose bulging when there is a blockage in it and the water can't run freely through the hose). If you ignore symptoms because a doctor can't see a reason for them (yet), then you'll ignore the opportunity to heal the trauma underneath them before they become so pronounced they eventually do become disease your doctor can see. It is quicker, easier and less expensive to treat symptoms as early as possible. You don't have to wait for a fully-fledged disease before you acknowledge an issue to be dealt with. Why not just do the following exercise on a regular basis, and consult a therapist or other type of healer (if your regular health care practitioner cannot see an issue and cannot help you) to work with issues that seem to need more support to release them if needs be?

Other symptoms of unresolved trauma include depression, a sense of not feeling really alive or well and present in your day-to-day life, a sense of anxiety you cannot quite pin down to anything in particular, or even a fully-fledged phobia, no matter how 'understandable' or common or how rare and 'odd' that phobia might be.

Another sign of unresolved past trauma is a sense that you keep ending up in the same relationship patterns or life situations, again and again, just with 'different players'. Leaving one employer to find yourself in a new job with an employer who has the same issues as the old one, or likewise, from one relationship into another and finding the same situation repeating itself, are examples. These things are nothing at all to feel ashamed of – the bulk of the human population is in a state of unresolved emotional trauma to some degree and not completely here and now in the present moment. That's okay because it can be changed.

This exercise will help you change that within you, so you can live in the now – and take advantage of all that life has on offer. Otherwise it's a bit like sitting down at a feast – you don't eat anything because you are so busy remembering what you had for breakfast two days ago, you don't even smell the delicious fragrance of the meal placed in front of you. That's a waste of a wonderful opportunity for nourishment and delight.

Getting ready:
This is quite a powerful exercise with three parts, so it's important you are not going to be dragged out of it before you get a chance to finish. Putting twenty minutes aside for this exercise, plus, if possible, an additional ten minutes to rest and replenish afterwards is ideal. It's sort of like giving yourself time to digest a good meal by not getting up and rushing around immediately after eating it.

You'll need to minimise possible distractions. That means turning off your phone and email, hanging a sign on the door if needs be. Or if you live in a busy and active house, where getting some time to yourself is something of a miraculous occurrence, then you'll need to either lock yourself in the bathroom or put yourself in your car and go for a drive to a quiet location where you can simply be in your own space and complete the exercise without interruption.

If you are in the car (or the bathroom!), getting comfortable may not be quite as easy as if you were able to curl up in your favourite lounge chair, but please take a moment to get as comfortable as you can in whatever environment you are in.

Make sure you have adequate covering, as it is not unusual to cool down when you begin to relax and do inner work such as what you will be guided to do through this simple exercise. You might also heat up, of course, that is possible, but if you have layers you can easily add or remove during your exercise, your physical comfort won't become a distraction for your focus. Changes in body temperature can indicate emotional release from the body. This is fine. You can expect that your body temperature will adjust itself back to 'normal' at the end of the exercise.

The exercise:

<u>Part 1</u> – **Reclaiming the Lost Self: Shining the Torch Beneath the Trapdoor**

Start by saying aloud: "Within me is great courage and strength. I have survived and I am now ready to thrive. Fear shows me where I need to step up. I am ready to see clearly, to let go of the past, and to live my life with more happiness and peace than ever before."

If you need to repeat this statement more than once to really start to *feel* the truth of it, that is fine. Take your time and if you can, say it with a gentle and relaxed tone.

Relax and close your eyes. Visualise, imagine, feel or pretend that you can sense a warm and loving feeling in your heart. That feeling is like a glowing sun inside of you. It feels good, with just the right amount of warmth and light.

If at any time during this exercise you feel concerned or in need of comfort, you can remember this warmth and light of the sun within you, shining brightly, happily, easily.

Turn your back to that sun within. You sense its warmth and light at your back and that feels good, comforting, like a friend who 'has your back'.

With the sun behind you, you can now visualise, imagine, feel or pretend that you can see some darkness before you. You are safe to see this darkness. You only have to turn and look at the sun if needs be, and you'll be surrounded by light.

Visualise, imagine, feel or pretend that the sunshine behind your back and in you is gently shining through you, all the way down your arms and into your hands. You can hold up a hand to send sunshine into that darkness if you wish. If you need more light to see into the darkness, send more light. You have a ready-made 'torch' in your hands and you are perfectly safe and in control.

Relax and take several slow, deep breaths.

Visualise, see, feel or pretend that you are now moving into the darkness, using the 'torch' of your hands if you need more light.

You hear or sense a distant knocking sound.

Approach the sound.

You see a trapdoor. The knocking sound is coming from beneath the trapdoor. You feel an inner push to open it and see what lies beneath. What do you feel?

When you are ready, open the door and shine the light in.

What you see is *you*. What part of you has been locked away in there? Is it your strength? Your anger? Your gentleness? The child within? The part of you that dreamed of a different life? This part of you may seem tired or broken, angry or afraid. You may or may not clearly see this part of you, and that is okay.

Explain in your mind, or even use words aloud if you wish, that you have come to take this part of you home now. That part of you never needs be lost and alone again. You are not afraid of this part of you and it doesn't have to be afraid of you – or anything – anymore. Tell this part of you that everything is going to be okay now.

Using the light in your hands if you need to, reach out to take the hand of this lost part of you. Guide that part of you back with you now, out of the darkness forever, and into the light of the warm sun.

Part 2 – Releasing Unresolved Trauma: Cellular Shower and Shaking Like a Wet Dog

You and this new-found part of yourself stand in the light of the sun now.

A gentle shower of rain begins to fall, yet the sun is still shining. It is a sunshower! The rain is light and feels soft on your skin. You can see sunlight and rainbows through the rain as it falls, soft and golden over you and this new-found part of you.

This is a special type of rain. It cleanses you from the outside and on the inside. Notice that the rain washes away whatever you no longer need or want. It clears the past gently and thoroughly from you and this new-found part of you.

Visualise, imagine, feel or pretend that there is a loving smile on your face and in your heart. The other part of you can feel that too.

When you are both ready, that lost part of you will move into your heart, becoming one with you again. This feels good and is relaxing. It is like coming home.

Now it is time to renew yourself as the cleansing rain has ended.

Visualise, imagine, feel or pretend that every cell in your body has a tiny wet dog living in it. Everyone of those tiny wet dogs are now shaking off the excess water, twisting wildly and shaking all the water off their fur! It's fun!

Each little dog in each tiny cell starts at the top of his head, with his ears and jaw flopping about, and twists and shakes all the way down to his bottom. Even his tail shakes off water! His jaw is loose and his joints are relaxed, and all that water flies off him, leaving him happy, clean and dry. Every cell in your entire body is clear and you feel great.

Relax for a few moments now and enjoy this tingly feeling.

Part 3 – Face Everything and Rise: Using Fear to Push Up Higher

You feel good, shining, clear.

Before you is a mountain. It might be a small mountain, more like a hill, or a huge peak. What you want most and best of all is at the top of that mountain. You feel confident and patient as you look at the mountain, and you begin to climb it, one step at a time.

You notice some ledges jutting out, some tree branches here and there perhaps, even some rocks. When you see something in your way, you turn it to your advantage, using it as something to grab hold of to hoist yourself up higher. You use it as a step to push up.

You are climbing that mountain and you know you are going to make it.

Feel the sense of inner confidence and peace this knowledge brings. No matter how long it takes, or how many things get in your way, you are going to make it. You feel good. You are okay to keep going. You are going to get there.

Choose to visualise, imagine, feel or pretend that you are at the top of the mountain now. Allow yourself to feel good, to relax, to feel that something important has been accomplished. You are proud of yourself. You have done well. It feels good.

When you are ready, simply open your eyes and you have completed your exercise. If you wish to relax and 'digest' the experience, simply rest for ten or so minutes before going about your daily activities.

You can repeat this exercise every two or three days (or even daily) for two weeks if you are going through a particularly difficult time where your fear seems very real and very hard to overcome.

You don't need to necessarily push hard to have a breakthrough. Breakthroughs often happen when we finally let go of what we have been holding back within us – such as faith or courage. What this exercise will help you do is prepare you to let go of fear, release the past, and realise you have everything you need within you now to grab on to any challenge and climb to the top of your mountain.

EXERCISE 6: THE EYE OF THE STORM

Why you want to do this exercise:
When everything seems to be going crazy, and even when you think you might be going crazy, it can feel like you've been hit by a tornado and your life is thrown into chaos, crisis and confusion. Then it's time to reconnect with the still centre that always exists within you, no matter how wild the storm may seem. Getting into the calm eye of the storm will help you find peace even whilst things are in upheaval around you, which is one of the best ways to have enough energy to get through a challenge without being completely ravaged and drained by it.

Getting ready:
This exercise can be quick – just a couple of minutes, or twenty minutes or more if you incorporate a nap into the process.

Finding a quiet spot where you have privacy is helpful, as is turning off your mobile phone; although if you find it easier to relax by setting a timer for yourself, do that, at twenty minutes, or longer, if possible.

The exercise:
You are going get comfortable by sitting or lying down somewhere and making sure you have enough covers to keep warm. Allow yourself to settle.

You are now going to relax by closing your eyes and focusing on your breath for several moments.

When you are ready, imagine, visualise, feel or pretend that you can see a wild swirling tornado in the distance. You may hear or feel or sense the power and energy of that whirling tunnel of wind.

As the tornado whirls closer, you are pulled into it, through the wildness where everything seems completely crazy for a moment. Then suddenly, you drop right into the centre, which is quiet, even with the wildness all around you. You can witness the frenzy of the tornado, but you are untouched in the centre.

The stronger the storm becomes, the bigger that calm spot in the centre becomes. And the more that peace surrounds you. You feel very relaxed in the centre.

As your relaxation grows, the wild movement of the tornado begins to dissipate, until it quietens down altogether and there is only your feeling of relaxation all around you.

Breathe deeply and slowly. You have completed your exercise. You may wish to have a rest before returning to your day.

CHAPTER 8

Workbook Exercises for Crisis

. . . .

PRACTICAL EXERCISES TO FIND YOUR WAY THROUGH CRISIS INTO CHOICE

EXERCISE 1: COOL, CALM AND COLLECTED

Why you want to do this exercise:

One definition of being 'good in a crisis' is the ability to keep a clear head, especially when others cannot. This might seem like the sort of thing only relevant during the most dramatic situations in life, but I see the need for keeping a cool head every day. Humanity is in one big collective spiritual crisis at the moment, with fear arising for most people on a daily basis. Anxiety, uncertainty, doubt and fear are felt so often, and by so many, that it can be very difficult to not feel like you are drowning in the collective ocean of despair, along with so many others.

Being able to spot and become somewhat immune to the manipulative and disingenuous ploys of media and advertising is essential if you are to have genuine self-confidence and inner peace, to feel energised and not have to struggle through each and every day of your life. If you believe what you read in newspapers (if you read newspapers – personally I used them to line the kitty litter tray for my cat and packing breakables when moving house), you have to be careful. Think for yourself about whether you want to believe in the version of the truth being fed to you. Sometimes you will, but a lot of the time, you won't. If it makes you afraid, then it most definitely needs to be questioned. If you consume what is in most magazines or on most television shows without some sense of awareness about how these things make you feel, you'll struggle because you'll be taking in fear-based reality without even realising it. Like drinking those sugary-sweet alcoholic drinks, you'll wake up with a nasty hangover without even realising you were getting drunk.

Whatever you consume – whether it be food for the body, or food for the mind – will either raise you up or drag you down. If something fills you with fear, or doubt, or insecurity or pain, then it's not a great 'food' for you to take in. It will just make it more challenging for you to find peace of mind. Peace of mind doesn't mean you have to be all serious and not have any fun. Peace of mind is joyful. It is honest. It feels good. It is playful. It can also spot disingenuousness a mile away and sidestep it because the peaceful mind isn't particularly interested in being afraid. There's no point to it because anything fear pushes you to do can be accomplished with more happiness and effectiveness from a place of inner peace.

Sometimes I look at people who are yet to experience peace of mind, yet to realise there is a beautiful plan for their fulfilment unfolding in their lives every day, without exception, and that they are truly loved. They don't have to worry and yet they don't know that yet. I don't know how they make it through their day – let alone years and years of that inner sense of confusion and struggle, in so much inner pain, but pretending nothing is wrong and trying to just solider on regardless.

Then I remember the times when I was exactly the same. All I saw before me was struggle and I didn't know what the hell was going on in my life. And I remembered how I dealt with it at the time. I just assumed that was the way life was meant to be and it had to be that way. When we are in pain, we just keep going because that is all we know and we are strong. But there will be a moment when we choose to use our strength in a different way, and we ask an important, and freeing question. We choose to say, "But what if there is another way?"

To stop buying into what the world tells you, and instead to carefully ask the right sort of questions, is enough to take you from fear and stress into cool-headed cleverness. When you ask simple questions that have simple answers (such as: Is this good for me? No!), you begin to build up your common sense, your cool, calm and collected headspace where you are less immune to being whipped up into a fear frenzy by whatever latest tragedy the news has jumped on that day, or the otherwise contagious terror of those around you who haven't the presence of mind to wonder if perhaps there could be another response than feeling afraid. You can become a presence in your own life – and in the lives of others – that helps stem the tide of fearful reactiveness, and of despair. Your thoughtfulness and choice to step back and just say no to feeling afraid, to decide to look life square in the eye and say, "Let's do this together!" helps more than just yourself. You can become a calming presence that cools overwrought imaginations hell-bent on expecting the worst.

When I was a young woman in law school, my mother used to tell me I had plenty of common sense and that this was actually not so common at all. After a few years in law school, with a bunch of highly intelligent people, some of whom had no clue about the most basic matters of life, I came to agree with her. However, if you are smart enough to believe there is another way to respond to life than simply panic, stress or trying to play the game by the rules someone else has created, then you too will have plenty of common sense. It is an asset in this day and age when the sheer volume of information pouring into us daily can lead to overwhelm and a breakdown of the basic discerning function of the mind.

We need to remember to never assume what we see or read is true. Photographs are retouched, sometimes to create something that is completely fake. Quotations are not necessarily accurately researched. I found a cute little joke online recently: "The problem with most quotes on the internet is that it's hard to tell if they are genuine or not." This was reportedly said by Abraham Lincoln. It made me laugh, but it's also a reminder not to take things at face value.

To go from crisis mode to a cool head, the best questions to ask are simple. Is this true? Is this helpful? Do I need to hold on to this information? If you answer no to any of these questions, then it's best to drop it. There will be a more useful truth for you, and whatever you've been told so far, is not actually it at all.

This exercise can be used at any time you are in a crisis, or if those around you seem to be and you are wondering if you need to join them. It is a list of simple questions for you to ask and reflect upon. If you don't know how to answer one of the questions, just continue through the list, and then take a break. Don't try to force an answer to come. You'll find as you get used to cutting through all the fuss that tends to come with a crisis, you'll get very quick and skilful at answering these questions. Some answers will come to you immediately, clear as day. Others will pop into your mind some time later. Sometimes the answer will be that you stop worrying, even if you aren't sure why. You just realise you don't have to stress about what is happening, that if you need to do something, you'll feel it, and if not, then life is doing its part to sort things out.

Once you have your answers, then it's time to take the next step, which is to act on the truths you have uncovered. That means trusting in your answers and not having to understand how any action you take is going to work out. Just take the steps to act on what you have learned with trust that life will respond and assist you as you take those steps.

That's how you go from crisis to choice, from imagining the worst, to being cool, calm and collected, and therefore efficient and useful in the crisis at hand (which after this exercise, may not even seem to be such a crisis anymore).

Getting ready:

You'll need a pen and paper, or perhaps a journal if you keep one. If you prefer to take notes on an electronic device, like the notes feature on your mobile phone, that's fine.

This is a reflective exercise. That means you'll need to carefully read through the question and then listen for your inner answer. You won't have a right or wrong answer, you will have an approach that is going to be more effective and an approach that won't work as well. The approach that won't work as well is trying to force an answer you think is best. The more effective approach will be to treat this exercise a bit like you are going fishing. You cast the line with the question and you allow for the response to emerge out of you. That is a bit harder to do – unless you are familiar and skilled in this technique – if there are distractions around you. So if you can find a quiet, or semi-quiet space, where you are less likely to be interrupted (turning the mobile phone and email off for a moment can help), then that's great.

There is also a tip for this exercise – don't think too much! You want your answers to rise up spontaneously and naturally. If you get into analysis, starting to over think about things, you may make it all more complicated than it really is.

When I was learning how to be a barrister (before taking a career detour into the job of spiritual teacher) I had to learn how to argue both sides of a case. This would help me counter the arguments the opposing side would present and disarm their case. To my surprise, this was very easy to do. Arguing for one interpretation of the facts, only to then turn around and argue that those same facts meant something else entirely was very easy. It was so easy I found it quite disturbing. It seemed that rock-solid logical argument wasn't so rock-solid after all. I realised that if my mind could so readily concoct a story that said one thing one moment, and then the complete opposite the next, and found them both believable, then it wasn't going to be the best source of guidance for me. It was better to learn to listen to my heart, and let that guide my mind, rather than trying to logically argue my way to the truth of a matter.

The heart can't lie. It feels something or it doesn't. If you ask someone if they are in love, and they don't know, then they are listening to their minds, not their hearts. The heart says yes or no, that's it. The initial responses, the ones that just come out of you without thinking too much, that 'pop' out of you quickly and without your mind trying to talk yourself into thinking something else, are most likely going to be the answers of your heart. Your mind might be surprised at some of your answers. That's fine. It can be a good sign you are letting your heart, rather than your head, lead. When your heart leads, your head calms down and can do its job – acting on what your heart tells you – rather than try to work out something it is not equipped to work out (which is what you feel).

This exercise has two sections: firstly, to diffuse overwhelm by bringing you from your head into your heart, which will make it easier to hear your inner answers; and secondly, to offer calming questions that can help you let go of the drama and tune in to the quiet and wise voice of your heart to help you move through any crisis, one step at a time.

The exercise:
Have your pen and paper, or other note-taking tools, ready. Place them to one side, within easy reach.

Say this aloud: "I give myself permission to speak my truth. I will not judge, fear or censor myself. I allow myself to speak from my heart and I trust in my own inner guidance."

Relax and close your eyes as you focus on your breath, for at least five long, slow breaths in and out.

When you are ready, visualise, feel or pretend that you are moving from your head into your heart. You may like to visualise, feel, imagine or pretend that you are a softly-floating feather, or a smooth shiny stone, sinking from the head to the heart, slowly and surely, until you feel like you are resting in your heart.

This might be easy or very challenging for you. Take your time. Relax. There is no need to force this. If you feel you cannot do it, then pretend that you are in your heart by placing your hands over your heart and just breathing slowly in and out.

Now you are going to say: "The inner truth of my heart now helps me with … " Then describe your problem, crisis or question aloud, as simply and truthfully as you can.

Pick up your note-taking materials. You may wish to write the number of the question (rather than the whole question) and simply write your answer next to it. Your answer may be a simple yes or no. You may get an answer with a few more words or details than others. You may want to write your answers down, or say them aloud and then write them.

Gently focus your attention on your issue or crisis. Then ask and answer these questions aloud if possible, jotting down the number of the question and your reply. Don't stop to think or reflect on the answers yet, just go through each question until you have answered as many as you can in this sitting. That may be all of them. You can read the answers back to yourself at the end of the exercise. The point now is to flow without thinking too much.

1. Will this situation kill me?
2. Is there something for me to do in this situation?
3. If so, what?
4. When do I need to do this?
5. Do I need help from another person with this situation?
6. Do I need to ask for help or will that person come to me?
7. Is there something positive for me to learn from all this?
8. If so, what?
9. What quality or characteristic do I have within me that will help me succeed here?
10. Is everything going to work out somehow?

When you have finished answering the questions that you can, take your time to go back and reflect. If you still have questions yet to answer, step back from the exercise for anywhere from one to three days and then come back and repeat it, answering as many questions as possible.

You can repeat this exercise for one issue as often as you feel you need it, but do take a sufficient break in between. You want to let the answers of your heart filter up to your mind. Inside of you, is the wisdom to know what to do. But remember, accessing wisdom is like fishing with a line, not spearfishing! You have to give the answers time to find their way to you. You can't hunt them down by force.

If an answer is coming from your heart it will be truthful. It might not always be what you want to hear, but it won't make you afraid, it will help you feel confident and calm. If an answer makes you feel afraid then it has come from a fearful place in your own mind, not your heart. That is not something to feel bad about, but it is something to be aware of so you don't create fear through this exercise. If that is happening, you are in your mind, not your heart. The heart won't lie to you. If something isn't working, it will tell you. But it won't be afraid because it understands that when life provides a problem, it is because in finding the solution, we gain something worthwhile. The heart knows that this is how life works. So it is not afraid.

Learning to spot when your mind has stepped in – with complicated answers, fear-inducing answers, or panic or negativity – is part of the skill set you'll develop in doing this exercise. When you have at least one answer that comes from a loving and truthful place within you, make a note of it and pin it where you can see it regularly. This is your reminder that will help keep you on track to finding a solution, rather than getting stuck in the pain of the problem at hand.

If there are several things you need to do to put your answers into action, write a list. Make a simple plan of action you can check off as you complete your tasks. Keep the steps simple. Set a date that seems realistic for each of the items on your list. Keep your word to yourself by doing your best to finalise these items by the dates planned, but adjust them if needs be. If you need to write them in a day planner or diary, or as a reminder on your phone, fridge or mirror, do that.

As you check off the things on your list, you have completed your healing exercise. Although don't be surprised if, as you complete something, the next step shows itself and you have something else that needs to be done and added to your list. This is how you follow the breadcrumbs that life sprinkles on your life path, to make sure you keep going in the right direction to reach your best destination.

EXERCISE 2: IN THE DRIVER'S SEAT – WHAT IS DRIVING YOU?

Why you want to do this exercise:
There are fundamentally two forces in this world that can motivate us – love or fear. Even if you believe it doesn't matter how you get to where you want to be, so long as you get there eventually, the quality of the journey is actually just as important as the destination. There are certain things being motivated by fear cannot accomplish, that can only be accomplished when we are motivated by love. These are the things that draw more deeply on our courage and inner strength, that need a more creative and optimistic mindset to solve. These are the challenges in life that if faced with an open heart, will change us and our lives – sometimes most dramatically – for the better.

As we become more willing to embrace the challenges in life, we come to realise they actually do hold gifts for us. The more we embrace the challenge, the more we are open and receptive to the gift 'hiding' within it.

What makes it easier to embrace a challenge and benefit from it, rather than flee from it in fear and miss out on the gift it is trying to bring to you, is the state of your own mind. If you have fear in the driver's seat, you aren't going to enjoy your journey much. If you have love in the driver's seat, you will. It's pretty simple. The truths in life typically are simple. That of course, doesn't mean they are always easy to apply!

So this exercise will help you recognise the signs when fear is driving you, and how to shift gears so that love is in charge instead. When that happens, your life unfolds more easily because you are more open to what is happening. Sometimes what you have held on to from a place of fear becomes far easier to release and move past when you are coming from a place of love.

Love won't make you a martyr to everyone around you, nor a doormat. Love is gentle and kind, but it isn't a pushover! It's the most powerful force there is, and when you allow yourself to really feel it – not just for another person, which is what we typically think love is, but simply within your own heart – you'll experience a fearlessness you have never been able to experience before. That means things that once would have trapped you in indecision, self-doubt or fear, like guilt and shame, for example, won't have a hold on you anymore. Love is the liberating force without compare. If you think of love as a soft and fluffy pink cloud that can't be taken seriously, then you don't know what it really is yet. This exercise will help you begin to find out.

Getting ready:

Find a place where you can relax quietly and not be disturbed. If you need to have quiet music playing to help you relax, that is fine. If you need to be in your car or locked in a bathroom to get ten minutes private time, then that is fine too. One must be practical! You can do this exercise in the bath so long as you aren't so tired you are likely to fall asleep when you start to do the relaxation. If you fall asleep in a safer environment, such as on the sofa, that is fine of course. Just complete the exercise when you wake up. Sometimes you really do just need a rest, and you can come back to this exercise when you are ready. Just make sure you do come back to it.

The exercise:

Lie back or sit comfortably and relax, focusing on the breath flowing in and out. Take your time and allow your breathing to settle deeper in your body, so that you are not only breathing in through your upper chest and lungs, but deep down into your belly. If it helps, you can place a hand on your lower abdomen to notice when it rises and falls slightly as you breathe in and out.

Do this for at least five breaths, or however long feels right for you.

Now you are going to visualise, imagine, feel or pretend that you are in a car. This is a nice car that you like to be in. You might notice the colour, smell, feeling or details of the car, or it might just feel good to be in.

You are on a curving road, in this car that you like being in.

You see in the distance a beautiful place you would very much like to visit. You'd love to go to that place! It will be so good when you are there. You are so happy you are going there. You feel excited and also peaceful.

You push the button that says 'drive' and your car begins to head towards that beautiful place.

There are two other buttons on your car. One says 'fear mode' and one says 'love mode'.

You press the 'fear mode' button. The car slows down. It only drives in circles. No matter how much you see that lovely view and want to get to it, in this mode, you can't get anywhere new, only where you have already been. The circles you drive in get smaller and smaller until you aren't moving at all.

What is this like for you?

When you are ready, press the 'love mode' button instead.

Your car springs to life, heading instantly towards that beautiful place in the distance. Your car drives on through new and interesting places, and that beautiful place you want to visit is getting closer and closer with every passing moment.

What is this like for you?

Relax and enjoy the journey for as long as feels good.

When you are ready, open your eyes. You have completed your exercise.

Whenever you find yourself stressed out or afraid, take a moment to repeat this exercise and relax. It all happens much more easily that way.

EXERCISE 3: SWIM SAFELY IN YOUR OCEAN OF EMOTION

Why you want to do this exercise:

If you kept eating meal after meal, without giving yourself a chance to digest it properly and eliminate it, your system would slow down and you'd feel sluggish and after a while, very unwell. You need the digestion process to transform the meal into useable energy, so the food you ingest can become fuel. Your body knows how to do all this. It takes in the food you eat, responding instinctively by releasing the appropriate enzymes and triggering the digestive process.

There is a saying that 'a healthy digestive system can digest a rock'. Whilst I don't exactly suggest testing this assertion for yourself, the idea of it is helpful. When your digestive system is healthy, you can process even less than pure and organic foods, though obviously the healthier the food, the less strain on the digestive system. But it's good to know that if needs be, the body knows how to deal with an occasional naughty treat or slightly off meal.

Your body not only processes physical food, but emotional energy too. Your life experiences are like the food you take in. Your emotions are naturally-occurring instinctive responses to what is happening in your life. Some life experiences are 'lighter' than others, and easier to digest – like a quick snack we probably don't even require much rest to digest and just 'eat on the run' without thinking about. Some life experiences are more like a rich, heavy meal with many flavours and components and will require much more time and energy to digest.

It is usually so in such cases where the emotional digestion gets a bit sluggish. Unless you are naturally emotionally intelligent, grew up in an emotionally healthy and functional environment, or have done some work on yourself through personal development or therapy, then dealing with your emotions might be a challenge. They can be a challenge even if you have the benefit of those three head starts in life!

If you are having a 'heavy meal' of an experience in life, it's very likely a complex emotional response will be triggered, just like a greater variety of enzymes would be needed to digest a rich meal compared to a simple snack. This is where we can get stuck. If you feel a mixture of fear and excitement at the prospect of a big change in your life, a mixture of sadness of letting go and happiness of something new, grief and joy, loss and gratitude, hope and doubt, confusion and trust … well, unless you are well-versed in the subtleties of your own emotional life and, perhaps even then, you may not really know if you are coming or going, or how to 'digest' what is happening to you. The result can be feeling so emotionally overwhelmed that you just shut down completely, unable to process the experience and get the benefit of it by turning it into food for your growth.

If this happens enough, you would sadly become one of those people that live their life in a reactive state, refusing to grow and evolve and becoming closed off from life and missing out on so much that life is trying to give to them.

The pain of facing up to, feeling and releasing old emotions is far less than the joy and freedom that comes to you when you do. The pain of avoiding facing up to your emotions is far greater than dealing with them and getting on with your life. This is especially the case over time as unprocessed emotions can accumulate, creating more for you to deal with later on in life. It can become like carrying an increasingly heavy burden inside of you.

Eventually it can even become disease because enough emotional energy has been pushed into the body and not allowed to come out. It has to come out somehow though, and disease is a way for your body to try to release old emotional energies. Sweeping dirt under the rug (or pushing your emotions down where you can't feel them clearly) doesn't create a clean floor (nor emotional health and peace of mind). It just serves as an appearance of a temporary fix, which will still need to be dealt with eventually.

The good news is that you can begin connecting with your emotional energy – and benefitting from it – right now. For some people, feeling emotions is a scary prospect. If you are used to living in your head and having everything you think make logical sense, then opening up to your intuitive, instinctive, emotional side – which everyone has – might feel quite foreign to you.

I remember when I began doing some deeper work on accessing my emotional intelligence. It was a strange and sometimes quite annoying world because it constantly flowed, changed and moved. I wanted it to be simple, with one feeling at a time that I could deal with, and then it could all just be done.

What I ended up with was an ever-shifting sea of feelings and at first I just got really mad about it. How was I supposed to handle all that? I didn't know at the time I would come to enjoy that ever-changing sea within me, just like I enjoy the changing moods of the ocean or the weather. I didn't realise at the time that the more I explored these emotional currents, the more I would learn to swim in them without necessarily feeling like I was drowning.

It can take a while to become a good 'emotional swimmer'. You'll still feel your emotions and sometimes be very deeply moved by them, but you'll find you can learn from what they tell you (such as anger telling you a boundary needs to be set, or fear telling you that you are breaking through a comfort zone into unknown territory, or sadness telling you that something needs to change, or guilt telling you that you need to forgive yourself, or shame telling you that you need to love yourself, as some examples). Your life will improve, as will your health on mental and physical levels too. So will your relationships and your sense of purpose and clarity in your life.

Yes, there are many benefits to learning to swim in your emotional waters, so let's go through a guided exercise to help you build your emotional intelligence, and learn to swim in those emotional waters of yours without fearing getting caught in a rip or becoming lost at sea.

Getting ready:
You have two options for this exercise – you can do it in a relaxed, seated (or lying down) position in a quiet room, or you can carry it out in or near water, and that could be in a bath, shower, or lying by or in the ocean (or other body of water). The only safety precaution with the second option is that you want to be sure you stay relaxed and not fall asleep because that could be unsafe. So if you are tired or feeling that you might fall asleep, then the first option might be better for you. Or if you are tired, but the second option appeals most, then rather than being in the water, choose to be near it instead, such as sitting by a lake, waterfall, pond, aquarium, fountain or the seaside.

The exercise:
Sit or lie comfortably.

Close your eyes or soften your gaze and keep them slightly open, whatever feels best for you.

Focus on your breath. Feel the breath flowing in and out, and allow yourself to relax. If you have been unconsciously holding your breath, or breathing shallowly, you'll notice that as you focus on it. Respond by allowing your breath to become slower, deeper and more even on the inhalation and exhalation. If you feel comfortable with this, you may even want to pause between the inhalation and exhalation, and the exhalation and inhalation, for just a second or two.

Breathe and relax for as long as you need – at least five breaths – and when you are ready, you can continue on to the next step.

You will now visualise, imagine, feel or pretend that you are floating on top of an ocean.

You feel when the ocean is still. You feel when the ocean rocks you from side to side with the rise and fall of the waves. You feel when the currents of the ocean are cool or warm beneath you.

Relax now for as long as feels good and simply observe, feel, or listen and watch.

If you have a fear of the ocean, imagine or pretend that you can let it go by becoming even more relaxed. The more relaxed you are, rather than trying to force it out, the more effective it will be. Fear makes us tense, so the more we relax, the more easily we will discharge the fear. If a big wave surges, relax into it.

You are safe in this ocean. It is a part of you. Let it move or be still, and relax as you bob on the surface.

When you are ready, say this affirmation: "My emotions are my intuitive instincts. I trust my feelings. They help me know what is true and what to do."

Relax and breathe in and out, slowly and deeply.

You have completed your exercise.

You can come back to this exercise whenever you feel you don't understand something you are feeling, when you are afraid of tapping into your emotional truth about a situation, or when you feel stuck in a 'negative' emotion and unable to 'get free' of it. You can also use it to gain more energy and peace if you feel tired or drained.

EXERCISE 4: TAMING THE DRAGON

Why you want to do this exercise:
There's a turn of phrase to describe the situation when you are angry with a person. It is that 'someone's got your goat'. It's not exactly clear where this expression originated, though there are theories that goats have been used to calm other animals – horses before a race to ensure a better race performance, and cows in a barn to ensure greater milk production. So the idea is that if someone pinches your goat, they would undermine the success of your ventures, sort of stealing the calm that leads to best performance and production.

In the personal growth and self-help field, this would be called 'giving your power away' to another person. That is what happens when you believe another person is capable of making you unhappy, for example, or angry, or is in any way in control of your emotional wellbeing. Now this might seem obvious to you if you have already explored personal growth, but if you are new to all that, then it might seem like your goat actually can be stolen by someone else. You might regularly feel happy and then connect with a particular friend or family member who seems to suck the joy right out of you, leaving you feeling tired and depressed, or angry and frustrated, and then you are quite unable to remember why you were so happy in the first place! In those instances you might believe that other person does have power to control your emotional state.

However, what is happening in those situations, is that you are giving your goat away to the person in question. You are giving them permission to dictate your emotional responses. Perhaps not consciously, but if you feel like another person has power over your emotions, then this is what is happening, even if you aren't intentionally saying, "Hey, you get to be the boss of me."

We can give permission to another person to be our judge, jury and executioner when we allow someone else to make us feel bad about who we are as a person and how we choose to live our lives. We are going to bear the consequences of our actions – for better or worse – whether another person likes our choices or not. Giving permission – even subconsciously – for another person to judge us, doesn't help anyone.

Sometimes we give permission without realising we are doing so because it happens so sneakily. We might feel guilt or a misplaced sense of responsibility to try and make someone feel happier, and so we allow them to emotionally manipulate us because we find it difficult to bear the thought of standing up to them and saying no, even in a loving but firm way.

Maybe you are scared that if you stand up to a person, they won't love you anymore, or they'll cut you out of their life. Perhaps that fear is an accurate assessment. Perhaps that person is only willing to have people around them they can manipulate or control. Whether your instinct is correct or not, you are still in a position of allowing someone to try to manipulate you because you are afraid and not trusting that if life takes someone or something from you, it will eventually deliver a worthy replacement!

Maybe you are allowing people to infect you with their drama because you have the mistaken belief that if you love someone, you have to be miserable when they are miserable. Or you just go along with the moods and whims of someone you have decided is more worthy of your respect than yourself because you lack self-confidence to trust in your own feelings. That could be someone in your life such as a partner, parent, employer or even possibly a child.

To 'claim your goat' and claim your calm, to not unconsciously give another permission to manipulate you emotionally, is a huge step towards feeling happier in your life, no matter what is going on. If you have been unconsciously caught up in allowing others to manipulate your moods and emotions – perhaps for a long time – then saying no and choosing to just feel happy, no matter what, can feel very rebellious. You might even wonder if you are breaking a law somehow! When you are going against something you have done and have taken for granted for so long, even if it is a good, healthy and moderate change you are making, it can feel like you doing something wrong, even when you are doing something very right. You might have a lot of resistance until you face the feelings sneakily causing you to place another in a position of power over you. You might feel as though you are the world's worst and most selfish person as you 'dethrone' that other person who has become quite used to sitting in judgement over you. The people who once were manipulating you, and now can no longer do so, might call you a terrible and selfish person, and accuse you of not caring anymore. You need to really hold on to your goat then!

Once you give yourself permission to be happy, even if others around you are unhappy, you'll realise that instead of feeling like every time someone is drowning in their own misery or negativity, rather than diving in there and drowning along with them (not helpful for either of you), you'll be able to remain where you are and throw them a lifeline – your smile. This takes me to another expression – 'let your smile change the world, don't let the world change your smile'. This sums up the opposite of letting someone 'get your goat'. It also gives you the opportunity to be a happier and more positive person more often, and the opportunity for others to join you, if they wish.

To really get this, you also have to give up goat-stealing from others. Trying to control how another person feels to make them feel guilty or ashamed if you are having a tough time, to take out your anger on another person, or to try and control them with your opinions or beliefs are all attempts at goat-stealing from other people. This is not 'good karma' and it will keep you trapped in goat-stealing from others and them goat-stealing from you. You either stay in that manipulation mindset – manipulating and being manipulated – or you choose to claim your goat, give up goat-stealing from others and instead, learn to disengage from the drama around you, and choose to honour the excellent

Polish saying, 'not my circus, not my monkeys'.

In this exercise, 'the dragon' is the drama that another, or even you, are going through. You can either let it steal your calm or you can use it as an opportunity to grow your cool, calm and collected heart and deal with what needs to be dealt with. This doesn't mean you have to have a boring life where nothing happens! Some people get addicted to drama. If they don't have some crisis or tragedy happening constantly, they become uncomfortable.

People with drama addiction aren't interested in growing through a crisis. They just want to use it to gain attention or sympathy. They will milk that drama for as much attention as possible, and when it runs out of steam, they'll be in yet another drama before you can blink twice! What they need – although quite possibly giving this to them might evoke a tantrum in response for a while at least – is someone who doesn't see them as a victim, and who believes they can, if they choose, live a happier life where they are responsible for their own goat, and don't need to try and steal yours!

Despite what drama addicts may believe, drama isn't interesting. It's actually repetitive and boring. It's not about excitement and living well, it's about avoiding growing up and taking responsibility for your own happiness. The juicy, fun, exciting stuff happens when you are willing to embrace life and go with what unfolds. It is not about trying to blame another person or even to blame life when things don't seem to meet your immediate need for attention or whatever else you might think you should have in that moment. This can be hard to outgrow, but the moment a person realises they are worthy of being loved and cherished, and that the world doesn't revolve around them, is the moment they can become a more useful, creative, loving and loved human being.

Learning to 'tame the dragon' means that you don't allow drama – yours or another person's – to get the better of you. Getting stuck in why things won't work or change, getting negative and believing there's no point to anything – these sorts of despairing dramas won't help you. If you feel them but don't want to feel them, that's a good sign you are willing to whip that dragon into shape. If you want to burrow down into those feelings, then you are going to be stealing goats and causing havoc to your own happiness, not to mention the happiness of those around you.

However, we all have choice. That's fine. Happiness – as pleasant as it is – is not always an easy choice for people. We might think we have to be thinner, richer, more successful, healthier, more in love or more of *something* before we can just choose to be happy. Learning to be happy in a famine, instead of only during a feast, is something we can all choose if we wish. Some of the highest rates of happiness have been measured in the poorest of countries; Tanzania comes to mind as an example. This doesn't mean you can't be living a materially abundant life and be happy, but it is a timely reminder that it's not necessary for your life to be 'perfect' for you to choose to be happy. Sometimes realising that is enough for you to tame the dragon and give up a drama addiction (or drama-addicted people in your life) permanently.

When you are ready to be happier, to choose that for yourself, to know that it's a more effective, more pleasant and overall better way to attract love and affection into your life than through drama, then it's time to do this exercise.

May your dragon-taming skills flourish!

Getting ready:
You'll need a place that is private and quiet if possible, though you can have some music playing in the background, provided you feel that helps you relax and focus and does not become distracting.

The exercise:
Sit comfortably. Close your eyes and focus on your breath flowing in and out for however long it takes for you to begin to relax, but at least for five long, slow breaths in and out.

When you are ready, you are going to visualise, imagine, feel or pretend that you are sitting by a camp fire.

You may see, sense or feel, or even hear, the crackling of the flames. That camp fire helps you relax, and your breathing naturally and easily becomes slower and more even.

Close your eyes and relax by your camp fire for however long feels good, but for at least five long slow, deep even breaths.

If you are finding it hard to breathe in a relaxed way and really let go, you can place one hand over your heart and one hand over your belly to help you come out of your mind and into your body, so you can begin to really relax.

When you feel very relaxed, you are ready for the next part of the exercise.

You will now visualise, imagine, feel or pretend that the flames of your camp fire are becoming flames from the nostrils of a large dragon.

You might see this dragon clearly, or need to pretend that it is breathing fire out of its nostrils.

You are curious about this dragon. Even if it might try to intimidate you or scare you, you know it cannot harm you.

You notice by your side a wand made of gold. You know this belongs to you, even if you have never noticed it or seen it before.

Now you lift the wand and you notice what it feels like in your hand. Is it heavy or light? Is it plain or does it have designs on it?

When you hold this golden wand you feel confident and relaxed, and the dragon bows its head to you, stepping forward so you can jump on its back.

Whatever direction you point the wand, is the direction the dragon will go. You can point the wand upwards and fly in that direction on the back of the dragon if you choose. You can point it forwards and move forwards, and so on. You might wish to do complicated twists and turns, or keep it simple and fly in one direction for a while.

Relax and fly with the dragon for as long as you wish. How do you feel when you are riding this dragon? Can you enjoy the experience more when you know you are in control of the direction this dragon will take?

When you are ready to return, point the golden wand down to the earth, and you'll return easily and swiftly. Thank your dragon and let him or her return back into the flames of the camp fire.

Place down your golden wand by your side again and close your eyes.
Relax by the camp fire for however long you need, breathing deeply and slowly.
When you are ready, open your eyes. You have completed your exercise.

EXERCISE 5: QUICK TRICK – FROM REACTIVE TO CENTRED

Why you want to do this exercise:
This is a quick and effective exercise to help you in those moments where you feel like you have lost your centre. When you've lost your centre you will feel out of control or not really know what you feel, or not seem able to make a clear simple choice or decision. It can also feel like you are being pulled in too many directions at once and not knowing which way to go. If you feel overwhelmed with demands and are unable to be productive or get *anything* done whilst trying to do *everything*, then you have lost connection to your centre. Other symptoms of not 'being in your centre' are: a feeling of disconnection; anxiety without a particular reason; increased fearfulness or a sense of unease; physically bumping into things and becoming unusually accident-prone; or feeling confused or uncertain about what you really want or need. Sometimes when people are out of their centre, they feel they have forgotten something, that something is not quite right, but they cannot necessarily say what it is. It is a niggling feeling only relieved when you click back into your centre again.

Being centred requires that you feel grounded enough in mind and body so you can really feel connected to yourself and the present moment. This exercise will help you get into that state so you know what your inner feelings are telling you, have more energy, see things more clearly and are able to make more constructive choices that feel right for you.

Don't worry if you feel like you aren't as centred as often as you wish. Some days, or even weeks or months, will have you feeling you are more often off your centre than in it. Part of how we grow is learning to gently, patiently and persistently bring ourselves back to centre again and again. That practice is how we get good at it. Then we can spend more time in that centred state, and know that if something does ruffle our feathers so to speak, we can be sure we can bring ourselves back to that state when needed. We can become a bit like those inflatable punching bags that have a weight at the bottom, so when you hit them, they right themselves back to centre every time. Eventually you'll become so good at bringing yourself back to your centre that you'll feel like you live in that secure place within yourself most of the time, and if you do have an off day or off moment, you'll come back to your grounded sense of self more quickly.

Getting ready:
You can do this exercise anytime and anywhere provided there is somewhere to sit and some privacy. And provided you don't need to be focused on something else – such as driving a car or chopping vegetables! You really need to give yourself some minutes of 'me time' to do this exercise properly. If you can't find five minutes to do that for yourself,

then it's no wonder you are having difficulty feeling centred!

There's a saying that 'you should meditate for twenty minutes a day, unless you don't have enough time, in which case you should meditate for forty minutes'. Whilst I am only asking you give yourself five minutes here, you'll get what I mean. If you feel you don't have time to do this, then it's all the more important you *make* the time by setting a priority to do this for yourself.

You can do this exercise daily. That can be especially helpful if you are going through a phase in your life where you have a lot happening and the days feel like they fly by and you can't quite believe it's already dinnertime, for example.

It's best to do this exercise during the day as it will bring you energy. If you try to do it immediately before sleep, although it will help calm your mind, you may find it a bit too stimulating physically. However, if you have insomnia because you cannot seem to stop thinking, it may actually help you fall asleep more easily. Try it at different times of the day or evening to feel how it works best for you.

The exercise:
Stand with two feet flat on the ground. If this is physically difficult for you, then sit comfortably, but with your back as upright as possible (without becoming tense), with your hands resting on your legs.

Focus on your breathing. Breathe in and out whilst starting to slow down your flow of breath. This will help you to relax. You want to be relaxed, but not resting or sleepy. If you need more energy to wake you up a little, breathe a little deeper in and exhale with a little more effort, but don't force your breath to the point of becoming tense.

You will now become aware of your right side. Push a little into the ground with your body weight, especially on the right side. You might focus on your feet on the ground or your hands on your legs, leaning slightly towards the right side of your body.

Bring yourself back upright, so that you feel more evenly balanced in the centre.

Now you are going to put your attention onto your left side. Use your feet on the ground, or your hands on your legs, to push down a little as you lean towards your left side.

Bring yourself back upright, so that you feel more evenly balanced in the centre.

Repeat this process again. Notice how you move from the centre, to the right, then back to the centre, and to the left, then back to the centre again.

Now repeat it at least one more time. This time you are going to count the seconds you stay in each position. When you are in the centre, stay there for at least five counts. When you move to the right and the left sides, you will only stay there for three counts at the most. You will always stay a little longer in the centre than off to the right side or your left side.

Now, if you are standing, sit down. Lean back and relax.

You are going to visualise, imagine, feel or pretend that you are an ancient tree with a thick, powerful trunk, strong and upright. You are grounded with roots that run deep into the earth. You have many branches that reach up and outwards too. There might be rain and wind that cause your branches to move a little, but your trunk and roots remain firm.

It feels good to be this tree – strong, grounded and secure. Relax for as long as you choose, but at least three long, slow breaths in and out.

When you are ready, open your eyes and you have completed your exercise.

EXERCISE 6: SEEING THE SIGNS

Why you want to do this exercise:

If you had a best friend who loved you absolutely, was super-smart and well-connected, knew what you needed and what would truly make you happy, and wanted to help you get there *and* was powerful enough to know all the right people and help make things happen for you, wouldn't you want to accept their help when offered? Well that's what life wants to be and do for you. You have to allow it, by paying attention and noticing the advice given. Whether or not you follow it is totally up to you and that's fine. You have to decide for yourself how you want to live, but big road signs – especially at major points in the journey – will always be there for you.

Life is so attentive and helpful that before you even know you need to ask a question about which road to take, you've been given nudges in the right direction. When you eventually ask your question about which way to go, the signs become more obvious because you are paying more attention.

To see the signs life gives you more clearly, you need to learn how to look through the eye in your heart, rather than the eyes in your head. Sometimes the eyes in your head will tell you that you are just being silly, or reading too much into something, or convince you there are no such things as signs at all. Or perhaps the eyes in your head will see something and then try and figure out what it all means – should you interpret it as a sign to pause, or to go a different way, or should you interpret it as a sign to move ahead? You might feel even more confused than what you were before you recognised a sign. And you don't need to be.

The eye in your heart is capable not only of recognising a sign, but of feeling the truth of its message at the same time. There is no room for doubt or uncertainty or questioning or confusion, because you just feel it, recognise it, know it, all at once. *After* that, your mind may step in and try to convince you otherwise, but it will be like a drop of water trying to drown out a wave because when you see with your heart, there is such a sense of 'getting it', of just *knowing* what is true and what you need to do, that you cannot forget it.

From a spiritual perspective, we would call going from the eyes in your head to the eye in your heart, the same thing as moving from your intellect to your intuition. Some people think that being an intellectual means being super-smart, but there are different kinds of intelligence, and sometimes what is logical is nowhere near as brilliant and helpful and miraculous as less rational, but more instinctive and gutsy intuitive insights.

Some people believe that irrational, illogical ideas are dangerous, silly or stupid *if* they view them through their intellect. The intellect wants to make sense of everything, to be able to see it and touch it, before it is accepted as real. The intuition is a different sort of intelligence. It is willing to take leaps and risks based on what feels right. These are the passion projects that turn into far-reaching and highly successful businesses and the apparently inconsequential choices that change the course of your life and destiny. The successful and inspiring Oprah Winfrey has been quoted as saying that her career developed as it did because she trusted her intuition, rather than only making logical business-minded choices.

Logic belongs to the intellect, and the intellect is great for taking tasks, organising them and getting them done. It is sort of like your car. The intuition is for getting inspired, getting glimpses of the journey and making decisions about the route. It is sort of like the trip planner. They work best together. It's sort of like 'let your heart lead, but take your head with you'. If you do it the other way around, you will break your heart again and again, shutting down its voice with 'can't', 'shouldn't', 'too risky', 'no long-term prospects', 'that field is too competitive' and more. If you only operate on intuition and don't then put those insights into practical steps *and* take those steps, then it's a bit like sitting at a road sign that points you in the direction you know you want to go, but you never actually walk along the path.

If you try to let the intellect lead, you won't even see the sign. You'll miss the easier options that come along to try and help you, and you'll try to do things the way you think they should be done rather than what is actually going to *work well and best for you*, which, coincidentally, is not so often the way you expect.

Intuition can take leaps whereas intellect can only take steps. They each serve a purpose, but to see and read the signs in life accurately, you'll need to rely on your intuition.

This exercise will help you strengthen your intuition. It is not something you can force. Remember the idea I expressed earlier in this book that intuition is more like fishing on a line and you have to wait for the fish to bite rather than hunt them down like a spearfisherman? Well this exercise will teach you how to be in that state where the fish will want to nibble at the line. And it will show you how to throw that line in the first place.

It is a quick and simple exercise you can do anytime you feel you need a sign from the universe about which way to proceed, or what you need to know about anything happening in your life.

And don't worry if you don't think you are an intuitive person. It's been my experience that people are more intuitive than they give themselves credit for. It is more about learning to realise what is already happening within you and paying attention. This exercise will help you get to that place. The more often you do this exercise, the more receptive you will become to your intuitive wisdom. It's a bit like programming the setting on the car radio so that when you get into the car and turn on the engine, the radio always pops up at that station automatically. When you do this exercise, it's like setting the station – you are able to hear the broadcast whenever the radio turns on without having to think about it. When you go to make a decision, you'll be prepped to receive your inner intuitive insights rather than a bunch of logical arguments for this way and then the opposite way that leave you none the wiser.

Finally, some people are quite nervous about opening up their intuition. They worry they will start hearing or seeing things they don't want to know. I can tell you this – there are many things in the world you are exposed to on a daily basis that you don't want to see or know, at some level, although you might have become a little numb to that. You have emotional and psychological material thrown at you daily, much of it being fear-based because that is what tends to prevail in the media. When you open your intuition, it is true you are opening up to yet another source of information, but this is not fear-based at all. If what you are sensing is frightening, it is not intuition. It is the mind masquerading as an intuitive insight.

Intuition comes from the heart. When it is genuine, there is nothing that could be more comforting. Even if it is telling you that you need to go ahead and take a step on your path that you feel is rather challenging, you will feel comforted, secure, willing. Intuition is life-changing and heart-healing medicine. It is nothing to be afraid of, and has everything to recommend it.

Getting ready:
You'll need a quiet and restful place, preferably where you can sit comfortably and not be interrupted.

You may wish to have a pen handy to jot down any insights that may come to you during the session. However, this is not an exercise that has a purpose of getting a specific answer at this time. It is about strengthening your intuitive muscles so they are ready to receive when the time is right for you.

If an intuitive knowing or insight comes to you during this exercise, that is a bonus. What you want to be aiming for during this exercise is to feel as relaxed as you can. That will be enough to allow your intuitive self to make its presence more felt. Then answers can come when the time is right. That might be immediately. It might also be hours, days or even weeks later.

The exercise:
Sit comfortably and relax by closing your eyes and noticing the flow of your breathing.

If you are having trouble really feeling your breath and relaxing your mind to focus on your breath, then you may like to place one hand over your upper chest and one on your belly, and notice that as you breathe in, your hands rise slightly. As you exhale, they will naturally lower slightly.

Let yourself relax and be with your breath flowing in and out. It can help to imagine the words 'let go' as you breathe out.

Stay with a gentle focus on your breath, and perhaps the words 'let go', as you exhale until you begin to relax, at least for ten breaths in and out.

You are now going to visualise, imagine, feel or pretend that there is a pleasant-feeling golden light that glows softly in the centre of your chest. It feels good, like love, peace and happiness.

It helps you to relax and feel really good. You notice that the golden light glows a little brighter as you breathe in. As you breathe out, it grows a little wider. Let that golden light grow to whatever size feels right for you as you relax and feel good.

You are now going to visualise, imagine, feel or pretend that deep in the centre of that golden light is a beautiful eye. It is the most beautiful eye you could possibly imagine. This is the eye within your heart.

You know this eye can see you. It gazes at you gently, with love. What does it feel like to be gazed at with so much love? Can you receive this, knowing you are worthy of it?

As you relax and breathe, you feel the golden light glowing within your chest and the loving eye within that light. It feels pleasant and healing.

When you are ready, say: "The eye within my heart sees clearly. It guides me through my intuition. It's easy for me to feel my intuition. I trust my intuition and I naturally rely on it. It tells me everything I need to know, when I need to know it."

Repeat this statement several times if you need to do so to really feel and believe in what you are saying.

Then simply close your eyes and relax for as long as feels good.

When you are ready, open your eyes and you have completed your exercise.

When you have done this exercise, you may have some clear feelings or ideas come to you. If you feel like jotting down some notes now, or in several hours or days time, do so.

After doing this exercise your intuition is heightened. It is good to note the ideas or thoughts that come to you in that state. A typical experience of intuition is that what you are perceiving can sometimes seem so obvious you don't know why you didn't realise it earlier. Yet when you try to think of it again later, you might not be able to remember it! That is because intuition is a naturally expanded state where you have more awareness. It feels obvious at the time, just as if the road ahead would be more obvious if you were seeing the whole pathway from above, looking down. You have a greater perspective and the way ahead seems clear. However, once you are back down walking the road again, it's not as clear as it seemed from that heightened perspective. So write down your intuitions, even if you think they are obvious. Looking back later on, you might be so grateful you did, as you 'rediscover' your earlier insight again.

EXERCISE 7: CONTRACTION OR COURAGE?

Why you want to do this exercise:
One of the first things that crisis tends to do is push us out of the immediate pain or shock of what is happening and up into our heads. Instead of staying with the feeling, we tend to plot a course of action to respond as quickly as possible. Sometimes that is helpful in the case of a genuine physical emergency. In that situation, figuring out that you'd better call for reinforcements, finding the number and placing your call as quickly as possible for the appropriate services, is a good idea.

The difficulty is when a crisis is of a different kind, somewhat longer-lasting, and therefore requiring more than one single decision on your part to get through it. Those kinds of crises could be long-term illnesses or other situations that seem to drag on for longer than you would like. They can perhaps feel more like a marathon than a sprint. They have the tendency to wear you down and push you into your head as a way to cope with the sense of prolonged stress or feeling that you are being 'cooked' by life, perhaps in something akin to a pressure cooker.

If a crisis feels like a never-ending onslaught of stress and strain, after a while your courage and best intentions to 'grab the bull by the horns' and move through it bravely might wobble. So you need to remember two things. Firstly, no matter how intimidating something might seem, you are given only what you can handle and what will help you get to the best possible place within yourself and in your life. Secondly, contraction (pulling away, resisting, shutting off, shutting down, going into your head rather than staying with your feelings) is not going to get you closer to the resolution of the crisis.

When things seem to be complicated, or even when they seem simple, it's helpful to keep your response as simple as possible. If something feels complex, or seems difficult, it's likely your mind has got in there and made it more complicated than it needs to be.

In law school one of our professors used to say that lawyers are trained to find problems where there aren't any! I think human beings can do this more generally when we allow our minds to get too carried away. If we really understood that life is working itself out every day, and in our favour for the best that is possible for us, we would relax, trust more, think less and do more. Whilst we are working that out, the best thing to do is to learn how to feel for the truth underneath the constant doubts or plans of the mind. This exercise will help you do just that. Then instead of pulling away in contraction, you can open up with courage, and life can more easily help you get through even the most long-lasting or stressful crisis.

Getting ready:
A quiet place, where you can sit comfortably and not be disturbed, is ideal for this exercise.

You may want a pad and pen, journal, or electronic note-taking device (like a mobile phone with a note-writing feature), just in case you get inspired with an insight and want to write it down.

The more you learn to trust your intuition, the more insights you'll get, even when you don't expect them. Making a note of them is a good habit that will help you be more in tune with your intuitive wisdom within, which in turn makes it easier for you to relax and trust that whatever comes your way, you can handle it, even if you aren't sure exactly how. When you need to know something, you'll know it.

The exercise:
Sit comfortably and relax. You can do this by focusing on your breathing. If you are breathing in a shallow way, with your shoulders rising and falling as you inhale and exhale, rather than your torso gently expanding and contracting, and your belly softly rising and falling as you breathe, then you may like to place a hand on your ribs and another on your belly to help you slowly deepen your breath. Remember to exhale as fully as you can without forcing it.

Close your eyes and relax there for as long as you need.

Now you are going to visualise, imagine, feel or pretend that you can make a circle around you. This is easy to do, and the circle curves around you naturally.

You are now going to fill your circle with whatever feels good. That might include: love, happiness, peace, fulfilment, satisfaction, nourishment, joy, connection, success, health, abundance, wellbeing, passion, confidence or courage.

You can do this by imagining or pretending that you can put a feeling into your circle, or a 'picture', or a colour. Or you can do it by gently speaking, saying, "I put LOVE in my circle. I put JOY in my circle … " and so on, until your circle is as full of good things as you would like.

Now you are going to relax and imagine that very gently, as you breathe out, your circle expands. Breathing in, you soak up all the good things in your circle. This gives you energy, which you gently send into your circle to make it – and all the good things in it – grow a little bigger when you exhale.

Breathe in the good things, breathe out and increase the circle and all the good things in it.

Allow your circle to become as big as feels good. Don't worry if you get enthusiastic and your circle bursts like a balloon! You are only going to be covered in good feelings. If that happens, you may like to start again, and breathe a little slower to make your circle expand to the right amount for you – not too little and not too much.

Feel how nice it is to relax in your circle for however long feels good. If you want to nap, do that.

When you are ready, open your eyes and have a good stretch. You have completed your exercise.

You can complete this exercise anytime you want to feel good, and anytime you feel you are pulling away and closing off from life – be it a particular person or situation – and you'd rather be brave and move through it than try to avoid it, so you can have a good resolution.

EXERCISE 8: COLLAPSE OR CLIMB

Why you want to do this exercise:
Sometimes life will leave you feeling a bit flat, or possibly feeling squashed under the great big weight of a huge challenge! There are times when you really need to rest and recuperate to recharge your batteries. Many exercises in this workbook, including the previous three exercises, will help you do just that. If you feel exhausted, then take some rest, and choose to do one or more of the previous three exercises (not all at once necessarily; you might choose to do one or more per day) and work up to this one.

When you feel ready, you can then move on to this exercise. If you already feel 'up for it' then of course, just do this exercise. It is to help you give up fatigue and find the good sort of fight within you, the sort that is like the surfer putting in an effort to paddle to catch the wave rather than trying to swim against the tide. This sort of fight is what gets you in the right place at the right time, working *with* life and trusting that if there is a challenge before you, even if that challenge is in the form of a crisis, then there must be some value in working through it, and something good that will come of it for you.

This simple exercise is going to put you in touch with the wise warrior within. When you find yourself in need of an energy boost (provided you aren't trying to push yourself as a substitute for enough rest), this will help. When you need to remember how powerful you are – on those days when you might feel like you've gone twenty rounds in life's boxing ring, and come out of that a little worse for wear, this will help you find your confidence again. You are an amazing human. You have been through SO much in your lifetime already, and survived it, and you are reading this book to find a better way to live, so you are smart too. You just sometimes need reminding exactly how much power there is in you. We often think of that as brute strength, but physical strength is only one expression of power. Power of the spirit will win over any other sort of power every time, because power of the spirit never lets you give up until you get what you want!

Getting ready:
If you are the sort of person who can hug trees and exercise in public places, and not worry what others might think of you, then you can do this exercise outdoors (and maybe attract some curious new friends or at least inspire some passers-by to be a little less uptight and feel more free to just be themselves). However, if you are going to be distracted by having others around (and personally, even though I am comfortable being myself, this sort of healing work I prefer to do in private when possible) then find a space with some privacy, so you don't need to worry about being interrupted or distracted. If you can find an outdoor space in nature with some privacy, then that is a perfect combination, but the exercise will work for you if you do it indoors too of course.

The exercise:
Stand with your feet about hip width apart. Keep your knees almost straight but not 'locked'. Put your hands either on your hips or lightly let your arms rest by your sides, whatever feels most comfortable.

First, you are going to become as aware of your feet as you can.

If you cannot do this stand due to injury or any other reason, sit comfortably and use your hands pressed onto a hard surface, such as a book or table, instead. Through this exercise, you will do the same process I describe, but use your hands (and palms and fingers) instead of your feet (and soles and toes).

Imagine, visualise, feel or pretend that you can feel four sides of your feet. First you will feel your toes, the 'front side' of your feet, by gently and slightly moving your body weight forward a little to feel your toes pushing into the ground.

Next you are going to sense the 'back side' (in a non-cheeky sense, if you'll excuse the pun) of your feet, at your heels. You will do this by slightly and gently moving your body weight as though you can lean more into your heels, feeling where they push into the ground.

Next you are going to sense the outside of your feet, perhaps allowing the body weight to roll outwards just a little, to sense the outside edges of your feet as they touch the ground. You may feel your ankles move slightly to allow this to happen.

Finally, you are going to sense the inside edges of your feet, underneath the arches, where they touch the ground. Roll your body weight a little so you can feel the inside edges of your feet pressing down. If your arches are high, you might not have a lot of physical contact with the floor – if any – but you can still feel the inside edge of your heel and ball of the foot, and the edges your big toes, touching and pressing into the ground.

Now you are going to move in these four directions, getting used to the front, back and two sides of your feet. Take your time. Move in whatever order feels good. Rock and roll on your feet a little if you wish. If you are feeling energised, you can bounce, hop, dance, or jump if you wish, provided you stay aware of how your feet connect to the ground.

Now you are going to imagine your feet are like taps that can open. They can push stuff out – just like water flowing out of a tap.

Imagine, visualise, feel or pretend that you are turning on the tap and allowing anything you don't need (whether you know that that is consciously done or not) flow out of your feet into the earth. This can become fertiliser for the earth. You can let it go. Stay with that process for several breaths.

When the taps are no longer 'emptying', you are going to imagine, visualise, feel or pretend that your feet are now like gentle suctioning cups that pull good energy up from the earth. It feels good to receive this from the earth – all the healthiness, the naturalness, the balance, the power and the good feeling that nature has, gently and helpfully rising up into your body, by way of your suctioning feet.

Stay with that process for several breaths.

Now you are going to say this, aloud if possible: "I am strong, I rise. I am courageous, I rise. I believe in myself, I rise. I am supported by life in all ways, I rise."

Imagine that the connection between your feet and the earth is very strong now. So strong that if someone tried to push you, you wouldn't fall over! Feel how good and supportive that connection feels. You may even feel a bit stuck, but don't panic, that will pass.

When you are ready, either sit down and rest, or go and move about physically for several minutes.

You have completed your exercise.

You can do this anytime you need to find the strength to keep going. It's sort of like using the energy of the earth to flush out the engine of your car, to do a refuelling so it can keep driving.

CHAPTER 9

Workbook Exercises for Confusion

. . . .

PRACTICAL EXERCISES TO FIND YOUR WAY THROUGH CONFUSION INTO COMMITMENT

EXERCISE 1: CRYSTAL CLEAR MIND

Why you want to do this exercise:

Sometimes mental overwhelm sneaks up on you. You'll be feeling well, perhaps quite positive, and then all of a sudden you'll notice that isn't the case anymore. Perhaps you are suddenly exhausted, or distracted and unable to complete a simple task. Maybe things just suddenly seem too much for you to handle and you feel afraid or anxious, or you start sweating or finding it hard to breathe easily, without knowing why. Or you just feel that you aren't being productive, that your efforts are 'all over the place' and you aren't getting things accomplished.

These are symptoms of mental overload, too much information going in, and it needing to be discharged so the symptoms can stop and you can feel in control and able to function more effectively again.

This exercise is for those days (which, let's face it, might well be *most* days) when the mind seems to be a little busy, trying to sort out a few too many things, or has you feeling a bit like a dog chasing its own tail around and around (which stops being funny eventually and doesn't get you anywhere).

Getting ready:

Your best setting for this exercise is somewhere peaceful and quiet, with minimal chance of interruption. So that means mobile devices switched off, or at least onto silent, and put out of view for the exercise. It also might mean locking a door or putting up a 'do not disturb whilst door is closed' sign, or simply taking yourself off in your car to have some solitude whilst you complete the exercise. Just make sure you stop driving, and pull over and park somewhere, before you start the exercise!

The exercise:
Sit quietly and focus on your breathing. If there is noise or distraction around you that you cannot control, then focus on how easy it is with each breath to put some space or distance between you and the distraction. It is like it just gets further away from you with each gentle breath in and each relaxing breath out.

Do this for however long feels necessary for you to begin to unwind and relax into your own space.

When you are ready, you are going to close your eyes and visualise, imagine, feel or pretend that there is a beautiful clear lake before you.

Your lake might be between some snow-capped mountains in a crisp, cool and refreshing landscape, reflecting back a silver-grey sky, or perhaps it is in a forest landscape, reflecting the rich green foliage of the trees. Or your lake may be in an open clear setting, reflecting a clear blue sunny day or even a shining moonlit night.

Allow your lake to be whatever feels good.

There may be some breeze or activity within or around the lake. A bird might fly above and you may hear its call. You might see the passing clouds reflected on its shining surface.

Suddenly your lake becomes very still. There is just silence and stillness, so strong that you can feel it. It feels very healing, restful, peaceful.

The stillness of the lake fills your mind with peace.

When you are ready, slowly say: "My mind is filled with peace. My mind is open. My mind is relaxed. I feel so relaxed. I feel so relaxed. I feel so relaxed."

Repeat that statement as many times as you wish.

Then just relax for as long as feels right for you.

When you are ready, open your eyes. You have completed your exercise.

EXERCISE 2: YOUR INNER CRITIC

Why you want to do this exercise:
Although it's not quite the same as having multiple personalities, healthy human beings do have what are known as 'sub-personalities'. These are the characters that live within you every day, from the child within (that gets a kick out of funny animal antics and has a laugh), to the rebel teenager (that feels a thrill when breaking a rule and getting away with it), to the serious adult (that decides you really do have to get up and go to work today) and the inner critic (that tells you that you really could improve yourself in every single way). You also have something of an inner cheerleader (that encourages you and hopefully drowns out the voice of the inner critic, at least sometimes) and an inner seeker

(that is looking for something, even if it isn't always clear what is being sought). These different parts of you all have their own voice and their own impact on your quality of life. When you have healthy sub-personalities that mostly get along with each other, you'll be living a life that is fairly healthy and happy too. When those sub-personalities get out of control, angry, hurt or annoyed with each other or with the world, then you can feel downright awful within, and more afraid, confused and lacking in self-confidence than you need to be.

So let's take an example of a child that makes what he thinks is a masterpiece for his overworked, stressed-out parent. In truth, the masterpiece is a lot of brown paint (the child wanted to include as many wonderful colours as possible on his pièce de résistance!) smudged on a piece of paper.

The parent, worrying about some issue or other, sees this 'work of art' but doesn't realise exactly how important it is to the little boy. They don't notice his pride in sharing the picture with them, and distractedly just say, "Yes, that's great – well done," before tossing it on the back seat and forgetting about it because the more adult issues on that parent's mind really do need to take precedence in that moment. The parent could be proud – distracted, but proud – but the little boy who doesn't understand all that is crushed! His wondrous work of art, tossed onto the back seat.

He waits to see if the parent will pick it up and put it on the fridge door, a sign that he has done a 'good job'. This doesn't happen. The parent rushes on with the rest of the many things that need to be done that afternoon, and the little boy – unknown to the parent – begins to develop a critical inner voice. *That wasn't good enough. That's why it wasn't on the fridge. You aren't very good. You aren't good enough. You can't paint. You don't deserve to have your picture on the fridge.* And so on.

Those painful feelings of rejection and criticism – whether intended or not – begin to grow, and the inner critic within the child gets a voice, a place at his 'inner table' where decisions are made. If situations like this happen enough, that inner critic might become quite powerful (and it is a powerful voice in most people until they know they can change that situation as an adult).

Let's say that the little boy seemed sad and his other parent tried to cheer him up. "Don't worry about that, it's just a picture! Go and play outside instead!" That parent wants to make him happy. It's a kind intention, but the little boy hears that his passion for his picture is meaningless and what has value is to be active instead.

So the inner critic can have you believing you really aren't talented when perhaps you actually are, and in the very thing you believe you are least gifted in! The inner critic might be the voice that stops that young boy from enrolling in art classes. Even though that is what makes him excited and happy, he'll think it's worthless. His inner critic might start telling him that anything that makes him excited and happy, that really captures his heart, is best avoided because he will just suffer rejection and disappointment, all the more so than if it was in relation to something he didn't care about. So he might pour all his energy into sports instead, perhaps becoming very good at them, whilst his heart is left on the sidelines yearning for easels and oil paints! Oh how sad! Depression, anxiety, 'unexplained' fits of rage, violence on the sporting field, or even self-sabotaging behaviour of missing practice or cracking under the pressure of competition and denying himself absolute success in his sporting pursuits – these are all ways for the truth of what is happening for that boy to come out.

The thing with the inner critic is that it *is* trying to help protect you from pain. The difficulty is that it doesn't do a very good job of it. It ends up causing pain by preventing you from really living from your heart and taking risks. You don't have to hate your inner critic or try to pummel it into silence. You can love it, you can appreciate what it has done for you, but you will need to make sure you don't allow it to run your life. You can give it specific (and limited) tasks such as proofreading an email for spelling errors, or deciding whether or not to re-use a service provider who has been a bit lacklustre in performance or customer service. These are things the inner critic can do well – pick out what is not working and show it to you. You don't want that inner critic picking at you 24/7 however and undermining your confidence. You are not supposed to be perfect; you are supposed to be you and taking a journey where you stuff things up on a regular basis, learn from those 'mistakes' and do things differently next time. That's growth. That's life. The inner critic tends to believe that only perfection is acceptable and that's just not realistic or even helpful most of the time.

The best way to shift the inner critic from running (and ruining) your life, to helping you deal with the practical issues it is better suited for, is to begin to question instead of to accept criticism. This doesn't mean you are going to become obnoxious or arrogant. It just means you are going to become kinder – and happier, more loving and at peace with yourself.

This might sound like a huge task, but it will probably be some of the most enjoyable 'spiritual homework' you are ever given (apart from the homework I always like to give which is to remember to make time for some fun in your life – something which hardworking people can forget sometimes).

The way you question criticism is a two-step process.

When you notice yourself saying something critical, mean or judgemental to yourself (aloud or in your mind) you *really* notice it. That's the first step. It's like catching yourself in the act, so to speak, with your hand in the cookie jar. You 'catch' yourself in critical mode. If you call yourself an idiot or stupid or fat or tired or not fit enough, not attractive enough, not smart enough, or even if you just get frustrated and angry with yourself, even if you aren't sure why exactly, you really let yourself *notice* it.

Whether or not you think you have a 'good reason' for the criticism is completely irrelevant. You can be motivated by love (and encouragement) or criticism (and fear). This exercise is about shifting from inner critic to inner cheerleader, to boost self-esteem and encourage you to take the chances that are going to give you the most out of your life. If you are humiliated, lacking in self-esteem and cowering because you never think you are good enough, then the critic has been getting away with far too much. Being bold, brave and open to life is going to feel unnatural and difficult for you in that case, and it doesn't have to be that way.

I endured over a decade of such intense self-criticism that I felt pummelled, exhausted and completely victimised. It felt like I had a sadistic madman living inside of my head, determined to make me feel as terrible about myself as possible. There were days when I just wept at the amount of hate I felt in that internal critic's voice. It took me many years to learn how to stand up to it and overcome it. It was a process involving the two steps I am sharing with you here.

So the second step is that once you have 'caught' a criticism, you respond to it differently. That doesn't mean agreeing with it! It doesn't mean saying, "Well yes, but … at least I am trying etc." The inner critic doesn't need you to encourage it! What it needs is polite thanks for trying to help, but a firm response that that's enough now. You do not need to argue with the inner critic. You do not need to earn the approval of the inner critic (if you haven't already guessed, the job of the inner critic is to NOT approve, and trying to make it otherwise would be a bit of a waste of time and energy).

The different response in you is going to come from an encouraging, comforting part of you that can build up your self-esteem and self-confidence to live your best life rather than wear you down with impossible demands for perfection. That is going to replace the role of your inner critic (and leave that free to do your book-editing or write an annoyed letter to a consumer tribunal about inadequate product labelling).

You will need to learn to trust this encouraging voice, to let it respond to any criticism, fairly and strongly. Some people believe that you need criticism in order to grow, but whilst there is constructive criticism that says, "Okay, we've tried something this way. It could work better, so let's try it another way," the sort of destructive criticism directed at you as a person rather than about changing your behaviour, doesn't have a place in a healthy relationship with yourself or with another. The encourager in you urges you to keep experimenting and trying until you get to what works. That is a more effective way to grow and develop as a person than from a place of never believing you are good enough. I know what that did to me, and I see so many people who are still crippled by the inner critic. They are capable of so much and they don't know that about themselves because the inner critic voice drowns out the voice of encouragement that would have them try – and win! – so often.

So how would your encouraging voice respond to an inner critic's statement? Here's an example. This time, instead of a young boy and his burgeoning artistic streak, this example is of a young woman who has difficulties in choosing a partner for a relationship who truly loves and respects her.

Inner critic speaks: "I am so stupid! I can't believe I am back in this situation again! What's wrong with me? Why can't I find love? There must be something wrong with me! If only I wasn't this shape! I need to lose weight, otherwise I am always going to be alone."

Or her inner critic might blame the men she has become involved with, saying something like, "All men are so selfish! They only want to use me and they aren't respectful or interested in me as a person, only in what they can get *from* me! No wonder I can't find love. There are just no good men out there."

Either way, this critical voice is not particularly helpful (or true).

The encouraging voice (hearing the inner critic's voice) can respond in a more helpful and truthful way. It might say something like, "I love you. You are doing so well. I love how brave you are, to keep opening your heart. You are a good person. You are an attractive person. You have so much to offer. I love spending time with you. You mean so much to me and I want to take good care of you. I want you to be happy, but if you feel angry and sad right now, that's okay too. I am listening to you because I care. I love you."

If you are not used to a loving and encouraging voice, then you won't realise just how powerful and valuable it is. You might think it's all fluffy nonsense that doesn't do anything helpful at all. But this voice encourages the woman to love, care for and respect herself. When she is doing that, rather than 'looking for love in all the wrong places', she will be attracted to men who also want to love, care for and respect her. She will feel more worthy and valuable. She won't be so desperate for affection that she'll get into relationships that are not genuinely caring, loving or respectful. She will start to feel more loving from within herself so she will begin to recognise when others are loving and respectful to her, as opposed to using her. She will become more emotionally intelligent and able to make better choices for herself. All that from an encouraging rather than critical attitude.

For a while, when you start to use an encouraging rather than critical voice, it may be difficult. You may have to work out what an encouraging voice would say if you are not particularly used to that kind of positivity in your life. I had the benefit of being much loved as a child, and yet when I started to do this work for myself I felt clueless as to what a loving voice inside of me would say to the endless demanding drive for perfection that existed as my inner critic's voice. I just didn't know how to stand up to it, how to overcome its relentlessness.

What worked for me was keeping it really simple. I found that simple messages, often repeated, eventually added up with a good effect. In the early stages I scoffed at that voice. My comments such as, "I love you, I am proud of you," didn't mean much to me. *So what?* I would think. *That doesn't change anything!* It didn't seem helpful at all. But in time, I grew to believe in those comments, to feel more loved and more proud of myself whenever I said yes to a challenge and had a go, especially when it was something I wasn't so confident in, when I wasn't sure I could do it perfectly. Those were the times I was especially proud of myself. Soon I responded well to those encouraging words, and I tried more and more things, lived more and more outside of my comfort zone, and began to really resolve the issues my inner critic could never resolve for me. I realised love would accomplish way beyond what fear ever could. But we have to have patience, and trust and be willing to give it a go, not just try it for five minutes and then give up and go back to the familiar way of criticising ourselves and everyone else. Sometimes, as the song goes, we just need to try a little tenderness. It can go a long, long way.

All you really need to ask yourself is this: is the voice you are hearing or feeling making you feel loved, happy and good about yourself and your life, or not?

If it is already a positive, encouraging voice, doing you good, then you don't need to work on it. Just keep listening. Some people might worry that they are kidding themselves, like a permissive parent who smiles indulgently at their child who is running wild like a crazed animal, destroying everything in sight and making life hell for all they encounter, whilst sighing dreamily about how 'spirited' their child is. That isn't loving or encouraging, that's deluded! Being able to see when behaviour isn't healthy or working for you is part of self-respect and self-love. You can say, "I love you," to yourself and feed yourself nothing but chocolate biscuits (and I've been there!), but you aren't loving yourself really. You are denying yourself the nourishment you need and you'll be making yourself unwell. That is not love. That is self-harm hiding in an indulgent attitude.

The inner critic telling you that you are stupid is not going to help, because you aren't stupid, but that behaviour isn't going to make you happy or well. You need the encouraging voice that tells you, "You are worth more than this. You are deserving of good health so I want to give you food that is delicious and makes you feel good, not tired and depleted. I can see that by wanting to eat chocolate biscuits you want to feel happy and have some pleasure in your life – so I am going to find ways for us to have that pleasure and feel good because you deserve those things." Then there is a chance to change the behaviour from a place of feeling good about yourself rather than hating yourself or thinking you are useless.

If you try to fuel change in your life from a place of negativity you'll end up finding it harder than it needs to be. It can drain your energy and leave you feeling like a whipping post rather than a person who deserves love and respect. We are all here to grow and evolve as best as we can, and having some compassion for ourselves and others allows us to do so much more of that, and find it more enjoyable along the way too. Life can be hard enough at times. I don't believe there's any virtue in making it any more difficult than it needs to be.

Getting ready:
You have a choice how deep you want to go with this exercise. You can complete it seated in one chair, but if you want to explore these sub-personalities within you more deeply then you may like to choose to do a more active version of this exercise. That will involve you having three different places to sit or stand. One place will be for you, one will be for the encouraging voice within and one will be for the inner critic. (That last one doesn't need to be an electric chair by the way. The inner critic can be helpful when kept in check.) When you are sitting in each chair, you will visualise or pretend that you are becoming that part of you – either yourself, your inner critic or your inner encouraging voice.

Pretending to be the inner critic might be easy for most people to connect with, but the encouraging voice is going to be less familiar for many people. You may need to use your imagination and, like an actor playing a part, draw upon whatever positive experiences you can find of kindness and goodwill in your life experience to imagine what an encouraging voice might say to you. Whatever positive memories you have of feeling loved and supported will come in handy as you learn to tune in to this part of your personality. It is within you, even if you find it awkward or feel a bit silly trying to express it at first. It will become much easier and much more believable with practice.

You'll want some privacy during this exercise. It will help you focus and not get distracted, and also, you won't worry about looking like a crazy person if you choose to do this exercise by standing up, moving around and talking aloud. Believe me, you might sound and look a little crazy, but it will be the good sort of crazy that will help you become even more sane and happy in your daily life. A bit of good crazy in the right way, and at the right time, can prevent the unenjoyable sort of crazy – depression, despair, self-destructive behaviour – from making its way into your life later on.

The exercise:
Sit quietly in your chair and relax. You may like to close your eyes and rest for several moments.

When you are ready, say: "I love myself and accept myself. I do not have to be perfect or always 'make sense' straight away. I am willing to listen to all the parts of me and find the best way for all of me to be happy."

Then relax. You might like to put your hand over your heart and another hand over your belly. Focus on breathing slowly and deeply in, and then slowly and fully exhaling. Notice how your hands rise and fall slightly as you breathe in and out. Continue this breathing for at least five breaths.

Now you are going to visualise, imagine, feel or pretend that you are 'following' your inhalation and moving inside of yourself on the breath, just as if your breath in was a wave you could ride on. It's so easy for you to do this. It takes very little effort to just float inside of yourself, like you are walking into a big room deep in your body.

With each exhalation, you gently but firmly push the day-to-day world a little further away from you. It feels good and relaxing to do this.

Breathing in, you walk deeper into that room inside of you. Exhaling, you feel more free to go within and leave the day-to-day world behind for a little while.

You now see two extra chairs in your inner room. In one chair sits your inner critic. In the other chair sits your inner encourager.

You say this to them: "I am glad we are all here. We are going to work together to help everyone get what they need and want. I am in charge of this process."

Now you face the encourager and say: "Your job is to remind me of what I can do. You can help me feel positive and to keep trying until I get what I want. Thank you for doing this. I trust you."

You may visualise, imagine, feel or pretend that your encourager accepts your statement.

If you are not using one chair for all parts, you may go and sit on the chair (or stand in the space) you choose to be the 'place' your encourager sits (or stands). Now allow your encourager's voice to speak through you in response. That response can be out loud if you wish. That can be very powerful.

If you don't know what to say, allow your encouraging voice to say this to all of you: "I love each one of you for all that you are, and I will accept the job of helping each one of you to get what you need and want. You are all part of my team and I love you. I will help you and I will guide you. There is no need to worry or fear anymore. All will be well."

Notice how this feels.

When you are ready, return to 'your' seat (or space). If you are using one seat for all, simply bring your attention back to yourself.

When you are ready, face the inner critic and say: "Thanks for doing your best to keep me safe and to protect me. I appreciate all you've done for me and now it's time for you to alert me when something or someone is not as they seem. Don't worry if that doesn't seem like enough. It's an important job and you'll do it well."

If you want to, go and sit in the chair (or space) allocated to your inner critic (if you are not using one chair) and allow them to respond. If you don't know what your inner critic can say, allow it to say this to the group: "I want the best for you. I will do this job for you and use my critical powers to help us all get what we want and need. Thank you for including me."

Notice how this feels.

When you are ready, return to 'your' seat (or space). If you are using one seat for all, just bring your attention back to yourself.

Finally, you are going to visualise, imagine, feel or pretend that all three of you are in a circle. You are working as a team. You all want to help each other. Each part plays a role and each part can help make your life better. Allow yourself to feel supported, trusting and loved as much as you possibly can. It will become easier to do this with practice.

When you are ready, bring yourself back to the 'here and now' by standing up and walking about the room, noticing the time and the date and generally 'grounding' yourself in the present moment.

You have completed your exercise.

There will be shifts and insights that will come after this process has been done over the coming days and weeks. Some things you will notice, other things will be more subtle, but effects will take place. If you want to continue to integrate the inner critic and encouraging voice within, it can be a good idea to repeat this exercise again within a one to three week period. This process can happen quickly, but it is also common for it to take several weeks or months before you really feel the change, so don't give up. It is so worth it to keep going with this exercise until you feel a breakthrough. It will happen for you. And you do deserve it.

EXERCISE 3: EVICTION!

Why you want to do this exercise:
Ninety-nine times out of a hundred, the voices you have running in your mind are at worst, just a little wounded and in need of lots of positive reinforcement and loving encouragement to turn a negative attitude into a more helpful one. The voice that tells you 'why bother' and 'you'll fail' can be responded to with a 'maybe, but I am going to give it a go anyway' voice, so you aren't held back by those attitudes, and in time, they will begin to change in response to the go-get-'em approach you choose to have towards your life.

However, there is that one per cent we need to be aware of and respond to with a harder line of a 'no tolerance policy'. In my work, these are the sorts of voices that come out of people who have absolutely no interest in wanting to grow, heal or learn anything. They either aren't capable or willing, or are simply disinterested.

For many years, falling into the 'trap for young players', I tried to help people who were expressing such a voice. I figured if they were coming to me for help, then they must want help, right? No. Saying that you want help and being willing, ready and interested in receiving it are two separate things. Saying you want help, but expecting another person to take responsibility for you, your life, your issues, your perceived problems and anything you feel is wrong in your life is something else altogether. It was a draining, exhausting, drama-inducing and destructive experience. Eventually I realised it was also futile. It got the other person nowhere and brought me down. So I stopped. Do I still have goodwill and a desire for people who are more interested in spreading fear and negativity to have a better life? Of course. But I have become a little wiser about choosing to listen to my intuition and offering my energy to those who are going to use it. Otherwise it's like throwing precious seeds onto dry and infertile soil. Better to place them in soil that is ready for them and can use them, then there can be a beautiful garden rather than a waste of seeds on hard cracked earth. That earth needs tilling, or perhaps resting, but not seeds. That's the right thing, perhaps, but at the wrong time.

Within each one of us, there may be a voice or characteristic like this. For most of us, it's subtle and we don't buy into it, chalk it up to a bad mood occasionally and move on. But for others, it has more of a grip, and the more that person believes in it, becomes afraid or negative, the more powerful that grip becomes. Then that person is not so interested in living well, or in others being happy, but more interested in fear, in promoting fear, in instilling fear and negativity in others. It's sort of like an emotional or psychological version of a virus that wants to spread and infect as many others, gaining more hosts, as possible. If your psychological and emotional immune system is good, then you aren't going to fall prey to that. You'll either avoid such negativity from affecting you altogether, or you'll fight it off pretty quickly and easily, if you do suffer from a bout of the blues, and come back to feeling happier and more optimistic again.

We can build our immune systems, so to speak, at that level through all the work in this book. You may well be surprised at exactly how negative we can become without realising it; and certainly, you can be stunned at exactly how happy and free even the most negative and tired person can become when they give themselves permission to take a journey like the one you go on through this book.

I have gone from extreme fatigue and depression, self-hatred and utter bleakness, fear, anxiety and despair (experiencing all these symptoms at once, I might add, and for many years at that) and was able to learn how to come to a place where I didn't feel miserable every day, where I could process negativity and let it go, and where my emotional 'resting heart rate' was one of peace more often than not. I think that in a strange way, the extent of my own suffering was a gift. I know that, given where I was in my life and how I felt, if I can transform into a relatively happy and peaceful person, then anyone can do so, if they choose that for themselves. So even if you feel you struggle to find peace because you are so sensitive for example, and therefore easily prone to 'catching negativity' from a variety of sources, or even if you think you cannot feel peace and contentment inside of you for some other reason, I know that this is simply not true. You are capable of it. We all are. You just have to take the steps necessary – one at at time – and not give up until you get to where you want to be.

Part of that process means that if you stumble across a part of yourself, a voice in your head or a feeling that is so utterly overwhelming, that it pushes you towards suicidal thoughts, for example, feeling that you are worthless or that your life is worthless, then a different sort of intervention is needed. These sorts of feelings are far more common than you may imagine, but that doesn't make them any less of an indication that genuine help is needed and as quickly as possible. These sorts of feelings are not bad or shameful, but they are a sign that something has got a hold of you that isn't healthy and needs to be sorted out. You are given a life to live it. It's meant to be a gift you receive, and what you do with that life is the gift you give in gratitude for it. If you are doubting yourself, your value, your life, then somewhere along the line, something has become distorted. It needs to be untwisted so you can be well again – emotionally and psychologically, as well as physically.

Positive reinforcement and encouragement are useful when there is a willingness and ability to change. So for an over-zealous inner critic, who really is trying to help you stay safe, there is a possibility that great positive healing can happen simply through a reprogramming of that part of you (such as in the previous exercise). But for suicidal thoughts, or a type of darkness within your heart and mind that you cannot seem to get a hold of but causes you inner distress and mental anguish, a more toxic force is at play, something that is not actually trying to help you, but trying to harm you. It is a destructive or predatory force. That is a part of nature, so there's no need to be afraid of it, but we do need to deal with it intelligently and appropriately. A shark is a shark, and there's no use being nice to it and imagining that's going to turn it into a goldfish. It'd be like patting a grenade and imagining it is a kitten, and then being surprised when it blows your hand off, instead of giving you a playful swipe. That's just not an appropriate way to deal with the situation.

So if you – or a loved one – are struggling with the sort of voice in your head, or feeling in your heart, that has you questioning whether you want to be alive, whether you have any right to live a life free from fear and suffering, or that keeps you in a constant and crippling sense of self-doubt, fear or inner anxiety, despair and recurring sense of unpleasant darkness, then this exercise will help, but it is only one step. I would also suggest that getting professional assistance in a personal context a good idea too. Professional assistance might be finding a therapist or counsellor who can help you work through what is happening, and help you as you find the strength to stand up against that negativity within (or around you, if you feel the source of this pain is actually from a toxic relationship, living environment or workplace, for example). It can take time to realise you are allowed to do this and to learn how to do so persistently and effectively, so that eventually, the negativity will cease to sway you and cause pain. That therapist or counsellor will be like your coach for learning new skills to deal with the darker side of human existence. We aren't meant to live permanently in or with such darkness, but sometimes, if we are on a big life journey, we will (probably unintentionally) take a tour of duty through some very dark places within ourselves or within life. That's okay, provided that we equip ourselves for such a journey. A professional helper can be our tour guide, preventing us from becoming unnecessarily lost or caught up in less-than-desirable exploitation or manipulation by the underbelly-dwelling locals. That tour guide can help us find our way out of the dark again when it is time too, wiser for the experience and vastly more capable of dealing with any future encounters with darkness within us or around us, with more understanding, awareness and firmness. It is never wise to deny the darkness within, but it is very smart to learn how to avoid it getting the upper hand in your own mind, or at least how to dethrone it when it does get a bit too prominent in your inner world of mind, body and soul.

This exercise is the dethroning. But please, do note that if you find it is not enough for your particular experience of pain to resolve itself, then be bold enough to seek the further support of a skilled therapist or counsellor. In that process, you could learn something wonderful that could change your life.

Darkness can be intelligent and seem to retreat when you are feeling strong, only to come back to you when you are feeling vulnerable. It's sort of like a good-for-nothing ex who seems to sense when you are lonely and between relationships, and then starts calling again 'out of the blue' to lure you back into a dysfunctional relationship! Sometimes no amount of kindness and encouragement is going to help toxic behaviour become healthy. Sometimes the best way to promote healing in yourself and another is to refuse to indulge or enable it, and *just say no*. If you have any trouble saying no in any part of your life – towards your own bad habits or the people in your life who seem to perhaps take more from you than they should – then this exercise will be great for you too.

So whether you are doing this to boost your assertiveness more generally or to deal with specific darkness or negativity within you, this exercise will help build more confidence in your own empowerment and ability to choose what you do allow, and do not allow, to take up space within you and your life.

Game on!

Getting ready:

It is best that you do this exercise in a place that feels safe for you. That might be your home, or a place in nature, or at a friend's place or therapist's office. A relatively safe-feeling environment is best for this exercise because you are going to be standing up for yourself. You want to feel you are doing this with at least your feet on stable ground, even if you feel your intestinal fortitude wobbling a bit at first.

You *will* gain more power and sense of your own empowerment as you do the exercise, but starting from a very wobbly place might make this exercise a little difficult for you. That being said, if you really lack confidence, that is actually okay. Everyone has their I'd-rather-hide-in-bed-till-this-is-all-over days (or weeks, or months sometimes). You can still do the exercise, and it may well be enough to get you feeling fighting fit and in no mood for nonsense, which is great. However, if you find that it doesn't help your anxiety during the process itself, then that's okay too. It just means it's time to step back, and perhaps do the next exercise, 'Priorities of the Heart', instead, coming back to this one when you feel a bit more robust and ready for it. Help from a counsellor or therapist could be very useful too. You might even want to go through the exercise, with them reading it to you.

The exercise:
In a comfortable, quiet place, where you won't be disturbed, sit back and close your eyes.

Relax and focus on your breath.

It feels good to breathe in. It brings you energy and vitality.

It feels good to exhale. It releases tension and allows you to feel more relaxed.

Do this for as long as feels right, to help you relax and let go on the exhalation, whilst feeling some positive energy flowing in with your breath.

You are now going to visualise, imagine, feel or pretend that you can see the most vulnerable 'you'. That might be part of you that is afraid or tired, unwell, or just in need of reassurance and love. It might be a child you sense or see within, or just a feeling you have.

Visualise, imagine, feel or pretend that you can put your arms around that vulnerable part of you and hug it. You may wish to physically give yourself a hug whilst you do this.

Say aloud, in soothing tones: "I am safe. I am protected. I am loved."

Repeat that statement and hold the hug, or the feeling of a hug, for as long as feels right for you.

When you are ready, you are now going to visualise, imagine, feel or pretend that there is a very powerful and unconditionally-loving presence around you. This might be an angel with a sword, or a powerful warrior who protects you, or it could be an invisible but powerful spirit being, or it might even be you feeling strong and courageous.

That loving protector wraps around you now, as though you are being held in a protective and safe hug, just as you have hugged the vulnerable part of you. You may wish to physically give yourself a hug again as you imagine, visualise, feel or pretend this. You can now relax back into your seat as though you are settling into that hug.

Say aloud, in soothing tones: "I am held. I am safe. I am protected. I am powerful. I am loved."

Feeling the feelings, hugging and being hugged. If you are a person familiar with touch, and comfortable with it, this will be easier for you perhaps than if you are a person who is unfamiliar with touch and being held. If you find the idea of being held difficult, then simply hold your hands together rather than hugging your whole being, and feel as though your hand is being held by another, in a loving and safe way.

Visualise, imagine, feel or pretend that the vulnerable you now feels safe. You are feeling more confident and loved, and you know that your protector will remain with you always from now on.

Now you see, imagine, feel or pretend to see a wonderful looking chair. It is more like a throne really! Perhaps it is ornate and golden, or big and plush and comfortable. It might be a big lounging chair, or an upright, velvet-padded, elegant chair with a high back. This chair is whatever looks most beautiful and appealing to you at the moment. It can be as simple or spectacular as you wish.

That chair is your inner throne.

On that inner throne is something other than you. It might be a dark spot, or a dark person, or a symbol, animal, or even some sort of creature. Whatever it is, you are unafraid. You are relaxed and you know that chair belongs to you. YOU get to choose who sits on it, and when and for how long. *It is your chair. You are in control of that chair.*

You, with your protector and your vulnerable self held safely within, calmly and firmly speak to whatever is on your chair. Say in a calm, quiet, firm voice: "It's time for you to leave now. This is my place. You do not belong here. You may not return. Go in peace."

Repeat this three times.

Your chair becomes empty.

Go and sit on that chair now. Claim it for yourself. It is where you are meant to be.

What does it feel like on that chair? Can you get used to being there?

Say the following aloud: "I am ready, willing and able to sit upon my inner throne. No-one and nothing else is allowed to take my place. I call for wisdom, protection, courage and love to be by my side and in my heart at all times. All is well within me now."

Repeat the above three times.

Relax upon your chair now for however long feels good.

Now, put your right hand on your right knee, and your left hand on your left knee, and sit up as straight as you can. Feel how your posture is strong. Feel how you have strength within you.

Anytime you need to 'remember' your throne and you upon it, you will be able to take this posture – sitting up straight with right hand on right knee, and left hand on left knee – and immediately reconnect with the feeling of you seated upon your rightful throne, empowered and loved.

Sit in this posture for however long feels good and when you are ready, simply stand up and move around, and come back to the 'here and now'. Notice the time and the date to help ground you. You may also notice that you have more energy and feel stronger.

You have finished your exercise.

EXERCISE 4: PRIORITIES OF THE HEART (WHAT REALLY MATTERS TO YOU)

Why you want to do this exercise:
An exercise I have asked participants in my workshops to do in the past is about gaining some insight on their priorities. If you don't know what really matters to you, how can you make it a priority in your life? And if you don't make it a priority, then you are essentially saying that what matters to you, matters least, which means that you are making the priorities of other people more important than your own. This is not noble and self-sacrificing, because what matters to you, really does matter. You are meant to be you, as fully and completely as possible, not someone else. You can only really be you if

you figure out what that means and live accordingly. This is the path to genuine happiness and fulfilment. Whilst it might feel good to satisfy the passing urges of other people for a while, eventually something in you is going to snap – in a sudden uprising of anger, a disabling depression or some other 'sign' from life that you need to quit trying to please everyone else and claim your own life, and live it from your heart.

So the exercise I have used in the past is to ask people to write down the most important things to them, what really matters, inspires their hearts, makes them feel that life is worth living and what fills them with the most enjoyment, passion or delight. Even if the things on their lists are dreams rather than things they have already experienced, that is okay.

Once they have completed that – usually around five or so items on a list is good – I ask them to make a tally of how much time they tend to spend on those five things. That might be how much time they spend thinking about them, and how much time they spend acting on them.

Often enough, people are pretty shocked at how little they give to what matters the most. If needs be, I ask them to write down the five things they give most of their energy to – mentally and emotionally (in terms of thinking or worrying) and physically (in terms of action). That can be a bit of a wake-up call for most people. Feeling a bit sheepish about not really taking their own selves seriously enough to make their desires a priority, some intentions are set and actions carried out for lifestyle changes.

What else you will notice as you get into this exercise is the difference between inherited values and current values. This is the difference between the things you've been told by your parents, by society, by the media, that are important. Inherited values may have little to do with what really means something to you and more to do with the agendas (conscious or not) of others. Inherited values need to be questioned. It doesn't matter if it was right for your forebears; it may or may not work for you now. If your forebears lived through the Depression when food was scarce, fighting others for resources might have made sense for survival; yet, if that doesn't relate to how you live now, in a time of relative plenty where you know you can put food on the table, that old value isn't going to work anymore. Even if you have lived in a time of scarcity, it might not work for you now; you might see more sense in building co-operatives and working on community gardens and sharing in resources for financial reasons and to limit waste. This is a different value, on community and connection rather than suspicion and distrust. You have to choose how you want to live, and by that decision, you will then make further choices about who you invite into your life, and to what extent, and to whom you give a wide berth.

If status is important to your family, but to you, artistic expression is what makes you feel happy and alive, then you are going to live a very different sort of life if you decide to give up chasing a high-powered career and put time, money and energy into creating art. I have met too many miserable people with 'great careers' to know that pursuing a career others think will make you happy and safe is not a recipe for happiness or fulfilment (and therefore, leaves you feeling most unhappy and unsafe because you aren't taking care of yourself by finding out who you are, loving yourself and living with respect for who you are as a person).

Your values are not as moral as you might think; in fact, they aren't a moral issue really. They are a heart and soul issue. They are about what you would get up for on a day when you didn't want to get out of bed. They are about what you would work for on days when you are tired and don't want to work. They are about what would bring you joy, motivate you with meaning, or make the heartache of failure or disappointment bearable, because you love or care enough about what you value to not give up when the going is tough, maybe even for a long time. Your real inner values are what inspire you to live into the fullness of your character, to find out just how strong, brave, daring, creative, resourceful, determined and powerful you really are – because what you value is the stuff that you'll be willing to grow for, to reach for, to be uncomfortable for … anything less than that is too easy to give up on. You've got to really know what you can love and value if you are going to find out how amazing you are as a person – and you have so much that is incredible within you. You've probably already discovered a lot of that and you may not have even touched upon what you really value yet. Imagine what you'll find out about yourself when you do!

Even if you already know your values, you might like to go deeper with this exercise. You may even like to make the lists I mentioned in the beginning of the description of this exercise, especially the one on what you spend most of your time thinking about. If you have a dream, and you spend most of your time fearing it will fail (because you are human, and humans have an odd quirk of dreaming beautiful dreams and terrifying nightmares hand in hand), then you might want to become more aware of that so you stage an intervention and replace those fearful thoughts with prayers for help and prayers of gratitude. It will be a better use of all that energy of yours.

This exercise is meant to get you thinking and moving in the right direction. You can use it anytime you feel you have lost your way, become uncertain about what you are really meant to be committing to, or are overwhelmed with too much happening and no real sense of clear priorities. When you come back to what really matters to you, what will feel the best thing of all to attend to in that moment, and you respect yourself enough to actually act on that insight, then you'll find that you not only become more productive, but you'll feel happier and more loving and at peace with yourself and the world too.

Getting ready:
You'll need either a pen and paper (or journal) or some form of note-taking device. You might not write many lists, but sometimes the act of actually writing something forces you to slow down and *think*, to get clear and make a commitment because everything is laid out before you in black and white. Writing it down means you can't pretend that you don't know, or that it isn't true – which happens more easily if you just think of something true but are uncomfortable and forget about it by distractedly thinking about something else. Writing stops you from getting away with that. It is a step towards commitment because it makes it more real.

If you can have a relatively peaceful space where you won't be disturbed, that is helpful. Music in the background that relaxes rather than distracts you can be a good idea, especially if it has a slow tempo, which allows your breathing and heartbeat to relax and your intuitive, insightful mind to open up more easily.

The exercise:
You are going to write some lists.

Your first list: WHAT I'VE BEEN TOLD IS IMPORTANT.

It doesn't matter if you believe it or not, but write at least ten things on this list that you've been told are important. That might include family, friends, love, health and money. The reason why I want you to write more than five things on this list is because if you go deeper, you'll get more out of this exercise.

So here are some other things to consider as possible things you've been taught or told (directly or indirectly) as being important: status, how you look, owning a house, driving a certain car, being seen to be rich, having a degree, being a 'tough' man, not being vulnerable or weak, not trusting others (because they'll hurt or use you), buying discount but not telling, not letting anyone know how much money you have, what size clothes you wear, how much money you earn, being nice, having people like you, being popular, having people afraid of you, being respected, being kind, being strong, being a leader, staying out of the public eye, being seen and not heard, fitting in, standing out, being sexy or not too sexy, being popular …

Take your time. Think about what you've been taught.

Once you have at least ten things on your list, you can go over each item and either put a line through it, or a cross next to it, if it is something you don't hold as one of your personal values at this time in your life (even if you did in the past). Essentially, you'll see that some people could believe it and live that way, but *your choice is that you don't wish to do so*. Either you have already rejected that as a value in your life, or you are willing to learn how to let it go.

If there are things on that list you do value, *and* wish to keep as one of your values, then put a line underneath it, or a tick next to it.

You are now going to create a final list: MY COMMITMENT, MY VALUES.

You are going to write a list of the things you are willing to commit to – your real values, what really matters to you. This might involve some things from your first list, or you might want to dig even deeper.

You can do this by imagining that you are looking at your tombstone after you have died. What do you want it to say? What do you want people to know about you, about your life and how you lived? What would mean the most to you? One of my clients recently thought about this and she realised that what she wanted on her tombstone would be, "She cared." It was such a beautiful moment when she told me this; we both got a bit teary. It is also a value for her that she lives by. She really does care about people. What would you like your tombstone to say? Think about the words or actions you would be proud to have lived up to in your life.

Put at least five things on that list. These are the things that really matter to you now. You may revisit this exercise and update your list at any time, but as you really get to know yourself and go deep into your heart, you'll find certain values that will be with you your whole life. Some others may change a little, but at least one or two will remain the same. They will be a reflection of your true life purpose, the things you are meant to really 'get' and express this lifetime. It might take a few goes at this exercise before you find those, but they will come out eventually.

When you have at least five items on that list, you may want to pin it where you can see it daily – on the fridge, in your journal, by your computer. You may want to write at the top of the list: "I commit to … " and remind yourself that you can and will take action on what matters to you.

It can be a good idea to write a final list that changes regularly with steps you can take to commit to your values. It might be doing a course, or a regular yoga class, or affirmations, or reading a book, or telling someone you love them, or hugging your children, or making a monthly donation to a cause you really value, as some examples. You don't have to work it out all at once, but creating some steps from which to start is a great way to take your priorities and really make them a priority in your life – which will give you a surprising amount of energy and peace, more so with each step you take.

Finally, you can repeat this exercise at any time you meet a powerful personality in your life, get smitten or overwhelmed or confused about *your* purpose in life. Some people, sometimes without meaning to (and sometimes definitely meaning to), will pull you off your path for a while. You'll be dazzled perhaps, in love, admiring, sure that you've found 'the best thing ever', but eventually, you'll need to come back to your own truth, knowing that no other person has the answers to your own life! It is within you. You have to choose for yourself how you want to live, what feels truthful for you. Others might inspire you, but no-one else holds the key to the truth of your own heart. You do. You alone. Coming back to what matters to you is a way to set your feet back firmly on your own path, no matter if that path seems as shiny or impressive as another's path. When it is your path, it is perfect for you. That is just the way that human beings are designed, with an in-built blueprint to become all that each one of us is meant to be. As the saying goes, 'you were born an original, so don't die a copy'. Your path is more than good enough. It is what it is meant to be, and your heart helps you find the way.

EXERCISE 5: HEART LIGHT (LANTERN IN THE DARKNESS)

Why you want to do this exercise:
I hope that through this book you are learning that you don't need to understand things or to feel like you must control what is happening to you to feel safe and at peace. You might prefer to understand what is happening and feel in control of your world, but you know, it isn't necessary for everything to be working out for the best.

This simple exercise is quick and easy to do. It is that 'quick fix' for any time you feel completely in the dark – whether that be in the midst of a dark and heavy emotional onslaught of grief, fear or anger, for example, or managing to keep your chin up and getting on with your life, putting your time and energy into what really has meaning and value for you.

It can also be a simple remedy for any situation where you are meeting a fear head on or confronting a phobia. It is designed to bring you calmness, reassurance and comfort, so that you know, even when there is darkness in your life, and you have to find your way through it, there is enough light within your heart to always show you the way.

This is also a nice exercise to teach children or adults who are afraid of the dark or who find it difficult to fall asleep.

Getting ready:
The best place to do this exercise is in a darkened room, where you are unlikely to be disturbed, with a candle, where there is no danger of it being blown over (please take due safety precautions with open windows near open flames).

This exercise can be done by simply closing your eyes and visualising, imagining, feeling or pretending to feel the imagery I will guide you through, but the candle is an excellent prop to get you started.

Prepare your space, lighting your candle if you have one, and placing it where it can be easily seen whilst you relax. If you need a blanket or additional covering to remain warm whilst you start to relax (when your body may naturally cool down), have one handy.

The exercise:
Sit quietly and focus on your breath. Gaze at the candle if you have one; otherwise, you can close your eyes if you prefer.

Relax by focusing on the flow of your breath, breathing in and out, slowly and steadily, for at least eight counts. If it takes more for you to let go and relax, then do more. There is no rush. This whole relaxation process will only take minutes of your time.

When you are ready, in soft, quiet and yet confident tone of voice, say the following aloud, at least three times: "My heart holds the light that never goes out."

Continue to gaze at your candle, or close your eyes and make this exercise more internal now by visualising, imagining, feeling or pretending that you can see a candlelight flickering softly.

This is a special candle – it never, ever goes out. And it burns within your heart, creating soft warmth and light.

Notice this light. It feels reassuring and kind. As you adjust to 'seeing in the dark', the light becomes even more noticeable and bright.

You see the light always moving with you, and always shining just enough light for you to see one or two steps ahead of you, a bit like car headlamps in thick fog or rain.

The light is the right degree of brightness for you, enough just as it is to keep you safe and illuminate the path before you, showing you where you need to go. It will not show you too much so as to overwhelm you, nor too little so as to leave you 'in the dark' about what the next step for you could best be.

Rest and focus on the light – either of the candle or the candlelight within, for as long as feels good.

When you are ready, in a soft, quiet and yet confident tone of voice, say the following aloud, at least three times: "My heart shines the light that shows me the way."

When you are ready, place your hands together in a clasped position, and then open your palms and press them lightly against your chest, as if over your heart light. Say to your heart: "Thank you for showing me the way with love and truth. Thank you for being my light that never goes out."

You have finished your exercise.

EXERCISE 6: UNLEARN TO LEARN (INCREASING YOUR SPIRITUAL INTELLIGENCE)

Why you want to do this exercise:

Spiritual intelligence might sound like something that only monks who meditate for many hours a day can access, but spiritual intelligence exists within you and me. It is the ability to evolve. Spiritual intelligence is what enables you to take a life situation and make it work for you, to apply what you have learned and grow into a happier and wiser person because of it. It doesn't stop you from making mistakes (actually, I don't believe in mistakes so much as learning opportunities, which you have probably worked out by now) because they are how you grow. It does prevent you from mindlessly repeating things that make you miserable or stop you from getting what you truly want, and it does help you move towards your desires and dreams, changing you and your life, from the inside out.

When you build your level of spiritual intelligence, amazing things can happen in your life. You will actually feel you have changed and healed to such an extent that it is almost like you become such a different and improved version of yourself, that you are living 'another life within this life'.

The trick with spiritual intelligence is that you have to be willing to unlearn what you know. This can be hard at times, but is certainly possible. If you only focus on what you don't want to do, however, like giving up a habit that isn't so good for you, then the process can be more difficult than it needs to be. If you focus on adding, not just subtracting, it becomes easier. So you add a new habit that helps replace the old one, meeting the need of the old habit in a new and improved way. So if you smoked or drank to switch off your mind and relax, you would explore new ways to meet that need, because relaxation is a healthy need. As you develop those new ways, you also work on letting go of the old ways. You look for substitution and improvement, not just 'stopping' what you are doing to try to help yourself (even if the way it is helping you is not ultimately so helpful because of harmful side effects or compromise of your self-esteem because you are doing something you don't really want to do).

Spiritual intelligence happens when we meet a failure point in our lives. It's when something we counted on goes 'caput' and we don't know what to do, when the old ways cannot support us in getting through the challenge at hand and into the new life waiting for us. So we either stall and get caught up in fear of the unknown, failing to move forward, and become the sort of person that if you didn't see them in ten years, and then enquired about their life, everything would be exactly the same as it was ten years ago. They don't grow up or change, they don't allow life to guide them into new ways of being, thinking, behaving or feeling. They just refuse to engage. These are people who are still in the process of building their spiritual intelligence, their ability to evolve and grow. If you want to avoid the fate of being given a life but not really living it as much as you possibly can, then you'll need to build and use your spiritual intelligence. That means being willing to let go – or unlearn – in order to learn, and evolve.

It takes guts to let belief systems crumble – it can hurt a lot – and to reconstruct your world from the inside out. But every time you do it, you are letting go of layers of pain and holding back from life, which means you are becoming more trusting, more at peace, more willing and open to life, and you can receive that much more. It is a beautiful and graceful and blessed way to live – but yes, it takes courage and wisdom to live that way, and a daredevil streak of a risk-taker too!

This exercise is going to build your spiritual intelligence. It will work at a deep level of the mind, body and soul, and help you trust and understand that it's okay to grow. In fact, it's a good thing, even when part of that means destruction and letting go of the old known ways, leaving you – for a time at least – feeling like a plant that has been uprooted and yet to be put into safe new ground. In time, the shock of that transition will pass and your roots will greedily dig into yummy and more fertile new soil, and be happier and grow stronger and bigger because of that process.

When spiritual intelligence is from the heart, your reinvention into new cycles won't be on the surface, like a pop star changing a look or hair colour or image in a video clip. It will be the sort of transformation that really changes you as a person – not because you need to be different to who you are, but because you need to become *more* of who you are. You'll discover qualities and strengths within, you didn't even know where there. Often, the things you have considered you'd never do or be capable of are the very things that become your greatest strengths and assets. You'd be surprised what human beings are capable of developing in themselves if they are willing to give it a go. They can be the most beautiful flowering plants in the garden of life.

Getting ready:

You'll need a pen and a piece of paper or a journal. Consider the image below. You can write on this book, or on your piece of paper or in your journal if you prefer.

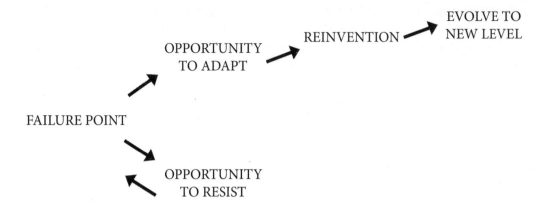

The exercise:

Consider an example where something in your life appears to be failing. It could be an idea, a relationship, a project or business.

Write it down under 'Failure Point'.

This doesn't mean something is wrong, but it does mean something isn't working the best way it could and it needs to change. There is a hidden blessing in there for you and you are going to find it!

Opportunity to Resist

We have free will. Growth brings us a lot of benefits, but it isn't always easy and sometimes we don't feel ready for it. Maybe we really need to know that something isn't going to magically improve or work out before we are ready to either let it go and move on, or not let it go, but find a different way to deal with the situation at hand so it can work out after all.

You'll get there eventually, but take this chance to get clear about what resisting the opportunity for change would look like. Mostly, it's just going to look like 'keep doing what I am already doing', which might be getting cranky at your partner, or continuing your business without taking any new chances on networking, marketing or developing your skill set. It might be to give up altogether, even though you still feel there is something worthwhile that could be developed if you were brave enough to put in the effort.

Choosing not to accept a failure point is often a case of denial – the refusal to recognise what is really happening (or not happening) and responding to that with a course of action. Whatever it would 'look like' for you to resist the opportunity to change, and instead to resist accepting or dealing with the failure point – write that down (under 'Opportunity to Resist').

Understand that if you keep doing what you are doing, you will keep getting the same results. It doesn't mean you have to give up on a long-term vision that can take time to grow, it means that to feed that long-term goal, for example, you'll need to adapt along the way, to find the things that really work.

Opportunity to Adapt

Now think about what you could do differently. It doesn't matter if it is the best idea ever, or just an idea, but come up with at least three things you could change in your attitude and behaviour that will be *different* to what you are doing now. Write these things down under 'Opportunity to Adapt'.

These are your opportunities to adapt. If something works well, you continue with it. If something doesn't seem to work, you let it go and come up with another idea instead.

The bonus with the 'opportunity to adapt' is that you don't have to figure it all out on your own. Life is very responsive. When we are willing to change, it will send us opportunities to act on and chances to take. So part of your opportunity to adapt is not only coming up with new ideas, but acting in new ways in your life situations. This can feel awkward and exhilarating! It will eventually become your new way to just be, and it will feel natural for you in due course.

Reinvention

You won't know what this looks like yet. This is the doorway to a new you and a new life. It is the result of you coming up with ideas that are different and acting on them, and also responding differently to the chances that life sends your way.

If you have already begun that process, then you can write some words that describe how you have grown and changed as a person, in how you are acting, but also in how you are feeling – more confident or secure, more vulnerable and risk-taking, more open, more connected, more uncertain and more successful perhaps.

If you have not yet begun to take your new steps, because you are still at the ideas stage, that is fine, but you can use your imagination to pretend you are already that reinvented, changed self. How might you feel different? How might you be different? Write some words down at the heading 'Reinvention'.

Evolve to a New Level

Finally, you are going to use some more imagination here and dare to dream.

How could a whole new level of your life look and feel? Write down some words or images that feel good and exciting to you under the heading 'Evolve to a New Level'.

What might success look and feel like for you in this situation you are working on? Even if you don't know how it can all work out or what it might look like, you can certainly still imagine what it will *feel* like. Write some feeling words at the heading 'Evolve to a New Level'.

It doesn't matter if it doesn't feel realistic *now*. The whole point of evolving is that what was out of reach for you in the past, becomes very much in your reach and available to you because you have grown capable of receiving it. If you are willing to grow and evolve, you may as well be willing to have big dreams and visions and to think really positively about what you'd like to experience in your life. You are willing to work for it, so be willing to receive the harvest too.

Review your work. Can you make a commitment to change, one step at a time? Yes? Then you have finished your exercise. You have also created a map for your change process.

Refer to it. Change your words as you go. Create new maps. Every time you 'hit a brick wall' in your life you can make a map to help you come up with your new plan for success.

This is making your mind work for you in a constructive way rather than in a self-defeating way. Every time you choose to try something new, a different approach, another way, you are building your spiritual intelligence. You are unlearning the old way and learning a new way. This is the best way for you to receive help from life, and the way you can turn any failure into a success. You clever thing!

EXERCISE 7: FROM CONFUSION TO SURRENDER

Why you want to do this exercise:
Confusion can be tough to accept. Yet when you are breaking through from an old way of doing things, and an old version of your life, into a new life calling you forward, you are going to be confused for at least part of the time. If there is big, radical, dramatic transformation and improvement taking place, then your confusion is quite likely going to be deep, rich and prolonged.

The good news is that there is a way to bear it with less pain and more grace, even – yes – enjoyment. This exercise will help you get there. Use it anytime you feel confused and in pain because of it. Remember, confusion is not bad, it's just you being pushed by life to make a commitment of some kind. When you mentally surrender, you are voting for more peace in your life and heart, and from that place, you can make the best choices about what you want to commit to and how. Confusion will eventually clear as you continue with your commitments, and you may even see a bigger picture about what is happening, and why, in your life.

Getting ready:
You'll need a quiet space to relax, where you will be unlikely to be interrupted or distracted. If you can do this in a room that is a little darkened, with enough light to read the instructions but not so much to keep the room very bright, that would be helpful for this exercise.

The exercise:
Focus on your breath and take some time to relax. You may be able to slow down your breathing a little as you relax. Instead of quicker, shallow breaths, your breathing can become deeper and slower. This doesn't need to be forced; it can happen naturally as you start to relax, and the more it happens, the more easily you will relax.

Take your time, close your eyes if that helps you to unwind, and focus on your breathing for at least ten breaths in and out.

When you are ready, visualise, imagine, feel or pretend that you are stepping into a dark place. Within that dark place is a kind and powerful person holding a lantern. This person is your inner guide. The lantern is symbolic in that your guide can help you find your way by the extra light shining in the darkness. It is safe to trust that person, and they are going to help you now.

Visualise, imagine, see or pretend that you are being led through that dark place. Your guide moves before you, holding the lantern to show the way, and you follow your guide, one step after another. If you stumble, your guide stops and holds the lantern so you can see to get back on the path again.

Relax and follow your guide. As you surrender and trust your guide to lead you, it might seem unfamiliar or awkward. You may even be scared that your guide might leave you alone in the dark. Your guide loves you and will not leave you. Your guide is patient and will give you as much time as you need to take your steps.

Relax, breathe and just keep taking one step after the other.

Eventually you and your guide take the last step from darkness towards a sunrise just beginning to break. Bright, clear, vibrant colours break across the sky. A new day is beginning for you. You have trusted your guide and made it through the darkness. This is your fresh new start.

Sit with your guide and enjoy the hope and beauty of the sunrise for as long as you wish.

When you are ready, if you have closed your eyes, open them.

How did it feel to surrender into being led? Was it easy for you? Or will you need to do this exercise again to learn how to let go and trust? Whatever your response to this exercise, accept that and work from there. That is how you'll grow. The easier it is for you to surrender to your wise inner guide, the easier it will be for life to lead you to where you need to be.

Say this aloud now, three times: "From confusion, I surrender, and my wise inner guide leads me to a new and beautiful place easily and with grace."

You have completed your exercise.

EXERCISE 8: CHANGING YOUR MENTAL OUTFIT

Why you want to do this exercise:
Imagine a piece of clothing that made you feel so good that you really believed you were the most beautiful or handsome creature ever when wearing it. If you took it off and put on old sweatpants, you might not feel quite as amazing (though perhaps very comfortable).

Our attitude or mental outlook is similar to a piece of clothing. Some attitudes will make you feel fantastic, others a bit sloppier. You can change your attitude – or your 'mental outfit' – and change how you feel as a result. You can choose to feel happier and more peaceful, more energised, more optimistic, more loved and more loving, simply by changing your mental outlook outfit. You have a lot more choice about how you think and what you feel than you probably realise.

Most of us have been raised to believe that how we react to something is truth. But that is a truth with a small 't', the kind of truth that can change – like it being Thursday today, which is true if I am in Australia, but not if I was talking about the United States where it would be night-time on a Wednesday. It doesn't mean it isn't true that it's Thursday – it just means it's a smaller truth, one that is relative. It depends on where you are at the time. How we react is a little truth. It can change depending on where we stand mentally at the time, how we choose to view things, and if we are willing to let go of our reactions to try on a different 'outfit' for a change.

This is actually not so hard to do when you get used to it. It's not just a case of the glass half full or half empty. At one level, you can simply be grateful that you have a glass of water, that you can see the glass, that the water is drinkable and wow, that's a lot to be grateful for – sight and good quality of living! That should be enough to make you smile. But you can go deeper into being a radical optimist and be truly rebellious at a spiritual level and realise the glass being half empty/half full is irrelevant because when it all comes down to it, things are going your way, no matter what appears to be – just like we saw in the story of the African king and his exceptionally positive friend earlier on. So even if you see that glass as half empty, it's good too.

When life wants to deliver something to us, it takes away whatever is in the way. A better relationship on its way to you? The old one has to go. A healthier body on the way? Then the old way of living has to go too, even if a health crisis is what is going to force that to happen. So it's all good, even if you don't know how that can be quite yet. Life is always helping you, and with a change of mental outfit, you become more willing and able to see that, which relaxes you and helps make life a more enjoyable journey, and the struggles something you are more willing to endure, with less fear, and more optimism … and look fabulous (in body and mind) whilst doing so.

Getting ready:
You can do this exercise as a guided visualisation, or you can get playful and use your actual wardrobe. It's totally up to you!

You'll also need a pen and paper or note-taking device such as the notes feature on your mobile phone.

The exercise:
Focus on your breathing. Relax and count to three as you breathe in. Pause for one count and then exhale as you count to three. Pause for one count.

Repeat – breathe in as you count to three, pause for one count, then breathe out for three counts, pausing for one count. Do this a few times until you feel more relaxed.

Now, visualise, imagine, feel or pretend there is (or actually find in your wardrobe) the oldest, most tattered piece of clothing you can find. It is the thing you feel is slovenly and you wouldn't want to be caught wearing outside the house.

Put it on – in your mind, or on your body – now. How do you feel? Give yourself a score out of ten for how you feel, with zero being not good and ten being amazing and like you could conquer the world. Write it down. If there is a word or feeling that goes along with how you feel, write that down too.

Visualise, imagine, feel or pretend there is (or actually find in your wardrobe) the most beautiful, special piece of clothing possible. It is the thing you would most want to be seen in, that you feel the most attractive in, that you feel suits you the most.

Put it on – in your mind, or on your body – now. How do you feel? Give yourself a score out of ten for how you feel, with zero being the lowest score and ten being the highest score. If there is a word or feeling to describe your experience in that piece of clothing, write that down too.

Do you notice that different pieces of clothing can bring out different emotional reactions in you? It is the same with your mental outfits. You are the same person, with the same talents and abilities, no matter what you wear; yet some outfits bring out the best in you.

Close your eyes now and visualise, imagine, feel or pretend that you have an 'anger outfit'. What colour is it? What does it look like, or feel like? In your mind, you can put that outfit on and experience it. You might imagine or feel that you want to stomp about and yell, or smash things.

When you are ready, change into a 'negativity outfit'. It might be bleak and depressing, your 'fat' clothes for when you feel like you are having an unattractive or bloated day and want to cover yourself up or not wear anything figure-hugging or tight. It might be droopy and ill-fitting, old, in need of a wash. How do you feel wearing it?

Imagine, visualise, feel or pretend that you can change your outfit now to a 'happiness and positivity outfit'. What colour is it? What does it look like, or feel like? In your mind, you can put that outfit on and experience it. You might imagine or feel you have lots of energy and want to do things like smile and laugh, or tackle an issue you have been putting off. You might feel more confident also.

What kind of mental outfit do you want to wear today? Imagine it and how you feel in it.

When you are ready, open your eyes. You have finished your exercise.

Remember, you get to choose the mental outfit at any time, any place. You can do this simple visualisation, imagining or pretending you have put on a new outfit in your mind, and allow your outlook and feelings to change for the better. Even if you are wearing sweatpants on your body, your mind can be sashaying about in a red carpet-worthy ensemble if you so choose.

CHAPTER 10

Workbook Exercises for the Other 3 Cs

· ·

PRACTICAL EXERCISES FOR THE OTHER 3 CS – CONSECRATE, CAPITULATE, CONTAIN

EXERCISE 1: CONSECRATION – SEEING THE GUIDING HAND OF LIFE

Why you want to do this exercise:

When you recognise that even behind the most ordinary of appearances, there is something special, sacred and spiritual happening (*even if you have no idea what it could be at the time*), you are consecrating your life. You are recognising that life and love are one and the same, and even tough love is still love. You begin to heal your relationship to life and realise you aren't being punished when things seem to go wrong, and if you can't work something out immediately, you aren't being stupid. (Well, most of the time anyway. We all have our occasional moments of utter stupidity I think, but if we learn from them, then that's actually being very smart.)

As your relationship with life becomes less suspicious and more accepting, you'll find you'll more easily start to recognise the silver lining in the clouds that pass through your life. Life seems less frightening, and more loving, because you feel less frightened and more loving.

Making life sacred is really just an attitude, a willingness to believe that beneath anything and everything is a guiding and loving hand, helping you take a particular path based on your own divine destiny, that inner evolution you are supposed to take this lifetime, to become all you were born to be.

This exercise will help you find that attitude and learn what it feels like. An adult learns best – in fact probably everyone learns best – when they can recognise a feeling. Ideas are useful, but what we really respond to and are moved by is emotion. It doesn't have to be intense emotion, but it needs to be felt.

Making connection with the sacred is something you have probably already felt many times in your life, maybe without even realising that was why you were feeling the way you were. When you have a sense that everything is going to work out somehow, when you have a moment where you feel like your soul is moved by the beauty of nature, when you laugh with delight at the antics of an animal or child, or when you simply touch the body of a loved one and you feel tenderness, affection and love – these are all 'everyday' moments where you are connecting with the sacred. Those sorts of feelings – love, affection, tenderness, pleasure, beauty, awe and inspiration, amusement and delight – increase as you consecrate life because you begin to see more of what life really is: love (sometimes hiding itself well, but always reaching out to you nonetheless).

Getting ready:

This is a soothing and gentle relaxation and guided visualisation (or imagination) exercise. So a quiet, not-too-bright room and soft non-distracting background music can work well. Turn off any potentially distracting electronic devices (such as mobile phones and computer email programs) and give yourself permission to really have some quality minutes here to switch off and feel some love!

As you will be relaxing, your body may cool down, so have a blanket or enough warm layers on you.

You can do this exercise seated if you wish, but lying down can be a deeply healing way to relax into the exercise.

This can be a good exercise to record and play back to yourself, to allow you to really let go. However, you can also read the instructions, and then relax afterwards.

The exercise:

Sit, or preferably lie down, to relax now. Close your eyes and breathe in and out, slowly and deeply, for however long feels right for you, but at least for five breaths.

You can place your hands on your belly, or over your heart, if that helps you to focus on your breath and relax.

When you are ready, say: "I am guided by the loving hand of life in all ways, at all times."

Repeat this statement softly, slowly, at least three times.

Visualise, imagine, feel or pretend that you are lying on the earth. It might be on the ground of a forest, or the sand of a beach. It could be in your garden, or on a soft rug on the floor of a beautiful place.

Visualise, imagine, feel or pretend that you can hear a heartbeat, soft, slow and ancient, arising from deep within the earth. You can feel and hear it as you lie on the earth.

It is so soothing. You feel like a baby in the safety of the womb, hearing the heartbeat of the mother keeping you safe and sound. Rest as you feel, hear or pretend to feel or hear, that heartbeat of the earth. Your own heartbeat may slow down a little to fall into rhythm with that slow and deep heartbeat.

When you are ready, visualise, imagine, feel or pretend that you can hear the breath of the earth as winds moving through trees and rustling their leaves. You might even be able to feel or hear, or pretend to feel or hear the trees on the earth breathing in and releasing oxygen as they breathe out.

It feels so good and relaxing to feel or hear the breath of the earth. Rest as you feel or hear, or pretend to feel or hear, the steady breathing of the trees, the winds rustling through their leaves. Your own breathing easily and naturally attunes to the breathing of the earth, becoming relaxed and strong.

Visualise, imagine, feel or pretend that you can sense the flowing of the waters of the earth – the movement of rivers, waterfalls and the ocean. Your own blood, and the fluid that runs along your spine, flows in harmony with the earth's waters. This feels so strengthening and also relaxing. Rest as you feel or hear, or pretend to feel or hear, the earth's waters flowing naturally, just as the waters in your own being flow naturally too.

Relax for as long as you need, then say this aloud at least three times: "I am connected to life. Life loves me. Life brings me what I need, when I need it. Everything I need is provided for me."

Rest and relax for as long as you need. If you fall asleep or nap for a while, that is fine.

When you are ready, simply open your eyes and you have completed your exercise.

Anytime you feel yourself forgetting life is sacred and loves you unconditionally (and if you are worrying, then you might have forgotten that at the time) you can remember the feeling of the earth's heartbeat, the earth's breath, the earth's waters, flowing and echoing in your body, mind and soul.

EXERCISE 2: CAPITULATE – WAVE THE WHITE FLAG

Why you want to do this exercise:
Capitulate means to surrender. It means giving in to what is happening but never giving up on the bigger picture. If you have ever tried (and I emphasise the word tried) to surrender, then you will know it is rather easy to say, "Oh, I've surrendered! I've handed that over to the universe to sort out," but somewhat more difficult to actually do.

Sometimes people do surrender quite spontaneously and easily – they just let go of the worry and actually feel a sense of peace about it, even though the situation is yet to resolve itself in their physical lives. Do they still want the situation to work out in a great way? Yes, of course. Do they still worry about how that is going to happen? No, because they have surrendered it.

This is the easiest way to know if you really have surrendered something, or if you have only 'sort of surrendered' (which isn't capitulation at all, because you haven't given in). You simply ask yourself, "Am I still worried about this?" If you are, you are still holding on. That's okay, it's not the end of the world, but it won't be the end of your problem either. It's better to let it go so that life can help you resolve it. Not much can happen if you have your worries held so tight to your chest that life can barely prise them out of your fingers and (1) start to untangle them and (2) begin to deliver the resolution to you (which you can then receive with open arms, if your arms aren't too busy holding on to your issue – do you see?).

Capitulation, or surrender, when it really and truly happens, actually feels pretty much the same as if your problem has just gone away. You could say that on a spiritual level, it has gone away. You have handed it over to life to sort out. You might be called upon to do your part, to respond to whatever opportunities to resolve it then come your way, but you have ceased trying to control it or force life to be other than what it is. The true feeling of peace that happens when you surrender, that sense of inner relief as you release the burden from your mind, body and soul, cannot be faked.

Surrender can be an absolute, where you simply hand it over to life and stop worrying altogether with unconditional trust that it is all going to work out perfectly. More often though, it is a process of letting go and then worrying once more, and needing to let go all over again. It's not as unconditionally trusting as absolute surrender, but that's okay. It's the beginner's approach to surrender! Sometimes, funnily enough, it's harder to surrender the shorter-term matters and easier to surrender the bigger-picture stuff. So you might surrender about where your life is headed overall, but struggle to capitulate on a mundane problem like trying to return an expensive mirror you bought online that doesn't actually look like the picture on the website at all (example from my own life, which worked out just fine, by the way). Whether your issue is a big one – about your career, or your child's safety in life, or some matter you've been trying to sort out for what feels like practically all of your adult life thus far which maybe money, or your body image or a health issue, or your love life – or if your issue is a small one, this exercise will help you learn how to give it up in the right way.

Every time you surrender, you are voting for peace of mind and earning spiritual brownie points. 'Spiritual brownie points' is the term I use to describe the 'good energy' you create when you trust life. Life likes it when you trust. It makes things easier for everyone. What if life was trying to get a message to someone, and you had the idea that you just wanted to tell a random person about a book you were reading? Maybe even this one! If you trusted, you would just do it. You wouldn't worry about whether that person might not be 'into all this stuff' or think you were weird. Instead, you would just say it, and whatever happened would be what happened. You surrender. You give in. You live with trust. And let's say that the comment sticks in the other person's mind. They read the book; it helps them. You randomly run into each other again, talk about the book, get a coffee and become best friends for the next forty years! Life accomplishes many things at once, and all the more so when we trust what is happening.

This exercise will help you capitulate, give in without giving up, let go because you trust it will work out. You'll do your part (stepping up to whatever it is that you can do) and life will handle the rest in the best way for all involved.

Getting ready:
If you have a white piece of paper and a pen (or crayons and coloured pencils) to write

with, that will be useful. If you want to get very creative, you can use crayons or paint, and work on a piece of white fabric instead of a piece of paper if you prefer.

If you have a room with some privacy that is great, but you can also do this exercise in a group or even with your children or other family members or friends if you wish.

The exercise:
Have your paper or fabric and writing tools ready.

Start by putting your hand on your heart and say the following aloud: "I choose to surrender into life's wisdom, love and power. I am so grateful and happy that my problems can be solved by life's generous and loving intelligence. I will do my part willingly. The rest I surrender with peace in my mind and joy in my heart. So be it."

Now it is time to write, draw or paint on your piece of paper or fabric. This is your 'white flag of surrender'. Whatever you choose to represent on this flag – using words, or symbols or pictures – you are going to 'hand over' to life. Don't be afraid to put the most challenging issues of your life on that flag.

To begin, write at the top or in the centre (or wherever feels best for you) in big letters, 'I SURRENDER', and then write or draw your issues or situations. There is no 'right' way to create your flag. Whatever works for you is just fine. Express yourself in as much or as little detail as you like. You might have one issue or many. This is your flag, your surrender, choose to include whatever you like. You might have positive dreams you want to surrender so they can happen more quickly and beautifully, as well as difficult issues causing pain that you want to let go.

Take your time.

When you are ready, and you have expressed what you want to surrender (and resolve) on your flag, it's time to stand up and wave that flag around! This is your sign to the universe, to life, that you are handing it over.

You might just wave your flag once, and it's done, or you might want to get into the experience and have some fun. Perhaps you'll put on some music and wave that flag in your own quirky and spontaneous 'flag waving dance'. Dancing like 'nobody's watching' can be great to help your body and mind let go.

How does your body feel when you surrender? Do you feel softer and more flowing in your movements? Do you tilt your head up and open your chest up to life? Or do you curl up and become quiet and peaceful inside, resting deeply?

Once you have 'waved the white flag' as much as you need to, you are going to sit down and put your hands over it. You are going to visualise, imagine, feel or pretend that a powerful 'waterfall' of white light is flowing down from the centre of the universe, all the way to *you*. It pours in through your head, down through your neck and torso and out through your arms, until it flows out of the palms of your hands and 'washes' all over your flag.

Any last worries or other aspects of holding on are washed away in this final 'white light rinse' of your flag.

You might feel something happening during this process, or nothing at all. Either is just fine; the effect happens whether you consciously feel it at the time or not.

Once you feel you have completed your final rinse, it's time to either store or dispose of that flag. You can put it away, you can throw it away, you can fold it up and put it in your journal, or in storage. If you feel you are ready to be 'done' with it (a good sign of surrender!), you can throw it away.

If you feel you might want to refer to your flag and do another white light rinse, if you 'pick up your problem' again in future, then put it in storage, and when needed, repeat your white light rinse.

You have completed your exercise.

It is absolutely possible to do this exercise once, and that will be all you will ever need to do on the matter, but it is also possible that it might take you a little longer to truly let go. It takes as long as it takes, and that's okay. Just remember to keep going till you feel total peace about the issues on your flag!

EXERCISE 3: SAFE TO LET GO

Why you want to do this exercise:
If you are a goal-setting, go-get-'em kind of person, then you have probably learned that you just have to 'make things happen' if you want to live a successful life. Hopefully, you have realised in reading this book that life wants to help you find the fulfilment you seek, but you have to learn how to let life help you. That means balancing hard work with letting go and allowing the fruits of your labours to manifest, and letting life's helping hand to intervene and assist on your behalf when necessary.

Even if you aren't a very driven person but you'd like to know the difference between working hard and trying to control everything (the latter being a recipe for undue stress and overwhelm) then this exercise will help you.

It is a good exercise to do anytime you feel overwhelmed, overloaded, or when simply trying to relax and unwind so you can 'switch off' from your day, or your week, and enjoy the present moment that much more. It is a 'present', after all.

Getting ready:
You'll need a comfortable and relatively quiet place to sit, as free from distractions as possible.

The exercise:
Close your eyes and relax, focusing on your breathing – in and out, in and out. Each inhalation and exhalation becomes a little deeper, and a little slower.

Imagine, visualise, feel or pretend that with each exhalation, your mind 'lets go' a little more, almost like you are prising the 'fingers of your mind' off whatever they have been holding on to. You feel your mind beginning to relax.

Now, visualise, imagine, feel or pretend that you are looking at a patch of healthy, rich soil in a garden bed. A seed has been planted deep in the earth and has been resting and preparing itself to grow.

You can't see that though. You wonder if the seed will ever sprout! You stare at the spot in the dirt. Nothing seems to be happening. You impatiently try to dig around to see if there is a shoot, but nothing is there. You are getting tired and stressed, so you lie down and have a rest instead.

As you rest, peacefully, the seed is growing, silently, invisibly, right next to you.

Relax and rest more deeply. The plant is now rising up and developing deeper roots beneath the earth and sprouting up towards the sky.

The more you rest and relax, the more the plant grows.

Open your eyes and notice how much the plant has grown whilst you were resting. You feel very happy about this and very relaxed. Notice these happy, relaxed feelings for a little while.

If you wish to rest further now, do that. The plant will continue to grow.

When you are ready to move on with your day, simply open your eyes and you have finished your exercise.

EXERCISE 4: BAMBOO YOU

Why you want to do this exercise:
These last three exercises are about containment. This one, *Bamboo You*, is about building a stronger container within your body. Your body is an amazing animal, able to grow and adapt, rebuild and heal itself. It even knows how to repair a broken bone. Amazing!

This exercise will help you learn to trust in the power of your body. It will also help you remember that strength is *not* about refusing to bend. If you refuse to be moved by a force greater than you (such as the force of life itself) you'll break. When you learn to be strong and flexible, you'll bend and adapt to what is happening around you, without losing your centre. This is how you can pursue your goals, and when life takes you on some interesting twists and turns, instead of giving up your dream, you will be able to find another path to get there instead. You can be like bamboo that grows fast and powerfully, has so many nurturing uses, and is *very strong and very flexible*.

The more you recognise this quality in you and your body, the more trusting you are going to be in yourself and in life. If you are afraid, you'll either collapse completely in the face of challenge (not enough strength), or refuse to give an inch and try to force things to happen how you think they should happen (not enough flexibility). When you trust, because you know you are strong enough to be flexible, you'll be willing to let life move you. The energy you would have once expended to try and resist life (like swimming against the current, it uses up a lot more energy than going with the flow) you can now put into working with what is, and turning that to your advantage. Strength and flexibility allow your body and mind to become more capable of handling change and challenge without becoming overwhelmed so quickly or tired out so fast. You can work smarter, instead of harder, using the same amount of energy, or less, to get further in your life. And you can do all this without having to think about it too much. You just learn to move in a different way, realising that it is safe.

Getting ready:
You can do this exercise seated, or if you have the ability to move, perhaps doing yoga or stretching, dance or any freestyle movement, you can do this exercise in that way.

So you will either need a chair upon which to sit, or a space within which you can move freely without knocking something over.

Having somewhere where you won't be interrupted is good too.

If you would like to have some background music playing, that is fine too. It could be something soothing and 'flowing' if you are planning on doing this as a moving rather than seated exercise.

The exercise:
Either be seated, or stand. Place one hand on your heart, and one hand on your belly if you wish. This can help you to connect with yourself and 'ground' yourself in the here and now.

Breathe in and out. Relax. Take your time to focus on your breathing, for at least several breaths, as you step out of the everyday world and into some 'quality you time'.

Visualise, imagine, feel or pretend that your spine is long and strong, like a tall bamboo plant. You feel so long and tall, as if you have grown an inch or more in height! It also feels like you could just keep growing!

You may do this whilst seated or moving physically, bending and waving slightly from side to side, and backwards and forwards slightly. Enjoy the freedom of this movement for as long as you wish. Can you sense the strength that is flexible, that can move freely? You do not have to become tense or force anything to be strong. You can relax and be stronger for it.

Finish your visualisation or movement in an upright position of your spine.

Relax and breathe in and out. Then say: "I am strong enough to adapt. I am strong enough to be flexible. I am strong and flexible, like bamboo!"

Relax for as long as you need, moving more or resting if you wish.

When you are ready, open your eyes and you have completed your exercise.

EXERCISE 5: CRADLED IN LOVE

Why you want to do this exercise:
Love is a powerful medicine for any ailment. It might not take away a problem, but it gives us the energy we need to tackle it. When you feel safe and loved within yourself, it's quite incredible just how courageous you can be in all areas of your life.

This exercise will bring you back to love. It helps to build a sense of inner security and strength which will support you as you deal with whatever is going on in your life. It is a good exercise to do anytime and every day if you wish. You might be surprised, with regular use, just how much this simple little exercise can change the way you feel and behave without much additional effort on your part.

Getting ready:

Have a comfortable place to sit or lie down, enough blankets or layers to be warm, and soothing background music if you wish.

It is good to switch electronic devices off, or at least on to silent mode so you won't be disturbed. If you need to also put a 'do not disturb' sign on the door, do that too. This is an exercise that is very much like going into the nicest cocoon you could imagine. You want to be able to relish that and really 'get into it' without worrying you'll have to deal with an it-just-couldn't-wait-for-twenty-more-minutes phone call, for example.

This exercise can be as short or long as you wish. It's up to you and how much time you have and how long you choose to stay in the process. Anywhere from two minutes to twenty minutes or more is a guideline for how much time is beneficial to carry out this exercise effectively.

The exercise:

Sit or lie down quietly and begin to notice in your body where you are holding tension or where you feel tightness or pain. Breathe in and out, slowly and deeply. Do not judge your body or any discomfort. Focus on the breath instead, maybe 'breathing into' parts of your body if you wish, but it is more than enough to just focus on your body and on breathing in and out.

Now, visualise, imagine, feel or pretend that you can sense your heart as a warm soft glow, humming peacefully in the centre of your chest. It feels nice – like being around the warmth and glow of a camp fire. If you feel too hot and want to be cool, that glow is a soft cooling glow. If you feel cold and want to be warm, that glow is a soft warming glow. You may see or sense or feel a colour or just the temperature.

Rest in that glow until you feel it has filled you up inside and radiates out, all around you, as though a caring person had wrapped you in a lovely soft blanket.

Relax. Breathe. Feel or pretend that you are being cradled in love, that warm soft glow from your heart that surrounds you now.

If you can think of people or animals you love, do that to help you feel the love in your heart if needs be.

Relax. Think, *I love you*, at least three times, and really mean it. You are a precious and valuable human being. You deserve love. Give that to yourself now, and really feel how your heart likes this and gives you back even more love in return. If you want to send the thought, *I love you*, to people you love, or to the animals, plants or the earth, then do that by just thinking it now.

Remain for as long as needed in this 'cradle of love'.

When you are ready, take your time and move slowly back into the 'here and now'. You will be surprised how relaxed you can become doing this exercise, and you don't want to suddenly start operating heavy machinery, chopping up vegetables or driving a car until you are really back and grounded again.

When you are ready, get up and walk around. Confirm the time and date to really ground yourself back in the 'here and now'.

You have finished your exercise.

Afterword

So what next? Keep going. Take your steps. Know that you are loved. You are safe. You are being loved by life into the fullness of all you can be.

There is so much within you that can come to life in the world. There is a fuller and more exciting, beautiful and creative life that you are meant to live – that is why you are here, in a body, taking this strange, wild and mysterious life journey.

Remember, that no matter what happens, it is love guiding you forwards always. If you want to change the quality of that love from tough to tender, then trust a little more. Trust yourself and trust life. Be open to what is happening and know that even though some days it's hard to believe it, life really does know what it is doing. And so, dear one, do you. Trust and live your life in love.

About Alana

When something is natural for you, especially if it has been that way since childhood, you can assume for a long time that it is natural for everyone. It took me some years to realise that my sensitivity, healing ability and natural conscious connection to the higher planes of spiritual guidance was unusual.

It wasn't long after that realisation that I stepped away from a career as a lawyer (spiritual law was always more interesting to me anyway) and I began my vocation as a spiritual healer and teacher.

From the earliest memories I have, I was always in conscious connection with Spirit. It has always been as natural as breathing to me and is probably the gift that I am most grateful for this lifetime – though I have gratitude for plenty.

As a young woman in my teens, I began exploring meditation and psychic work, and it was simultaneously like discovering a whole new world and one that I was somehow more familiar with too. In those inner worlds, I found a source of love, intelligence, humour and guidance that was incredibly kind and helpful. It changed my life. I wanted other people to have the opportunity to benefit from that loving guidance too, if they so chose. In my early twenties I began my work as a spiritual teacher and over the past two decades that has unfolded in some most beautiful and unexpected ways!

Now I live, breathe, write, sing, dance and create in honour of that loving guidance, to help its voice be heard in the hearts of those that are in need. This is the voice of the soul. It is the inner voice that honours you and all that you are, sees and encourages you to live with boldness and courage to become all that you can become.

You'll hear this voice in my books, DVDs, CDs and oracle decks. You'll hear it inside of your own heart, as though a tuning fork has been struck in the depths of your own being, and you'll realise that you don't need to be afraid. You just need to be alive and take your unique journey with trust. May you blossom and shine, dear one, into all that you can be, all that you are.

To find out more about Alana's work and consult her free online oracle, visit her website: **www.alanafairchild.com**

55 Keys
Tips, Tricks & Tidbits for Living a
Happy & Successful Life

Living your best life feels good for your body, your mind and most especially, your heart.

Your heart is smart. It knows what you need to become happier in life. Your heart has the answers for every question and knows how to guide you towards success and fulfilment. You just need to listen.

You can use the messages in this book to have a conversation with your own heart, tapping into the wisdom, courage and power within you.

These fifty-five tips, tricks and tidbits are morsels of wisdom to nourish you for the journey, from your head to your heart, into your happiest and most successful life.

100 pages, full-colour book with padded hardcover.
ISBN: 978-1-922161-54-3

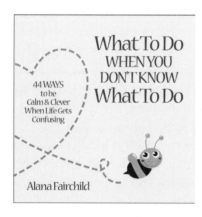

What To Do When You Don't Know What To Do
44 Ways to be Calm & Clever When Life Gets Confusing

Life can sometimes get confusing. Even with a positive attitude and a courageous heart, sometimes you will feel uncertain. How should you deal with the curveballs life throws your way?

When life gets confusing and you feel like you are lost at sea, this helpful little book will be your life raft, keeping you afloat, guiding you back to dry land.

Just take a deep breath, relax and open the book randomly at a page. You'll get your answer. And you'll know what to do.

100 pages, full-colour book with padded hardcover.
ISBN: 978-1-922161-55-0

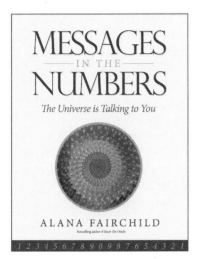

Messages in the Numbers
The Universe is Talking to You

You have wise spiritual guides from the spiritual worlds of Crystals and Ascended Masters. They are ready to help you on your path of spiritual growth now.

This book holds the key to decoding the secret messages in the numbers you notice around you – those repeating patterns on your phone, alarm, computer screen or the digital clock in your car, and even in significant dates, your house number or the number plates on the cars you drive past.

While it might seem like the Universe has far too much going on to attend to the various matters of concern in our individual human lives, in truth, within its infinite intelligence lie creative solutions for any difficulty you could possibly encounter. Included in that intelligence, is a benevolent streak of compassion. The Universe is not, contrary to our worst imaginings, entertained by our struggles in life, chuckling away with perverse humour at our misfortunes. The Universe is like your greatest cheerleader ever, urging you on to the right path, encouraging you to make the most fearless and loving choices, and guiding you towards your ultimate destiny, which is to experience a full, nourishing and soul-satisfying existence.

In short, the Universe wants to help you! And one of the ways it does that is by sending you messages through numbers. These are messages that the Universe wants to get through to you – to help you grow and live a happier, more connected and fulfilling life. Are you ready to hear them? It's easy! Let this super-practical guidebook help you interpret the messages in the numbers so you can receive the guidance that is meant for you.

Features simple guided meditative processes and sacred geometry images to help you connect energetically with each number's vibration.

232 pages, paperback.
ISBN: 978-1-922161-21-5

Crystal Mandala Oracle
Channel the Power of Heaven & Earth

In this stunning, stand-alone deck, you will work with the vibrant crystal mandalas by Jane Marin, as featured in Alana Fairchild's popular books 'Crystal Angels 444', 'Crystal Masters 333' and 'Crystal Goddesses 888'. Alana shares loving spiritual guidance from the angels, masters and goddesses to help you integrate the frequencies of the crystals and higher beings that are featured in each of the cards. The Crystal Angels will help you heal your body, mind and soul. The Crystal Masters will support your spiritual growth and help yousuccessfully pass through spiritual tests and initiations. The Crystal Goddesses will empower you to embody your spirit and express your soul purpose in the world.

This powerful deck will enhance your connection to the sacred worlds of higher beings and crystal energy, opening your heart to divine beauty and empowering your soul with loving consciousness.

Artwork by Jane Marin
54 cards and 244-page guidebook set, packaged in a hardcover box set.
ISBN: 978-1-922161-89-5

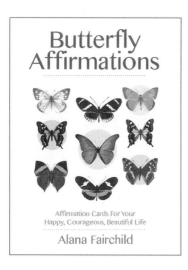

Butterfly Affirmations
Affirmation Cards For Your Happy, Courageous, Beautiful Life

Butterflies are creatures of hope. They remind you that struggles and endings are signs of something beautiful and new about to be born.

These cards contain affirmations to help you remember the courage and happiness within you. They inspire you to be wise, to be brave, to relax and to never give up on your dreams. Simply relax, choose a card and read the message. It will be what you need to hear right now. Let these 44 butterflies bring hope, healing and happiness into your life today.

44 cards packaged in a hardcover box set.
ISBN: 978-1-922161-65-9

Kuan Yin Oracle
Blessings, Guidance and Enlightenment
from the Divine Feminine

Kuan Yin. Radiant with Divine Compassion.

The 44 cards in this deck guide you to a place of inner peace and beauty. Her energy reaches out to you from each card. The messages, inspired by her presence and guiding voice, contain her wisdom to help us live a loving and enlightened life that is practical, spiritual and positive. The guidance in the messages and the practical exercises for each card nourish you on your spiritual path, help you realise that you are a divine Soul and learn to love, trust and live your highest destiny this lifetime.

Artwork by Zeng Hao
44 cards and 144-page guidebook, packaged in a hardcover box set.
ISBN: 978-0-9872041-8-9

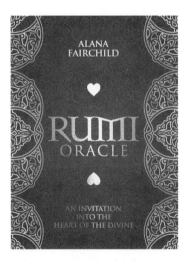

Rumi Oracle
An Invitation into the Heart of the Divine

Rumi speaks a sacred language that we understand with our hearts rather than our minds. He knows the heart is the gateway to divine union and he doesn't want you to play small this lifetime. He encourages humanity to live and love with absolute surrender, abandon and willingness to accept the mysteries of life.

Whether you have studied his poetry for years or are drawn to him only now, this oracle deck will strengthen and illuminate your connection with this beautiful and powerful soul who loves you with a fierce passion.

Rumi has a heart so open that the entire world that he loves so dearly can easily be held within it. His is a path of love. To dance in divine love with him, you need only be willing to enter your own heart. May the blessings of this spiritual brother lead you into the bliss of your own divine heart-centred nature.

Artwork by Rassouli
44 cards and 220-page guidebook, packaged in a hardcover box set.
ISBN: 978-1-922161-68-0

For more information on this or other
Blue Angel Publishing titles,
visit our website at:

www.blueangelonline.com